SIN IN VALENTINIANISM

SOCIETY
OF BIBLICAL
LITERATURE

DISSERTATION SERIES

David L. Petersen, Old Testament Editor
Charles Talbert, New Testament Editor

Number 108

SIN IN VALENTINIANISM

by
Michel R. Desjardins

Michel R. Desjardins

SIN IN VALENTINIANISM

Scholars Press
Atlanta, Georgia

SIN IN VALENTINIANISM

Michel R. Desjardins

Ph.D., 1987
University of Toronto

Advisor:
Prof. Heinz Guenther

Library of Congress Cataloging in Publication Data

Desjardins, Michel R. (Michel Robert), 1951-
    Sin in Valentinianism / Michel R. Desjardins
    p. cm. -- (Dissertation series ; no. 108)
    Thesis (Ph.D.)--University of Toronto, 1987.
    Bibliography: p.
    ISBN 1-55540-224-0.   ISBN 1-555540-225-9 (pbk.)
    1. Valentinians. 2. Sin--History of doctrines--Early church, ca.
30-600. I. Title. II. Series: Dissertation series (Society of
Biblical Literature) ; no. 108.
BT1475.D47 1990
241'.3'09015--dc19   88-10067
                                            CIP

Printed in the United States of America
on acid-free paper

Contents

Acknowledgments

I am most grateful for the support received while writing this dissertation. Fellowships from the Social Services and Humanities Research Council of Canada provided the necessary financial security. In addition, the members of the University of Toronto's Centre for Religious Studies—especially Muna Salloum, the heart of the Centre—provided continuous encouragement and fellowship over the years. Several scholars have generously made helpful comments on this work in various stages of its development. I think particularly of John Corbett, Peter Richardson, and Martin Shukster in Toronto; Louis Painchaud at Laval; Kurt Rudolph in Marburg; and David Griffiths, now in Japan but always close at hand. My supervisor, Heinz Guenther, graciously allowed me the freedom to develop my ideas. Above all there is Ellen, my wife, whose constant support enabled me to complete my work, and to whom I dedicate this book.

Abbreviations

AbhAkGottingen	Abhandlungen der Akademie der Wissenschaften in Gottingen
AGSU	Arbeiten zur Geschichte des späteren Judentums und des Urchristentums
ANF	The Ante-Nicene Fathers
Aug	*Augustinianum*
BCNHSE	Bibliothèque copte de Nag Hammadi, Section "Études"
BCNHST	Bibliothèque copte de Nag Hammadi, Section "Textes"
CCSA	Corpus Christianorum: Series Apocryphorum
CSEL	Corpus Scriptorium Ecclesiasticorum Latinorum
EThL	*Ephemetides Theologicae Lovanienses*
EstE	*Estudios eclesiasticos*
ET	*Église et théologie*
ETHDT	Études et textes pour l'histoire du dogma de la trinité
FRLANT	Forschungen zur Religion und Literatur des Alten und Neuen Testaments
GOH	Gottingen Orientforschungen, VI Reihe: Hellenistica
GCS	Die griechischen christlichen Schriftsteller der ersten drei Jahrhunderte
Greg	*Gregorianum*
HDR	Harvard Dissertations in Religion
HTR	*Harvard Theological Review*
JBL	*Journal of Biblical Literature*
JRH	*Journal of Religious History*
JTS	*Journal of Theological Studies*
LEC	Library of Early Christianity
LTP	*Laval théologique et philosophique*
Mus	*Le Muséon*
NHS	Nag Hammadi Studies
NovT	*Novum Testamentum*
NovTSup	Supplements to *Novum Testamentum*
NTL	New Testament Library
NVBS	New Voices in Biblical Studies
OLZ	*Orientalische Literaturzeitung*
PG	J. Migne, ed., *Patrologia graeca*
PTS	Patristische Texte und Studien

RAC	*Reallexikon für Antike und Christentum*
REAug	*Revue des Études Augustiniennes*
RSLR	*Rivista di Storia e Letteratura Religiosa*
RSR	*Religious Studies Review*
RTP	*Revue de théologie et de philosophie*
SBLDS	SBL DIssertation Series
SBLMS	SBL Monograph Series
SC	Sources chrétiennes
SCJ	Studies in Christianity and Judaism
SEphA	Studia Ephemeridis "Augustinianum"
SGKA	Studien zur Geschichte und Kultur des Altertums
SHR	Studies in the History of Religions
SJI	Sudien aus dem C. G. Jung-Institut
SR	*Studies in Religion/Sciences religieuses*
TextsS	Texts and Studies
TF	Theologische Forschung
TLZ	*Theologische Literaturzeitung*
TRu	*Theologische Rundschau*
TU	Texte und Untersuchungen zur Geschichte der altchristlichen Literatur
TZ	*Theologische Zeitschrift*
VC	*Vigiliae Christianae*
NW	*Zeitschrift für die neutestamentliche Wissenschaft*
ZTK	*Zeitschrift für Theologie und Kirche*

1

Introduction

1. INTRODUCTION

1.1

Sin is a prevalent notion in the writings of Christians during the first two centuries after the death of Jesus. In fact, from Paul to Origen virtually every Christian writer mentions sin, and several discuss it extensively.[1] If the death and resurrection of Jesus indeed broke the power of sin over humankind, as Paul already claimed, it surely did not break its hold over the Christians' imagination.

Valentinus and his followers have seemed to be the exception to the rule. The scholarly consensus is that sin was of no concern to this important group of second century Christians. This claim is supported principally by the fact that the patristic evidence for Valentinianism makes little mention of sin. This observation should have elicited surprise and further study from students of early Christianity. That it has not done so relates, in part, to the tendency in the scholarly community to adopt the heresiologists' viewpoint and to consider these "disciples of Christ" to be Christians "falsely so called." More importantly, though, it results from setting the Valentinians on a second century gnostic trajectory that has little or no room on it for sin. A fundamental tenet of Gnosticism is that the possessor of *gnosis* is freed from worldly constraints and is redeemed by nature, not by actions. Salvation for gnostics depends essentially on who one is and not on what one does. As the *Gospel of Philip* states, "He who has knowledge of the truth is a free man, but the free man does not sin" (77,15-16). Because of this antipathy towards the world the gnostic is seen to be only half-heartedly interested in ethical questions. From this perspective, then, one would not expect sin to play a role in the Valentinian conceptual system because the Valentinians were gnostics and gnostics were not concerned with sin. The patristic sources only seem to confirm this assumption.

1.2.1

This conclusion has gained a near-canonical status. Two factors require us to rethink it. The first is a truism among students of religion: there is often

---

[1] The linguistic evidence alone is revealing. Among early Christians, for instance, the Apologists use ἁμαρτάνειν, ἁμαρτία, and ἁμαρτωλός ninety times; both Irenaeus and the Apostolic Fathers, over one hundred times; and the New Testament, Clement of Alexandria, Tertullian, and Origen, each over two hundred times.

1

tension between theory and practice within a religious system. For instance, sin should be of no immediate concern to Paul because he claims that Christ has destroyed the power of sin and that salvation now comes through belief in Jesus as the Christ. Christians, being "in Christ," ought not to be affected by sin. Yet nobody would claim that sin actually does not play a major role in Pauline thought, or that all Christians in his communities considered themselves free from sin. Manicheism is a better example. As Kurt Rudolph tells us, here is a religion which, although decidedly gnostic, shows "an acute consciousness of sin."[2]

Many scholars have not distinguished between theory and practice in their analyses of second century Gnosticism. For some this has been by choice because they view Gnosticism more as a philosophical system than as a living religion. For others, it has simply been a continuation of the scholarly approach to Judaism and Christianity in the first two centuries C.E. that focuses on textual-critical matters rather than socio-political ones. The lack of information about gnostic behavior has understandably made most scholars wary of postulating an everyday side to Gnosticism not fully in accord with its basic ideology. But, while a thorough sociological description of second century Gnosticism may never be written,[3] it is important to realize that even from the sources we do possess there are clear hints that practice was not always in accord with theory. Rudolph's remarks again are *apropos*:[4]

> in theory, for instance, the gnostic conception of the world is really anti-cultic. All "hylic" (material) institutions are disqualified and regarded as futile for redemption. Strictly speaking this is true also of the cultic domain. Sacraments like baptism and last [sic] supper (eucharist) cannot effect salvation and therefore do not possess those qualities that are "necessary for salvation"; at most they confirm and strengthen the state of grace that the gnostics (pneumatics) enjoy already, insofar as they are retained. Only a very few branches however adopted this radical standpoint. . . . The majority, as is clear from the limited source material, practised a cult analogous to that of the mystery religions or the Christian church.

Most of the gnostic communities, then, in spite of some of their theories, appeared to have taken ceremonies, sacraments and prayer quite seriously,[5] and it is at least possible that the same holds true of sin.

---

[2] Kurt Rudolph, *Gnosis: The Nature and History of Gnosticism,* trans. and ed. by Robert McL. Wilson (San Francisco: Harper and Row, 1983 [1977]) 342.

[3] The best analysis from a sociological perspective is Henry A. Green, *The Economic and Social Origins of Gnosticism,* SBLDS 77 (Atlanta: Scholars Press, 1985). This is a revision of a thesis directed by R. McL. Wilson and completed in 1982.

[4] *Gnosis,* 218.

[5] *Gnosis,* 218–47.

1.2.2
    The second and decisive factor that demands a reappraisal of the view that
Valentinians were not concerned with sin is the occurrence of the term sin in the
majority of the Valentinian works from the Nag Hammadi collection. Armed
with this new and surprising information it becomes easier to detect that even
in the patristic descriptions there are indications that sin did play a role in Valentinianism. We can no longer claim that the Valentinians were not concerned with
this notion because, as gnostics, they could not be. In fact, they were.

1.2.3
    Two recent factors, then, demand a reassessment of sin in Valentinianism.
One is the discovery of a new and extensive source base comprising works which
are probably Valentinian and which in many instances include references to sin.
Only in the last decade have all of these works been available for study. The other
factor is the trend in the field of Christian Origins to examine what the religious
"man and woman on the street" thought and did. This has helped develop an
appreciation for the diversity in Judaism and Christianity in this time period. It
has also increased our awareness of the differences between social reality and the
stated theoretical ideals.[6]

1.3
    The primary purpose of this study is to determine precisely what the Valen-
tinians thought about sin and how this fitted into their conceptual system. Before
describing how we intend to proceed, two issues require elaboration. The first
concerns sources: which ones are available for an understanding of this second
century Christian movement, and how do we use them? The second concerns
what we mean by Valentinianism.

2. SOURCES

2.1.1
    The best full-length study of Valentinianism still is François Sagnard's *La
gnose valentinienne et le témoignage de Saint Irénée*, published in 1947.[7]

---

[6] Accounting for the social aspects of early Christianity has become a sub-discipline in
its own right over the last decade. To mention only the major books: John G. Gager,
Kingdom and Community: The Social World of Early Christianity (Englewood Cliffs, NJ:
Prentice-Hall, 1975); Gerd Theissen, *The First Followers of Jesus* [also called *Sociology
of Early Palestinian Christianity*], trans. by J. Bowden (London: SCM Press, 1978 [1977]);
Abraham J. Malherbe, *Social Aspects of Early Christianity*, 2d ed. (Philadelphia: Fortress,
1983); Wayne A. Meeks, *The First Urban Christians: The Social World of the Apostle Paul*
(New Haven: Yale University Press, 1983); Richard A. Horsley and John S. Hanson,
Bandits, Prophets, and Messiahs: Popular Movements at the Time of Jesus, NVBS 2
(Minneapolis: Winston Press, 1985); and John E. Stambaugh and David L. Balch, *The
New Testament in Its Social Environment*, LEC 3 (Philadelphia: Westminster, 1986).

[7] François-M.-M. Sagnard, *La gnose valentinienne et le témoignage de saint Irénée*
(Paris: Librairie Philosophique J. Vrin, 1947).

Sagnard found a certain consistency among the patristic portrayals of Valentinianism and stressed the significance and dependability of Irenaeus's description of this second century Christian group. Much has happened since this book appeared forty years ago. Of decisive importance has been the publication of the texts discovered near the Egyptian town of Nag Hammadi in 1945,[8] several of which appear to have been composed originally by Valentinians. The wave of scholarly interest in these texts reached tidal proportions in the 1970s and has since subsided somewhat.[9] Part of this included a reappraisal of the Fathers' accounts of their so-called gnostic opponents in the light of this newly-found "gnostic library." Sagnard would certainly write a different book today.

One of the enduring strengths of La gnose valentinienne is its sensitivity to sources. This is not surprising, for Sagnard, as a historian, was aware of how important it is to know what the sources are and to question how each of them should be used. What is striking about the many recent discussions of Valentinianism is the relative lack of concern for this issue.[10] What is also disturbing is the lack of sophistication sometimes shown by historians of early Christianity in their use of Valentinian sources. In this short section I delimit the full range of primary sources presently available for a study of Valentinianism. Then, as part of the discussion of how to use these sources, I examine more extensively their relative merits.

2.1.2

The Valentinian writings often served as grains of sand in the oyster bed of second and third century patristic literature, and in many instances it is still possible to recover those irritants with a reasonable degree of certainty. The major patristic works which contain this primary Valentinian material have long been isolated and, using Sagnard's list,[11] include the following seven: Irenaeus's Adversus haereses; Clement of Alexandria's Stromata and Excerpta ex Theodoto; Hippolytus's Refutatio; Tertullian's Adversus valentinianos; Origen's Commentary on John, which contains the fragments of Heracleon; and section

---

[8] A complete English translation of the Nag Hammadi texts has existed for a decade in James M. Robinson (ed.), The Nag Hammadi Library in English (New York: Harper and Row, 1977). Critical editions are also appearing in English (the Coptic Gnostic Library, under the general editorship of Robinson), German (the Gnostische Schriften of the Berliner Arbeitskreis für koptisch-gnostische Schriften, directed by Hans-Martin Schenke), and French (the Bibliothèque copte de Nag Hammadi from Laval, directed by Paul-Hubert Poirier and Michel Roberge — another French edition, edited by Michel Tardieu in Paris, Sources gnostiques et manichéennes, does not provide the Coptic texts).

[9] To appreciate the trends in scholarship, cf. the works collected by David M. Scholer in his Nag Hammadi Bibliography 1948–1969, NHS 1 (Leiden: Brill, 1971) and the annual supplements in Novum Testamentum.

[10] Cf. especially The Rediscovery of Gnosticism: Proceedings of the International Conference on Gnosticism at Yale, March 28–31, 1978. I. The School of Valentinus, ed. by Bentley Layton (Leiden: Brill, 1980).

[11] Sagnard, La gnose, 119–20.

33 of Epiphanius's *Panarion* which reproduces Ptolemy's "Letter to Flora." To these, says Sagnard, "on pourrait ajouter: Pseudo-Tertullien (*Adversus omnes haereses*), Philastre (*De haeresibus*), Épiphane ([le reste du] *Panarion*), trois écrits dérivant d'une même source . . . ; de même Théodoret."[12] To this group of later and derivative sources should be added Klaus Koschorke's recent collection of less familiar patristic material appearing to preserve some Valentinian sources. These range from Didymus's *Commentary on the Psalms* to comments recorded by the Second Tryllian Synod of 692.[13]

2.1.3

Another addition which now must be made to Sagnard's list is the evidence from the Nag Hammadi find. The problem here, though, is deciding which text to include—if any. This is a problem which cannot be resolved easily, or perhaps even satisfactorily. None of the 46 independent works to emerge from this discovery claims to be Valentinian or even to have been written by someone whom the Fathers have connected with this group, and the decision to call a work "Valentinian" rests exclusively on finding similarities between its content and the patristic descriptions of that group (with all their differences!). Obviously, this situation is far from ideal on methodological grounds. It has recently even led Frederik Wisse to take the challenging position that perhaps one should not attempt to isolate any Valentinian works at all from the Nag Hammadi collection. The fact that Wisse can argue such a case points to the hypothetical nature of any reconstruction.[14]

The range of tenable options on this matter is exemplified by scholars' treatments of *The Gospel of Truth*. This is a work which has a definite affinity to Valentinianism. For instance, one encounters terms such as aeons, the All, the Pleroma, Deficiency, Rest, and the distinction between three classes of people (pneumatic, psychic, and hylic). However, it also lacks much of the basic

---

[12] *La gnose*, 120. Sagnard does not pay much attention to these: "leur date tardive ne permet guère leur utilisation."

[13] Klaus Koschorke, "Patristische Materialen zur Spätgeschichte der valentinianische Gnosis," in *Gnosis and Gnosticism: Papers Read at the Eighth Annual International Conference on Patristic Studies (Oxford, Sept. 3rd–8th, 1979)*, ed. by M. Krause (Leiden: Brill, 1981). These are taken from the following: Didymus *Comm. Ps.;* Athanasius of Alexandria *Tomus ad Antiochenos*, c. 3; Oxford Papyrus P. Ash. Inv. 3; Epiphanius *Panarion*, 31,7,1; John Chrysostom *Sermo* I,3, *De virginitate*, c. 3, *De sacerdotio*, IV,4; Severian of Gabala, Fragm. on I Cor 15:47–49; Aphrahat *Homilia*, III,6; Julian the Apostate *ep.* 59; Ambrose of Milan *ep.* 40f.; Constantine's decree concerning the heretics; Theodosius II *On Heretics;* Theodore of Mopsuestia *Comm. on I Tim.;* Theodoret of Cyrrhus *ep.* 81; Timothy of Constantinople *De receptione haereticorum;* and the Second Tryllian Synod of 692 *can.* 95.

[14] Actually Wisse has gone as far as to question the very existence of a Valentinian group in the second century. See his "Prolegomena to the Study of the New Testament and Gnosis," in *The New Testament and Gnosis: Essays in Honour of Robert McL. Wilson*, ed. by A. H. B. Logan and A. J. M. Wedderburn (Edinburgh: T. & T. Clark, 1983) 138–45.

terminology of that movement: one looks in vain for a detailed list of aeons, for mention of the Sophia myth, or for a Demiurge—and the distinction drawn between him and the highest God. What is one to make of these omissions? Most scholars have situated this text somewhere along the Valentinian trajectory, yet even here there is a great deal of diversity. W.-C. van Unnik and K. Grobel, for instance, have placed it extremely early, arguing that the young Valentinus himself penned this work before his ideas reached maturity. Hans Jonas, on the other hand, has placed it later on the second century trajectory, insisting that the document presupposes a developed Valentinian system.[15] Other scholars have chosen simply to sever the connection with Valentinianism. Most notable in this regard has been Hans-Martin Schenke in his *Die Herkunft des sogenannten Evangelium Veritatis* (1958). The tendency now is to view it as more or less attached to Valentinianism.[16] Yet we have a work which can reasonably be called early Valentinian, late Valentinian, or non-Valentinian.

In spite of these problems and differences of opinion, it is possible to make a relatively safe voyage between the Scylla of over-confidence and the Charybdis of extreme skepticism by isolating a corpus from the Nag Hammadi collection that has clear Valentinian components—at least based on the patristic descriptions—and that is made up of works probably composed by Valentinians themselves in the second and early third centuries. Much more certainty than this cannot be expected. The following seven works, then, make a defensible Valentinian corpus from Nag Hammadi: *The Prayer of the Apostle Paul* (I,1); *The Gospel of Truth* (I,3/XII,2); *The Treatise on the Resurrection* (I,4); *The Tripartite Tractate* (I,5); *The Gospel of Philip* (II,3); *The Interpretation of Knowledge* (XI,1); and *A Valentinian Exposition* (XI,2).[17] To this core group may be added three other works whose Valentinian qualities are more questionable: the first and second apocalypses attributed to James (V,3–4) and *The Letter of Peter to*

---

[15] Cf. Jonas's comments following Robert McL. Wilson's paper delivered at the Yale Conference in 1978: "I still believe that this is more plausible than the view that the *Gospel of Truth* is an embryonic stage of Valentinian development. My case centers around πλάνη: I think that this makes little sense in the *Gospel of Truth* unless one endows it with personal, hypostatized powers of agency and makes it a figure like the demiurge or Sophia Achamoth" (in *The Rediscovery of Gnosticism*, I, 142).

[16] This breadth of opinion concerning the *Gospel of Truth* is summarized by Wilson in "Valentinianism and the Gospel of Truth" (*The Rediscovery of Gnosticism*, I, 133–45). Rudolph has recently called the *Gospel of Truth* "a homily which shows vague affinities with the Valentinian school" (*Gnosis*, 319).

[17] Included in *A Valentinian Exposition* are the fragments which follow it in Codex 11. Cf. Jacques É. Ménard's remarks: "Les trois fragments sur le baptême et les deux sur l'eucharistie (Bap A = 40,1–29; Bap B = 40,30–41,38; Bap C = 42,1–43,19; Euch A = 43,20–38; Euch B = 44,14–37) renferment une doctrine assimilable au traité précédent et, dans l'état actuel de la recherche, ils sont à situer dans le sillage d'un enseignement valentinien" (*L'Exposé valentinien: Les fragments sur le baptême et sur l'eucharistie (NH XI,2)*, BCNHST 14 [Québec: Les Presses de l'Université Laval, 1985] 84).

Philip (VIII,2). This selection is fairly consistent with scholarly opinion.[18] The hypothetical nature of the selection, though, warrants not placing too much weight on any one particular work.

2.1.4

This Valentinian corpus of the traditional collection deriving from the Fathers supplemented by the recent one from the Nag Hammadi Library must now be enlarged by two other candidates recently brought to light. Eric Junod and Jean-Daniel Kaestli's magisterial two volume edition of the *Acts of John* appeared in 1983.[19] The Valentinian affinities of this work have often been highlighted,[20] but never have they been presented with the thoroughness found in Junod and Kaestli's work. They have demonstrated that chapters 94–102 and 109 of the *Acts of John* are probably of independent origin, and almost certainly derive from Valentinian circles, maybe in second century Syria. The following year, Josef Frickel published his extensive analysis of the Naassene passage in Hippolytus (which extends in Book V of the *Refutatio* from 6,4–10,2). He concluded that the final redactor of this section (which he claims Hippolytus incorporated almost verbatim into his work) was a Valentinian—perhaps even Heracleon himself. It remains to be seen whether this thesis will be accepted, and whether one can indeed peel away as many redactional layers from this work as Frickel believes.[21] These two source- and redaction-critical studies, then, have perhaps expanded our base of Valentinian sources. Both the Naassene passages in Hippolytus and the *Acts of John*—or, more accurately, certain sections in them—must be examined as potential candidates for being Valentinian sources. The tentative nature of the claims, though, must not be forgotten.

2.2.1

Having delimited the primary sources for a study of Valentinianism one must assess their value. This is not an easy task. The scholarly tendency is to separate the Nag Hammadi material from that found in the Fathers and to view the two bodies of information in roughly the same manner as most NT scholars

[18] Henry A. Green would add to this list *The Apocryphon of James* (I,2), *The Exegesis of the Soul* (II,6), *The Authoritative Teaching* (VI,3), and *The Second Treatise of the Great Seth* (VII,2), while removing *The Second Apocalypse of James* and *The Letter of Peter to Philip* ("Ritual in Valentinian Gnosticism," *JRH* 12 [1982] 111). Koschorke ("Patristische Materialen," 122) would include the basic seven (having reservations about *The Treatise on the Resurrection*) while seeing some Valentinian elements in *The First Apocalypse of James* and *The Testimony of Truth*. Michel Tardieu, for his part, would include *The Testimony of Truth* and *The Apocryphon of James* and remove the two apocalypses of the same name. See "Le Congrès de Yale sur le Gnosticism (28–31 mars 1978)," *REAug* 24 (1978) 192.

[19] *Acta Iohannis*, ed. by Eric Junod and Jean-Daniel Kaestli, CCSA 1–2 (Brepols: Turnhout, 1983).

[20] For a discussion of scholarly opinion on this matter, see *Acta Iohannis*, 590.

[21] Josef Frickel, *Hellenistische Erlösung in christlicher Deutung: Die gnostische Naassenerschrift*, NHS 19 (Leiden: Brill, 1984).

now view Acts and the letters of Paul. Influenced by the arguments of John Knox, John Hurd and Gerd Lüdemann, scholars are increasingly basing their understanding of Paul on the evidence from his letters (the "primary evidence"). They use the deutero-Pauline letters and Acts critically, cautiously, and only after having drained the "primary evidence" of all its information.[22] The Nag Hammadi works, which allegedly come to us directly "from the source's mouth," are often seen as primary and given pride of place in any reconstruction of Valentinianism, while the sources found in the Fathers suffer the same fate as do the Acts accounts in any reconstruction of the life and teachings of Paul: they are to be consulted only after one exhausts the "primary sources," and their testimony is accepted with due regard for their redactional *Tendenzen*. In some respects Rudolph is a good representative of this modern position. In his recent and important study, *Gnosis: The Nature and History of Gnosticism*, he insists on "having deliberately given precedence to the original works today abundantly available, above all in Coptic, and less to the heresiological reports."[23] Rudolph's position would be unquestionable if the analogy with Pauline scholarship were more exact. As it stands, however, the situation facing the student of Valentinianism is more complicated.

2.2.2

The primacy of the Nag Hammadi sources is open to question on internal and external grounds. *Internally,* as has already been said, not one of these works claims to represent the views of Valentinus or to be Valentinian. There is a problem of circularity here. The Nag Hammadi works are designated Valentinian on the strength of the patristic accounts. Thus, the "primary sources" are only primary insofar as one accepts the claims made in the "secondary sources." This methodological problem has not received the attention it deserves. It also casts serious doubt on the primacy of this new source base. *Externally* there is the dual problem of dating and provenance. The receipts and fragments of correspondence which were used to pad the bindings of the codices help us to date their fabrication to *ca.* 350 C.E. As well, the proximity of the find to the Pachomian monastery, coupled with the mention of "monks" and "Father Pachom" in the bindings, makes it likely that the writings derive in some manner from the library of a monastery. As Rudolph suggests, Athanasius's ban on heretical books (in

---

[22] For a fine discussion of Pauline methodology see John C. Hurd, *The Origin of I Corinthians* (London: SPCK, 1965 [reprinted in 1983 by Mercer University Press, Macon, GA]), 3–42 (and xiii–xxi of the new edition). More recently there is Gerd Lüdemann's excellent work: *Paul, Apostle to the Gentiles: Studies in Chronology* (Philadelphia: Fortress, 1984 [1980]). They both acknowledge the pioneering work of John Knox in his *Chapters in a Life of Paul* (New York: Abingdon, 1950).

[23] Rudolph (*Gnosis,* 3) makes this point when contrasting his own work with Leisegang's (1924). In other respects, though, Rudolph reminds one of the older approach to Paul since he tends to use whichever source is suitable to his presentation. For instance, his description of Valentinianism is derived almost exclusively from the patristic sources.

his Paschal Letter of 367) could well have led to their burial.[24] According to R. van den Broek, "there is a growing consensus that the books were collected from various quarters by Pachomian monks who read them as edifying literature."[25] What we are probably dealing with, then, are Valentinian works still selected (and perhaps even altered) by non-Valentinians, and perhaps two centuries after their *floruit*. In addition, we have no way of knowing for certain when or where these works were actually composed, and how much modification had crept in over the years (even disregarding the important process of translation from Greek into Coptic—a problem which is absent from the Greek works of Irenaeus, Clement, Origen, and Hippolytus).

There is also no reason to assume that these works accurately represent the breadth of second century Valentinianism. For example, the emphasis on asceticism found throughout the entire Nag Hammadi corpus could tell us as much about the predilections of fourth century monks as it does about second century Valentinianism. Henry Green has voiced this point recently in his book *The Economic and Social Origins of Gnosticism*.[26]

> it should be emphasized that the Nag Hammadi library, if associated with the Pachomian monasteries, would have been biased towards the collection of ascetic works. Libertine behavior would have been considered heretical. Consequently, it may well be that just as the heresiologists were biased in their descriptions of the Gnostics (libertinism), so too the Nag Hammadi library may present a biased account of Gnostic tendencies toward asceticism.

---

[24] *Gnosis*, 43.

[25] R. van den Broek, "The Present State of Gnostic Studies," *VC* 37 (1983) 47. Armand Veilleux argues that the connection between the Nag Hammadi library and the Pachomian monasteries is not as firm as many assume ("Monachisme et gnose," *LTP* 40 [1985] 3–10). This view is supported by Louis Painchaud (in a personal letter), and by Paul-Hubert Poirier in "La bibliothèque copte de Nag Hammadi: sa nature et son importance," *SR* 15 (1986) 308 (a paper he delivered in Toronto in February, 1986). Veilleux's article is a helpful corrective to the assumption that the fabrication of the codices necessarily tells us something about who used them. Nevertheless, given the few remaining pieces to this Nag Hammadi puzzle, the best solution remains to link these codices in some manner with the Pachomian monastery.

[26] Green, *The Economic and Social Origins*, 226. Henry Chadwick alluded to this already in one of the plenary addresses of the Yale Conference of 1978: "One would not, of course, expect those gnostic texts that could be studied at Chenoboskion with reasonable impunity to be likely to favor libertinism, and therefore the picture of gnostic ethics to be obtained from the Nag Hammadi codices might be thought only to represent the nonlibertine standpoint" (in "The Domestication of Gnosis," *The Rediscovery of Gnosticism*, I, 15–16). On the asceticism of these monks, see now Philip Rousseau's *Pachomius: The Making of a Community in Fourth-Century Egypt* (Berkeley: University of California Press, 1985).

In conclusion, we can say that while students of Valentinianism are grateful for this chance discovery of texts from the Egyptian desert which has dramatically expanded our source base, to treat these newly-found works as primary in the same sense as we do the Pauline letters is simply not justified.

2.2.3

The Valentinian sources which are found in the patristic works pose another type of difficulty: what percentage of these sources is truly Valentinian and how much is patristic overlay? Indeed, many scholars have rejoiced over the Nag Hammadi find because they believe that finally it has given them access to sources which do not include commentary and reformulation. Underlying all of this—to state the matter directly—is the question: can we trust the Church Fathers' depiction of Valentinianism or not? To ask the question in this manner, though, is unfortunate for several reasons.

First, the Fathers ought not to be taken as a group any more than the New Testament writers are. The trust that one accords to these works varies from author to author and from narrative to narrative. Irenaeus's account of the Valentinians, for instance, is certainly more trustworthy than Theodoret's, and the narrative in the first book of his *Adversus haereses* is more useful for students of Gnosticism than his passing remarks at the end.

Second, trust is a relative matter, and we have to keep in mind that second and third century authors were not as concerned as we are today with verbatim reporting, or as Aquinas was with arguing a case. Recapturing the primary Valentinian material often will entail disentangling it from an author's redactional tendency. Students of the New Testament apply this principle to the book of Acts usually without despairing of ever being able to recover some Pauline elements or, more usually, to the Gospel texts with the hope of recovering at least some early traditions. In this regard, more studies are needed like Gérard Vallée's *A Study in Anti-Gnostic Polemics,* which sets out to examine some of the redactional concerns of three leading heresiologists: Irenaeus, Hippolytus (or the writer of the *Refutatio* if it was a different person), and Epiphanius.[27]

Third, it must be acknowledged that the Fathers have often reproduced the words of their opponents far more extensively and probably far more literally than the author of Acts ever did of Paul. For examples of this one need only point to the letter of Ptolemy to Flora embedded in Epiphanius, the exegetical observations of Heracleon which caused Origen such worry, and the remarks of Theodotus transmitted by Clement. To cast doubt on the basic reliability of Origen's quotations from Heracleon, for instance, is to be unduly skeptical.

Finally, lurking at times behind the questions of trust is a negative judgment concerning the merits of the Fathers' scholarship. To express the matter bluntly

---

[27] Gérard Vallée, *A Study in Anti-Gnostic Polemics: Irenaeus, Hippolytus, and Epiphanius,* SCJ 1 (Waterloo: Wilfrid Laurier University Press, 1981).

again: if they were so clearly outclassed intellectually, how likely is it that they ever understood the intricacies of Valentinianism? This issue, which frequently can be read between the lines in modern analyses, does not often surface in print. Thus one admires Rudolph for his openness on this matter. At one point in his *Gnosis* he claims that Valentinus represented "a high level of erudition" which, in many respects, surpassed his "petty [kleinliche] orthodox opponents like Irenaeus and Hippolytus."[28] Two remarks are needed here. Valentinus may indeed have acquired "a high level of erudition," but that is by no means certain. To be sure, we are told by Tertullian (*Adv. val.* 4) that he almost became head of the Christian community in Rome, that the beauty of his writings impressed even his critics, and that he had several learned disciples. But there is only a handful of fragments through which we can assess the "erudition" of this fascinating individual. More importantly, though, to call Irenaeus "petty" in comparison is to push the extremely limited evidence about Valentinus much further than it will allow and to be overly critical of Irenaeus's rather extensive literary output. The sources themselves provide nothing to suggest that Irenaeus was outclassed, that he could not understand the Valentinian position, and that consequently his description is untrustworthy.[29]

2.3

To conclude this section, we must ask how this evidence should be used. We have information deriving from two groups of sources. These sources are distinct, each having primary and secondary features; moreover, they are not homogeneous themselves.[30] The preceding discussion has suggested, to continue the earlier analogy, that the Nag Hammadi sources for Valentinianism are probably less "primary" than Paul's letters, while the patristic sources are in some respects more "primary" than Acts. There is, therefore, no need to ground an examination of Valentinianism exclusively on the evidence from Nag Hammadi — or even to begin necessarily with that group of sources.

It matters little with which group we begin this study, as long as we keep

---

[28] *Gnosis,* 210.

[29] One detects German and Protestant streams running through Rudolph's book. "Protestant" in his downplaying of the patristic sources, and his quest for a primary, undistorted stratum of Christian revelation. "German" in his adherence to the principal conclusion of the "religionsgeschichtliche Schule," that Gnosticism is not a development from Christianity but is also (and especially) a pre- and para-Christian phenomenon. (I think, for instance, of Simone Pétrement's recent book, *Le Dieu séparé: Les origines du gnosticisme* [Paris: Les Éditions du Cerf, 1984], which offers an alternative view of gnostic origins.) One could add, at least in terms of vocabulary, a Marxist stream. To give only one example from Rudolph's book: "Thus Gnosis can be largely understood as an ideology of the dependent petty bourgeoisie which however feels itself called to freedom on the ideological-religious plane" (292).

[30] This point must be kept in mind especially concerning the Nag Hammadi material. One need only compare the fragment from Plato's *Republic* (VI,5) with the *The Gospel of Thomas* (II,2) to appreciate the lack of homogeneity in the Nag Hammadi works.

them distinct and drain one of all its information before proceeding to the next.
We have chosen to start with the Fathers. Later in this study it will be possible
to assess, case by case, the degree of overlap which exists between the traditional
and the newer accounts. In fact, a few scholars have already found this overlap
to be rather extensive, at least between some of the major patristic sources and
texts from Nag Hammadi.[31] It remains to be seen how distinct these two groups
of sources actually are, and which turns out to be more useful in understanding
Valentinianism.

3. VALENTINIANISM

3.1
     The Fathers provide information about an opposing group which they call,
among other things, Valentinian. As we have seen in the section above, they also
have included passages from their opponents' works. From these passages and
from the patristic descriptions of Valentinianism it has been possible to add
other "primary" Valentinian sources from the Nag Hammadi Library—and
recently, by critical textual examination, to add another patristic passage and one
from the apocryphal Acts. Before proceeding to a detailed examination of these
sources, it is useful to describe in a general manner what we mean by
Valentinianism.
     Valentinianism is almost as difficult to describe as second century Chris-
tianity itself, of which it was a vital part. A good argument can be made for the
difficulty of distinguishing between Valentinian and non-Valentinian works, as
we have seen above. As well, the uniformity of the system and the possibility of
tracing its roots to Valentinus himself are far from certain.[32] One must also
recognize that "Valentinianism" is a theoretical construct based on works which
are essentially doctrinal in nature (whether heresiological or not) and which do
not necessarily reflect a clearly delimited social group. In spite of these
difficulties, I follow Sagnard in holding that the various patristic reports of

---

[31] In an earlier article, Wisse highlighted the differences between the Nag Hammadi
works and the evidence provided by the heresiologists ("The Nag Hammadi Library and
the Heresiologists," VC 25 [1971] 205-28). The end of the pendulum, though, can be
allowed to swing over to the other side as well, and one can point to recent works which
have emphasized the similarities. See Wilson, "Twenty Years After," in B. Barc (ed.),
Colloque international sur les textes de Nag Hammadi (Québec, 22-25 août 1978),
BCNHSE 1 (Québec: Les Presses de l'Université Laval, 1981). So also R. F. Refoulé,
Tertullien: Traité de la prescription contre les hérétiques, SC 46 (Paris: Les Éditions du
Cerf, 1957) 16-18; and J.-C. Fredouille, Tertullien: Contre les valentiniens, tome 1, SC 280
(Paris: Les Éditions du Cerf, 1980) 39-41. A middle position may well emerge after more
studies are carried out on individual works.
[32] The Fathers highlighted the diversity which they found among the Valentinians, and
viewed this as being proof of their error. A good example is Irenaeus in his Adversus
haereses (I,11,1): Ἴδωμεν νῦν καὶ τὴν τούτων ἄστατον γνώμην, δύο που καὶ τριῶν ὄντων πῶς περὶ
τῶν αὐτῶν οὐ τὰ αὐτὰ λέγουσιν, ἀλλὰ τοῖς πράγμασιν καὶ τοῖς ὀνόμασιν ἐναντία ἀποφαίνονται.

Valentinian teaching do indeed manifest a large measure of agreement and that the simplest way of explaining this agreement is to assume that there existed a movement one can call Valentinian, which derived at least the core of its teaching from Valentinus, who flourished in the mid-second century C.E.[33]

The Nag Hammadi works have not been particularly helpful in verifying the patristic claims about Valentinianism. However, this does not warrant acute skepticism about the existence of such a group. The Fathers' relentless attack on the Valentinian views enables us to presume that Valentinians must have existed,[34] and that they must have understood themselves as Christians. This is validated by the fact that the Fathers' description of Valentinianism coincides in some parts at least with the statements found in the Nag Hammadi works. The material affinity allows us to speak (albeit cautiously) of a Valentinian school, even though it is the patristic sources which offer the nomenclature and the overview.

Irenaeus's account of Valentinianism in the first book of his *Adversus haereses* (1,1-7,6) conveniently serves as our basic source for understanding the Valentinians. Sagnard has convincingly shown not only that there is a considerable amount of consistency in the patristic descriptions of Valentinianism, but also that this "Great Notice" which begins Irenaeus's account provides the best overview of Valentinianism—at least in terms of myth and philosophy, for the social underpinnings of the movement were of little concern to him. This is not to say that this overview is accurate in every respect or even that it should be the benchmark by which we judge what is authentically Valentinian or not. But it is a good place to start. The following is a summary of Irenaeus's "Great Notice." This particular form of Valentinianism will be called "classical Valentinianism" throughout this study.

3.2.1

The Valentinian divine world, or Pleroma, is composed of a core of thirty aeons or worlds which are arranged in pairs. The male-female pairing of these aeons, called syzygy (συζυγία), is a reflection of their completeness. A tripartite division of aeons is standard, the first eight (the Ogdoad) being discussed in more detail than the groups of ten and twelve which follow. The first pair, or Primal

---

[33] Sagnard, *La gnose*. Cf. especially his conclusions, pp. 562-67. Note also the remarks of Yvonne Janssens: "Suivant nos constatations, les documents les plus anciens de la gnose valentinienne: fragments de Valentin et d'Héracléon, Lettre de Ptolémé à Flora, *Evangelium Veritatis*, dans leur vocabulaire et leurs conceptions, manifestent de nombreux traits de ressemblance, suffisants pour conclure à l'existence d'une école que l'on continuera à appeler l'école de Valentin. Une grande liberté existe à l'intérieur de l'école; ses penseurs sont très personnels" ("Héracléon: Commentaire sur l'Évangile selon Saint Jean," *Mus* 72 [1959] 294).

[34] Tertullian vouches not only for the existence of the Valentinians, but also for their numerical importance: "Valentiniani, frequentissimum plane collegium inter haereticos" (*Adv. val.* 1,1).

14 Sin in Valentinianism

Dyad, are Abyss (Βυθός)—also called Progenitor (Προαρχή), Profather (Προπάτωρ) or even Father (Πάτηρ)—and Silence (Σιγή)—also called Thought (Ἔννοια) and Grace (Χάρις).[35] The Abyss is described as unknowable, invisible, and eternal.[36] At times it is considered alone, beyond the male-female pairing, but usually it is a male aeon "yoked" to Silence (*Adv. haer.* 2,4). Through her he emitted Understanding (Νοῦς)[37] and Truth (Ἀλήθεια), forming the basic Tetrad or the root of all things. From this pair proceed Word (Λόγος) and Life (Ζωή), who in turn emit Human Being (Ἄνθρωπος) and Church (Ἐκκλησία), forming the second Tetrad and completing the Ogdoad. Word and Life engender ten other aeons while Human Being and Church add the last twelve.

3.2.2

Only Understanding knows Abyss, and initially all the other aeons wanted to know more about their origin. For Wisdom (Σοφία), the last aeon, this desire turned into a passion (Ἐνθύμησις) which set into motion disorder in the Pleroma and, ultimately, the devolution of the divine being. To stop Wisdom from straying too far, Abyss, via Understanding but without Silence, emitted another aeon, Limit or Boundary (Ὅρος)—also called Cross (Σταυρός) and Redeemer (Λυτρωτής).[38] Wisdom's desire was separated from her and placed outside the Pleroma, in shadow and emptiness (σκία καὶ κενώμα—4,1), to become the "Lower Sophia" or Achamoth (Ἀχαμώθ).[39] She retained a pneumatic nature while being weak, "feminine" and formless because she was the product of Wisdom acting without her male pair. Understanding then emitted a new couple: Christ and the Holy Spirit. Christ taught the others that the Father is unknowable directly and can only be known through the Son, while the Holy Spirit brought harmony and peace throughout the aeons of the Pleroma (2,5). As an expression of their joy and *gnosis* all the aeons then joined in emitting a perfect aeon, Jesus—also called Savior (Σώτηρ) and All (Πάντα)—and his accompanying angels (2,6). The divine world was then stable again, with Wisdom's desire having led to an expansion of the original thirty aeons and the expulsion of Achamoth from the Pleroma.

3.3.1

This drama which was carried out in the Pleroma was enacted again outside the divine world. Christ left the Pleroma to give Achamoth a form κατ' οὐσίαν μόνον, ἀλλ' οὐ τὴν κατὰ γνῶσιν (4,1), but when he returned to his domain she longed for him and found herself barred from the Pleroma by the aeon Limit.

[35] *Adv. haer.* I,1,1: συνυπάρχειν δ'αὐτῷ καὶ Ἔννοιαν, ἣν δὴ καὶ Χάριν καὶ Σιγὴν ὀνομάζουσι.
[36] This is reminiscent of the 'Ein-Sof in the Medieval Jewish Kabbalah.
[37] *Adv. haer.* I,1,1: τὸν δὲ Νοῦν τοῦτον καὶ Μονογενῆ καλοῦσι καὶ Πατέρα καὶ Ἀρχὴν τῶν πάντων.
[38] *Adv. haer.* I,2,4: Διὰ δὲ τοῦ Ὅρου τούτου φασὶ κεκαθάρθαι καὶ ἐστηρίχθαι τὴν Σοφίαν καὶ ἀποκατασταθῆναι τῇ συζυγίᾳ.
[39] This no doubt derives from the Hebrew word for wisdom, חכמה.

Christ then sent Jesus and his angels to cure her of her passions, and he gave her a form "according to gnosis" (4,5). Her passions, stripped from her (as they had been from her mother), gave rise to matter (ὕλη), while out of her turning or "conversion" to Jesus came the psychic material and out of her purified self came the pneumatic fruits. Thus the world outside the Pleroma was filled and provided with a threefold nature. This triadic base is a fundamental feature of Valentinianism.

3.3.2
Out of the psychic material Achamoth created the Demiurge—also called God, Father, and King—who in turn created our universe. In his realm he established and oversaw seven heavens (the Hebdomad), which are not merely spaces but have an intelligent nature and are called angels. Achamoth, meanwhile, dwelt in the eighth heaven, also called the Intermediary (Μεσότης). Due to his ignorance of the divine world, the Demiurge naively and arrogantly considered himself to be the supreme being.

3.4.1
Human beings were created by the Demiurge, who formed them out of matter (ὕλη) and gave them a soul (ψυχή). At the same time, some human souls were impregnated by Achamoth with a pneumatic seed (5,5-6), giving them (the pneumatics) a triple nature. This also allowed the divine element to enter the Hebdomad. Humankind, though, remained ignorant of this fact, as did the Demiurge, and accepted the reality presented to it by the Demiurge; that is, of a universe guided by him, the alleged God and creator of all. Human ignorance of reality above the Hebdomad, and of the pneumatic element which has entered the world, allows the world to continue existing as it does, and facilitates the worship of its creator as the supreme God.

3.4.2
This situation was altered by a desire in the Pleroma to recover all the pneumatic particles and to rid itself of matter by bringing the world and the Hebdomad to an end. Valentinianism does not have the same apocalyptic urgency about the End Time as we find in many first century Jewish and Christian works, but eschatology remains fundamental to this system of thought. A radical transformation of the cosmos was expected in the near future (7,1), with the following scenario being the most common. Achamoth would ascend into the Pleroma and pair up with Jesus. Those human beings who possessed some of the divine were destined to abandon their hylic element in our universe, rid themselves of their *psyche* in the Intermediary, and, stripped to their pneumatic self, enter the Pleroma to join the angels who surrounded Jesus. The Demiurge's destiny was to replace Achamoth in the Intermediary, along with the people who lacked a pneumatic spark but who had chosen "the better path" (7,5). The πνευμάτικον, then, would be collected in the Pleroma, and the ψύχικον in the

Intermediary, but the σάρχιχον, including the people who had "chosen the worse," would be annihilated.

3.4.3

The Savior was given to the world to remind the pneumatics of the divine seed which lies within their soul and of the destiny which awaits them. He was to train others to choose the better path in order to survive the destruction and ascend to the Intermediary. This was Christ who was formed by the Demiurge and so given only a psychic nature, but who received the pneumatic essence of the Savior (Jesus) at his baptism (7,2). The essentials of Christianity, then, remain firmly rooted in Valentinianism: Christ is the Savior of humankind, in a world about to come to an end, and salvation is possible only for those who recognize his divine nature and the importance of his message.

4. OVERVIEW

4.1

The intent of this study is to determine what role sin played in Valentinianism. This is carried out by examining all of the primary sources, beginning with those found in the Fathers, then turning to the Nag Hammadi texts. In some respects, this study is both too large and too narrow in scope. Some might argue that we have bitten off more than we can chew by attempting to pull together such a wide and disparate collection of texts and to deal with Valentinianism as an entity. Others might ask why we have ignored all of the choice morsels by focusing on a relatively insignificant aspect of Valentinianism, especially when so much else needs to be explored. Both objections have some merit. It is our hope that an exploration of sin in Valentinian thought will prove to be nourishing in the end. In the meantime, a few explanations can be offered about our eating habits.

Valentinianism is not as well understood as scholars tend to assume. The state of affairs in part reflects the theological-philosophical approach which has usually been taken to the material. Studies are required on many facets of this important movement. Much still needs to be done to give bodies to these aeon- and Pleroma-filled "Valentinians." We need to ask, for instance, what distinguished a Christian artisan living in Lyon whom Irenaeus accepted from one whom he dismissed as Valentinian. Our ignorance about Valentinianism also reflects the tendency to place this movement on the gnostic trajectory, extending from pre-Christian times to the twentieth century, rather than encountering it as a vital second century Christian movement. The Palestinian Jewish/Hellenistic Jewish dichotomy has recently suffered severe criticism; so too must the gnostic Christian/non-gnostic Christian division be questioned.

We have chosen to use the term "Valentinianism" rather than "Valentinian Gnosticism" throughout this study. In part this is a matter of self-definition. These people considered themselves Christians, not gnostics, and if we are now to give them a label, "Valentinian" is preferable. Also, "Gnosticism" is too vague and ill-defined, and still carries with it too much accessory (negative or positive) baggage.[40]

It is in this broad second century Christian context that the use of sin in Valentinianism becomes especially intriguing. Sin itself may turn out to be relatively insignificant to Valentinians, but its surprising presence in the Valentinian texts from Nag Hammadi provides added incentive to reassess this movement. It is as though a few more letters were discovered in which the apostle Paul addressed churches he had founded (say in Petra and Bosra) and the recipients were identified as Jewish Christians. This might not change one's overall view of Paul, but it would surely force a reassessment of the Pauline material. A study of sin in Valentinianism, then, is an intrinsic part of the fresh examination of that movement which has begun after Nag Hammadi.

4.2

This study is in three parts. In chapter 2 we examine the Valentinian sources of patristic origin. The intent is to determine which texts provide information about sin and then to examine carefully what they say. Detailed exegeses of the relevant passages follow a broad survey of all the sources. In chapter 3 we do the same for the works from Nag Hammadi. Each of the works is treated separately and in context, and the patristic ones are kept separate from those from Nag Hammadi. In chapter 4 we summarize the results and set the Valentinian understanding of sin within the larger framework of Valentinianism.

[40] For a fine analysis of the sources dealing with Valentinian self-designation, cf. Anne M. McGuire, "Valentinus and the *Gnostike Hairesis:* An Investigation of Valentinus' Position in the History of Gnosticism," (Yale Ph.D., 1983) 11– 35. For a critique of the false labeling of some early Christians as gnostics, cf. Morton Smith, "The History of the Term *Gnostikos,*" in *The Rediscovery of Gnosticism,* II, 796–807. His following point is important: "By our academic prerogative, without considering ancient usage, we recognize certain schools as 'gnostic'; hence 'gnosticism' will be defined; and the resultant definition of 'gnosticism' will prove the 'gnostic' character of these schools" (798). For a recent survey of the ways in which Gnosticism has been understood over the centuries, cf. M. Tardieu's "Histoire du mot 'gnostique' " in *Introduction à la littérature gnostique. I. Histoire du mot "gnostique", Instruments de travail, Collections retrouvées avant 1945,* par M. Tardieu et J.-D. Dubois (Paris: Les Éditions du Cerf, 1986).

2

The Evidence from the Fathers

1. INTRODUCTION

1.1

Before the publication of the works found near Nag Hammadi in 1945, the literary remains of the Valentinians had to be unearthed exclusively from the Fathers. These patristic writings contain a wealth of Valentinian source material, but provide neither a uniform nor a positive portrayal of this group. As we have seen in the previous chapter, the evidence supplied by these patristic writers must be assessed critically. This is especially important because of the antagonism toward this group of "heretics" evinced by the heresiologists, one which in its hostility and one-sidedness is reminiscent of Paul's attacks on the Jewish-Christian "opponents" in several of his letters.

One of the most common anti-Valentinian charges was that these Christians often were licentious and considered themselves removed from moral considerations as a result of their possession of *gnosis*. Actually, one would expect the argument against the Valentinians to revolve around sin, at least in part, with one side claiming to be free of its power and the other saying that in fact these libertines were the worst of sinners. In other words, one would think that the Valentinians, emerging from a Christian matrix and faced with attacks on their libertine behavior every step of the way, would be forced to clarify their position *vis-à-vis* sin. Yet one finds no textual support for a controversy over sin.

1.2

The purpose of this chapter is to determine, from the patristic evidence alone, precisely what the Valentinians had to say about sin. The first task is to sift carefully through all of the evidence for Valentinianism which the Fathers provide in order to isolate those sources which can be of most use to us. The sources which do actually introduce sin into a Valentinian discussion are then analyzed in depth. As we shall see, the discussion of sin, while not extensive, is nevertheless worthy of examination.

2. A SURVEY OF THE PATRISTIC EVIDENCE
FOR VALENTINIANISM

2.1 Introduction

The patristic sources which contain the fragmentary Valentinian remains have been identified in the preceding chapter. Our concern now is to determine what these reveal about the Valentinian use of sin. Each of the sources identified by Sagnard is examined in turn, and this is followed by an overview of Koschorke's selection of later patristic material.

2.2.1 The Fragments of Valentinus

Valentinus seems to have had a long and active life. The quantity and quality of his writings impressed even his critics. Unfortunately, the search for Valentinus in some respects resembles the search for the pre-Socratic philosophers because only scraps of information remain about his life! His *opus* would fit comfortably on the heads of two or three pins, displacing few angels in the process. Roughly four hundred words are all that remain of Valentinus's own writings,[2] and these are scattered in fragments preserved by the Fathers. Our best information comes from the six fragments quoted by Clement in his *Stromata,* together with his supplementary comments. Two others derive from Hippolytus's *Refutatio,* while one is found in *De sancta ecclesia,* a work formerly attributed to Anthimus of Nicodemia but now shown to have been penned probably by Marcellus of Ancyra.[3] These nine fragments[4] have been conveniently reprinted in Walther Völker's *Quellen.*[5] Scholarly discussion of the fragments is extensive.[6] None of these fragments, though, or the contexts in which they occur, show any concern for sin. The absence of any reference to sin is not significant given the fragmentary nature of the evidence. It is also important to keep in mind that virtually all of the key aspects of the "Valentinian system" listed by Irenaeus do not actually occur in these fragments.

---

[1] For a reconstruction of Valentinus's career based on the few and often conflicting sources, see McGuire, "Valentinus," 76–90.

[2] The Greek text has 411 words presented as direct quotations and roughly 100 as indirect quotes.

[3] Concerning the authorship of *De sancta ecclesia,* see G. C. Stead, "In Search of Valentinus," in *The Rediscovery of Gnosticism,* I, 75.

[4] A tenth fragment may occur in a work attributed to Eulogius of Alexandria and quoted by Photius. A. Hilgenfeld includes it, but others do not. See his *Die Ketzergeschichte des Urchristenthums* (Leipzig: Fues's Verlag, 1884) 302.

[5] Walther Völker, *Quellen zur Geschichte der christlichen Gnosis* (Tübingen: Mohr, 1932) 57–60. He reproduces O. Stählin's text for Clement's *Stromata* (*Clemens Alexandrinus. Zweiter Band. Stromata I-VI,* GCS 52, 3. Auflage hrsg. von L. Früchtel [Berlin: Akademie-Verlag, 1969]); P. Wendland's text for Hippolytus's *Refutatio* (*Hippolytus Werke. Dritter Band. Refutatio omnium haeresium,* GCS 26 [Leipzig: Hinrichs'sche Buchhandlung, 1916]); and M. Mercati's edition of *De sancta ecclesia* (Rome, 1901, 96). W. Foerster provides an English translation of these fragments in *Gnosis,* ed. and trans. by R. McL. Wilson, 2 vols. (Oxford: Clarendon, 1972–74).

[6] Cf. Hilgenfeld, *Ketzergeschichte,* 293–305; Sagnard, *La gnose,* 121–26 (with a French translation of the fragments); and Stead, "In Search," 78–84.

2.2.2 The Letter of Ptolemy to Flora

This letter, preserved by Epiphanius (*Panarion* XXXIII,3,1-10), is attributed to a disciple of Valentinus. K. Holl's edition of the Greek text remains the standard one,[7] and it has been complemented by Gilles Quispel's translation and commentary.[8] It is remarkable that in this letter, in which Ptolemy gives a considerable amount of ethical instruction to a certain Flora, no concern whatsoever is shown for sin.

2.2.3 Clement of Alexandria's *Excerpta ex Theodoto*

There are 86 sections in this work, most of which reproduce the words of Theodotus. Some also are from other Valentinians. Clement has added his own comments, and these redactional elements at times are not easily distinguishable from the rest. The identity of Theodotus remains unknown, but no doubt he lived in the second century and, perhaps, in Clement's Alexandria. Sagnard's edition of this work remains the basic one.[9] Sin (ἁμάρτημα) is discussed once (52,2) in the *Excerpta,* and evil (πονηρία) several times (76,2; 77,1; 81,1-3). This concept clearly does not play a leading role in Theodotus's text as presented by Clement, but a closer examination is in order.

2.2.4 The Fragments of Heracleon

Clement claims that Heracleon was Valentinus's most celebrated disciple (ὁ τῆς Οὐαλεντίνου σχολῆς δοκιμώτατος).[10] Fifty-one fragments of his work survive, forty-eight of which are imbedded in Origen's *Commentary on John.* Cécile Blanc's outstanding edition of this work now presents the standard critical text, replacing Erwin Preuschen's.[11] The three remaining fragments come from Clement's *Eclogae propheticae* (25,1),[12] his *Stromata* (IV,9),[13] and Photius's *epistula* 134.[14]

---

[7] *Epiphanius. Erster Band. Ancoratus und Panarion Haer. 1-33,* GCS 25 (Leipzig: Hinrichs'sche Buchhandlung, 1915).

[8] *Ptolémée. Lettre à Flora,* SC 24 (Paris: Les Éditions du Cerf, 1949).

[9] *Clément d'Alexandrie: Extraits de Théodote,* SC 23, 2ième éd. (Paris: Les Éditions du Cerf, 1970 [1948]). Sagnard reproduces O. Stählin's text: *Clemens Alexandrinus. Dritter Band. Stromata Buch VII und VIII. Excerpta ex Theodoto. Eclogae Propheticae. Quis dives salvetur. Fragmente,* GCS 17 (Leipzig: Hinrichs'sche Buchhandlung, 1909) 124.

[10] Clement, *Stromata,* IV,9 (71,1).

[11] *Origène: Commentaire sur saint Jean,* tomes I (livres I-V), II (livres VI et X), III (livre XIII), et IV (livre XIX-XX), SC 120, 157, 222, 290 (Paris: Les Éditions du Cerf, 1966-82). When the final volume appears, this edition will completely replace Preuschen's *Origenes Werke. Vierter Band. Der Johanneskommentar,* GCS 10 (Leipzig: Hinrichs'sche Buchhandlung, 1903). I follow Blanc's renumbered text (Preuschen's pagination is in the margins of her work).

[12] Stählin, *Clemens Alexandrinus. Dritter Band.*

[13] Stählin, *Clemens Alexandrinus. Dritter Band.*

[14] Migne, *PG* 101, 984c.

These fragments have conveniently been extracted by Völker[15] and translated by Foerster.[16] Detailed commentary is available in Foerster's *Von Valentin zu Herakleon*.[17] Sin in these fragments is not mentioned frequently, but it does occur in fragments 10, 40 and 41 where it seems to have been an integral part of Heracleon's thought.[18]

2.2.5 Irenaeus's *Adversus Haereses*

An outstanding edition of the Latin and Greek texts of Irenaeus's *Adversus haereses*, with accompanying commentary and translation, is now complete in the *Sources chrétiennes* series.[19] Irenaeus wrote the *Adversus* to expose the gnostic way of thinking (Book 1), to refute it (Book 2), and then to present a positive description of the doctrine which is or ought to be preached by the Church (Books 3-5). In the first two books there is only one passage which attributes concern with sin to a Valentinian (I,21,2 — re: Marcus). This pericope is worth exploring because of its explicit reference to sin and the implication that remission of sins was of concern to the psychics.

2.2.6 Hippolytus's *Refutatio Omnium Haeresium*

This work, sometimes called the *Philosophumena*,[20] and probably written

---

[15] Völker, *Quellen*, 63-86. The Greek text of the fragments is also found (unnumbered) in Hilgenfeld's *Ketzergeschichte*, 472-98.

[16] Foerster, *Gnosis*, 162-83.

[17] Foerster, *Von Valentin zu Herakleon: Untersuchungen über die Quellen und die Entwicklung der valentinianischen Gnosis* (Geissen: Töpelmann, 1928) 31-44. He renumbers the fragments.

[18] In these three fragments, ἁμαρτία occurs four times, and ἁμάρτημα twice (or five times, depending on where one decides to end Heracleon's words).

[19] *Irénée de Lyon: Contre les hérésies*, Books 1 (SC 263-64), 2 (SC 293-94), 3 (SC 210-11) all edited by Adelin Rousseau and Louis Doutreleau; Book 4 (SC 100) by A. Rousseau, Bertrand Hemmerdinger, L. Doutreleau, and Charles Mercier; and Book 5 (SC 152-53) by A. Rousseau, L. Doutreleau and C. Mercier (Paris: Les Éditions du Cerf, 1965-82). A volume of tables and complete indices has been promised by the editors. This edition replaces W. W. Harvey's *Sancti Irenaei: Libros quinque adversus haereses* (Cambridge: University Press, 1857 — reprinted in 1965 by Gregg Press Incorporated, Ridgewood NJ). A. Rousseau has prepared a (slightly) revised one-volume translation entitled *Irénée de Lyon: Contre les hérésies; Dénonciation et réfutation de la gnose au nom menteur*, 2ième édition (Paris: Les Éditions du Cerf, 1985).

[20] The name of this work varies. The most common designation is the *Refutatio omnium haeresium*, a Latin translation of the title which one finds at the beginning of each book: κατὰ πασῶν αἱρεσέων ἔλεγχος. This Greek phrase has also led to the use of the title *Elenchos* (which Vallée prefers in his *Anti-Gnostic Polemics*). The title *Philosophumena* is taken from Hippolytus's own description of the work (IX,3), but he intended to describe only the Greek philosophical theories found in the first four books.

by Hippolytus,[21] is devoted first (Books 1-4[22]) to exposing the philosophical tenets of the Greeks, and then (Books 5-9) to refuting thirty-three allegedly gnostic sects by coupling each one with a previously mentioned philosophy. Book 10 provides a recapitulation and an exposition of the "true faith." Paul Wendland's critical edition has been superseded by Miroslav Marcovich's *Hippolytus.*[23] Two sections concern us in particular. The first is the bulk of Book 6 which exposes the Valentinian system, where we find "sin" placed once in the mouth of a Valentinian. Again it concerns Marcus (VI,41,1). The parallel to the passage in Irenaeus warrants a close examination. With the publication of Frickel's book on the Naassene passage in Hippolytus,[24] one must also consider the possibility that the final redactor of this gnostic document included by Hippolytus (extending from V,6,4-10,2) was a Valentinian who put his personal stamp on this work. An examination of this *Naassenerschrift,* though, reveals no concern for sin on the part of the redactor.

2.2.7 Tertullian's *Adversus Valentinianos* and *De Carne Christi*

Adversus valentinianos is a work in which Tertullian confronts Valentinianism directly and extensively. Jean-Claude Fredouille has now published the best critical edition.[25] Nowhere in this *Adversus* are the Valentinians said even to mention sin.

Some discussion about Valentinus and his followers — including an enigmatic Alexander — also occurs in sections XV and XVI of *De carne Christi.*[26] Sin

---

[21] This is the scholarly consensus on the matter, but the issue is far from resolved. For a judicious assessment of the matter, see Vallée's *Anti-Gnostic Polemics,* 41-44.

[22] Books 2-3 of the *Refutatio* are not longer extant. Book 1 has been known since 1701, but was initially ascribed to Origen. Books 4-10 were discovered in 1842 and published (with Book 1) in 1851 under Origen's name. It was not until 1859 that the work was attributed to Hippolytus. See Vallée (*Anti-Gnostic Polemics,* 41) for the relevant secondary sources concerning the nineteenth-century discussion.

[23] Wendland, *Hippolytus Werke. Dritter Band. Refutatio omnium haeresium,* GCS 26 (Leipzig: Hinrichs'sche Buchhandlung, 1916 — reprinted Hildesheim/New York: Georg Verlag, 1977); Marcovich, *Hippolytus: Refutatio omnium haeresium,* PTS 25 (Berlin: de Gruyter, 1986). A serviceable English translation was prepared by J. H. MacMahon in *The Ante-Nicene Christian Library.* VI. *The Refutation of all Heresies by Hippolytus* (Edinburgh: Clark, 1868 = *The Ante-Nicene Fathers,* V [Buffalo: The Christian Literature Publishing Co., 1886], reprinted in 1965 by Eerdmans). A better translation, and the one we use (unless otherwise noted), is by F. Legge: *Philosophumena or the Refutation of all Heresies,* 2 vols. (London: Society for Promoting Christian Knowledge, 1921).

[24] Frickel, *Hellenistische Erlösung.*

[25] Jean-Claude Fredouille, *Tertullien: Contre les valentiniens,* tomes I-II, SC 280- 81 (Paris: Les Éditions du Cerf, 1980-81).

[26] Jean-Pierre Mahé, *Tertullien: La chair du christ,* tomes I-II, SC 216- 17 (Paris: Les Éditions du Cerf, 1975).

is introduced in the context of a disagreement over the nature of Christ's *caro*, but Tertullian makes it clear that both he and Alexander actually agree that Christ's flesh was sinless (though they disagree over its nature). This is as close as we get to a Valentinian discussion of sin in Tertullian.

2.2.8 Clement's Other Works

Clement's writings are extensive, and they have been well edited by Otto Stählin, et al.[27] The *Excerpta*, we have seen, provides a considerable amount of information about the Valentinian thinker Theodotus. The question is whether other relevant Valentinian sections can be gleaned from the *Protrepticus*, the *Paedagogus*, and the *Stromata*. The first two turn out to be of little use. Although sin is mentioned frequently in these treatises, Clement is expressing his own opinion. Nowhere does he introduce the Valentinian view of this concept.

There are passages in the *Stromata*, though, which at first reading seem promising. These include the second chapter (11,2) of Book 2, where sin is mentioned within a section concerning Valentinus,[28] and the twelfth chapter of Book 4, which deals quite extensively with Basilides' view of sin. However, the description of Basilides is not connected in any way with the Valentinians by Clement, and in Book 2 it is the Basilidian view of sin again which is at issue.[29]

---

[27] Otto Stählin, *Clemens Alexandrinus*, 1.–4. Bände, GCS 12, 15, 17, 39 (Leipzig: Hinrichs'sche Buchhandlung, 1905–36). There are second editions of volumes 3 (1970, ed. by L. Früchtel and U. Treu) and 4 (1980, ed. by U. Treu); a third edition of vol. 1 (1972, ed. by U. Treu); and a fourth edition of vol. 2 (1985, ed. by L. Früchtel and U. Treu).

[28] *Clément d'Alexandrie. Les stromates. Stromate II*, SC 38 (Paris: Les Éditions du Cerf, 1954).

[29] The passage in Book 2 occurs in sections 10–11 (pages 40–41 in the Sources chrétiennes edition). These sections fall within a larger discussion of faith in this book which extends from 8,3 to 31,1 (following the fine division of the text by André Méhat, *Études sur les 'Stromates' de Clément d'Alexandrie* [Paris: Éditions du Seuil, 1966] 276–78). Clement believes that the acquisition of faith is in part a person's responsibility and that it must be freely chosen. In this context he criticizes the followers of Basilides and Valentinus for claiming that faith is something given from above to certain people (according to the former, to the elite; according to the latter, to the psychics only since the pneumatics have gnosis). In section 11 Clement remarks that repentance of sins and baptism become useless unless faith has been freely chosen. At first reading it appears that the Valentinians are included in this remark about baptism and sin (and the editors of the Sources chrétiennes edition, for instance, have organized the section accordingly). This would indicate that the Valentinians practiced baptism for the repentance of sins (at least for the psychics). However, a close reading of section 11 shows that, after introducing the Basilidians and Valentinians in section 10, Clement turns his attention away from the Valentinians. In section 11 the issue is what is wrong when faith is not freely chosen and is an indication of a superior nature (οὐκέτι οὖν προαιρέσεως κατόρθωμα ἡ πίστις, εἰ φύσεως πλεονέκτημα). According to Clement the Valentinians do not connect faith with possession of a superior nature.

Outside of the *Excerpta*, then, Clement seems to have provided nothing which is directly relevant to our inquiry.

2.2.9 Pseudo-Tertullian's *Adversus Omnes Haereses*

The text of this *Adversus*, once ascribed to Tertullian, is found in A. Kroymann's edition of Tertullian.[30] This short work (14 pages) presents a survey of heresies from pre-Christian times to Marcus and Colarbasus. Section 4 deals principally with Valentinus and is also the longest analysis of one person in this work. Nowhere in this section—or indeed in the entire work—is there mention of, or concern with, sin.

2.2.10 Philastrius's *Diversarum Hereseon Liber*

The critical text of the *Diversarum,* intended to provide a quick survey of heresies from pre-Christian times to Philastrius's own day, remains F. Marx's nineteenth century edition.[31] Of the 156 sections, 6 deal with the Valentinians (38–43), and once again there is no concern shown here for sin.

2.2.11 Epiphanius's *Panarion*

The *Panarion* remains a vast *terra incognita* for most scholars of Gnosticism, in part of course because of its date (late fourth century), scope (over 1000 pages), and nature of its arguments (extremely polemical). But what has impeded research on this fascinating work is mainly the lack of a translation of any significant part of the *Panarion* into a modern language.[32] The standard edition of the Greek text remains Karl Holl's.[33] The sections dealing with Valentinianism (31–36) do mention sin a few times,[34] but always in contexts which suggest that it was Epiphanius's concern, not the Valentinians. Indeed, with only the *Panarion* for a source, one would not think of exploring the Valentinian notion of sin.

---

[30] *Quinti Septimi Florentis Tertulliani. Opera. Pars III,* CSEL 47 (Vindobonae: F. Tempsky, 1906) 213–26.

[31] *Sancti Filastrii episcopi brixiensis: Diversarum hereseon liber,* CSEL 38 (Vindobonae: F. Tempsky, 1898).

[32] According to Vallée (*Anti-Gnostic Polemics,* 64–65 n. 8), a new edition of the *Panarion* is being prepared by P. Nautin to be published in the Sources chrétiennes series. A partial English translation by Frank Williams is soon to appear: *The "Panarion" of Epiphanius of Salamis, Book I (Sects 1–46),* NHS 35 (Leiden: Brill).

[33] *Epiphanius,* 3 Bände. The second volume (*haer.* 34–64) has been re-edited by J. Dummer in 1980.

[34] Sections 31–36, e.g., mention ἁμαρτάνειν four times (32.4.8; 32.4.9 [bis]; 32.5.3), and ἁμαρτία five times (32.5.3; 33.9.1; 34.19.4; 36.4.8; 36.6.2).

2.2.12 Theodoret's *Haereticarum Fabularum Compendium*

Theodoret, living in Antioch *ca.* 450 C.E., composed a synopsis of all the heresies from Simon Magus to Nestorius and Eutyches. This *Compendium,* more extensive than Philastrius's *De haeresibus,* is divided into four books, followed by a fifth which summarizes the heretics' views on twenty-nine theological issues, without mentioning sin. No modern critical edition of this work exists, and one must still use Migne's.[35] For our purpose, the important section is in the first book (chaps. 7–9), and there we find no concern whatsoever with sin.

2.2.13 Koschorke's Collection of Late Patristic Material

In all these later patristic sources there is not one mention of sin. It would seem that from the fourth century until the seventh sin was not something that was strikingly connected with Valentinianism. However, one must remember the qualification stated in the first section on the fragments of Valentinus: there is so little textual evidence in these instances that the absence of a particular concept is not surprising.

2.3 Conclusion

This survey of primary patristic sources available for a study of Valentinianism makes it quite clear that, from the Fathers' view of Valentinianism at least, sin was neither a major concern nor a contentious point of dispute. This negative result is important to keep in mind. Yet we do see that a concern for sin was in fact attributed to Valentinians by some of the Fathers. The works of Irenaeus, Clement, Hippolytus, and Origen all include passages in which the Valentinians are said at the very least to mention sin. It remains to examine these passages closely to determine what can be gleaned from this patristic evidence.

3. An Examination of the Relevant Sources

3.1 Introduction

All four of the major Greek-speaking Fathers who lived at the end of the second century and the beginning of the third have included at least some reference to the concept of sin being used by the Valentinians. The references are few and far between, but they are there and merit close examination. In this section, then, we examine the Valentinian understanding of sin in the following works: Irenaeus's *Adversus haereses;* Clement of Alexandria's *Excerpta;* Hippolytus's *Refutatio;* and Origen's *Commentary on John* (where most of the Fragments of Heracleon appear). The intent is to study each patristic reference

---

[35] *Theodoretus cyrensis episcopus. Opera omnia. Tomus quartus,* ed. J. L. Schulze, PG 83 (Paris: Migne, 1859).

to a Valentinian mention of sin, asking what can be determined from the passage itself and from its context in that work alone. The passages are deliberately kept separate and analyzed individually.

3.2 Irenaeus

3.2.1.1

At the very end of the first book of his *Adversus haereses* Irenaeus encourages us to imagine the following scenario: a savage beast (a few centuries later he likely would have used "dragon") is making destructive raids on a countryside which was formerly peaceful and united. The beast's success rests principally on its ability to keep its whereabouts secret and to strike when there is no effective opposition. Three stages are required to bring things back to normal. First, the hideout must be found and the beast exposed for all to see, then the creature must be destroyed, and finally the situation as it existed prior to the beast's arrival must be encouraged to flourish. Of these stages the first is fundamental, for once the beast is exposed the rest will follow in due course.

The gnostic heresy is the "dragon," says Irenaeus; the countryside it is attacking is Christianity; and he is the "knight"—but one who intends to conquer with the sharp edges of his quill. Books 3–5 of his *Adversus haereses* set forth Christianity's major tenets, and here he focuses on what he considers to be the unity and truth of the doctrines which he believes will shine even brighter once the gnostic threat has passed. Book 2 is a destruction, or refutation (ἀνατροπή) of the gnostic heresies. This is preceded by Book 1, the detection (ἔλεγχος) of the heretics' secrets, which Irenaeus considers to be the heart of his refutation.[36] This is not to say that even Irenaeus considers the ἔλεγχος simply to be a textbook summary of gnostic views. As we shall see, the structure and tone of the entire work make it quite clear that the ἀνατροπή has already begun in Book 1. Irenaeus understandably finds it difficult to smoke out the dragon with equanimity.[37]

---

[36] As Irenaeus says towards the end of Book 1: "sive adversus eos victoria est sententiae eorum manifestatio" (31,3). This quotation requires a comment on the language of the extant text of the *Adversus haereses*. Although Irenaeus wrote the work in Greek, it survives only in Latin manuscripts ranging from the ninth to the fifteenth centuries. The Greek text of some of the work—and most of Book 1—can be reconstructed from quotations in other Church fathers (i.e., Epiphanius, Hippolytus, Eusebius, and Theodoret). The Sources chétiennes edition has listed the Greek passages whenever possible, but has based its translation on a critically-reconstructed Latin text.

[37] Cf. Rousseau's remark: "nous tenons, de la bouche d'Irénée lui-même [9,5], le véritable objectif poursuivi par lui dans la deuxième partie du Livre. Il ne s'agit pas d'un simple exposé de «divers systèmes valentiniens», tel que pourrait le faire un historien du gnosticisme. Le but d'Irénée est *polémique*: . . . il veut que cet exposé même soit déjà, de façon virtuelle, une réfutation" (SC 263, 132).

3.2.1.2

It is from Book 1 that we derive most of our information about the Valentinianism known to Irenaeus. This book has a tripartite structure.[38] After a detailed analysis of Ptolemy's system (chaps. 1-9) we are led to a survey of the various Valentinian systems (10-20), and then to an examination of the pre-Valentinian roots which focuses on how all heresies can be traced to the theories of Simon Magus (23-31). The first two divisions concern us in particular. In spite of Irenaeus's insistence on the great variety of Valentinian positions, he considers Ptolemy's doctrine to be a good summary of Valentinian thought on the whole. Even more, it is thought to be its apogée (ἀπάνθισμα [flosculum] οὖσαν τῆς Οὐαλεντίνου σχολῆς — I, Pref. 2). This "Great Notice," as Ptolemy's exposé is called,[39] is then followed by a second part which can be seen (as Rousseau has argued[40]) as a triptych contrasting the Church's unity of faith (chaps. 10, 22) with the variety of heretical viewpoints (chaps. 11-21).

Near the end of the second major division of Book 1 comes the one passage in Irenaeus which attributes a concern with sin to a Valentinian: 21,2.[41] We will set this pericope in the context of chapters 10-22 by analyzing what Irenaeus wants to say in these chapters, how chapter 21 fits into the discussion, and what is said in 21,2 specifically.

3.2.2.1

The diversity of Valentinian thought and practice is what Irenaeus accentuates in chapters 10-22 as he shifts the focus from Ptolemy to Marcus. Just as Ptolemy was introduced in the early chapters as an example of the level of sophistication attainable in Valentinianism (a level which certainly does not impress the bishop of Lyons), so here Marcus is used to show how many kinds of Valentinianism one encounters . . . and how laughable some of them are. Including chapter 10 in this section, as Rousseau has suggested, helps to highlight Irenaeus's major concerns:

    a — the unity of the Church's faith (10)
    b — the diversity of the Valentinian doctrines (11-12)

---

[38] This tripartite division of Book 1 emerges so clearly from the text itself that scholars have tended to quibble only on exactly where the first division ought to end. Chapter 10 usually is tacked on to this first division — e.g., Sagnard, La gnose, 140-41. Rousseau's analysis has now made a good case for placing that chapter in the second division, taking it to balance the unity theme of chapter 22 and to set off the diversity of the heretical doctrines (see SC 263, 113-64). Rousseau also presents the best overview of this book, notwithstanding his occasional uncritical remarks about Irenaeus's "entirely accurate and true" portrayal of the Valentinians (e.g., pp. 149-50).

[39] Strictly speaking, this "Great Notice" extends from 1, 1-8, 4. For the fullest discussion of this crucial passage, see Sagnard, La gnose, 140-291.

[40] Rousseau, SC 263, 113-64.

[41] The parallel passage in Epiphanius is Panarion XXXIV,2,1-20,12.

c — Marcus and his school (13–20)
b′ — the diversity of the Valentinian (Marcosian?) practices (21)
a′ — the Church's credo *in unum Deum* (22)

Concerning Marcus, we are told something about his personal life (as a magician who is constantly taking sexual liberties with his followers; chap. 13), the distinctive elements of his teaching (grammatology and especially arithmology; chaps. 14–16), and his scriptural exegeses (concerning the Pleroma, chaps. 17– 18, and the unknown Father, chaps. 19–20).

3.2.2.2
In chapter 21 Irenaeus returns to one of the characteristic Marcosian concerns (see 13,6): the tradition of the rite of redemption (ἡ παράδοσις τῆς ἀπολυτρώσεως — 21,1), thought by Marcus to be the only true baptism, without which it is impossible to enter the Pleroma. Irenaeus focuses here on the diversity of their rites of redemption. These Marcosians, he gleefully announces, although they appreciate the necessity of this redemption, cannot agree on exactly how it is to be carried out: ὅσοι γάρ εἰσι ταύτης τῆς γνώμης μυσταγωγοὶ τοσαῦται καὶ ἀπολυτρώσεις (21,1). Variations emerge daily, he states (21,5), and he gives a representative sample. Some celebrate a pneumatic marriage in a bridal chamber (21,3). Others perform a water baptism while invoking a certain formula and expecting a certain response. There are variations on this formula and the responses, and now and then the formula is said to be pronounced in Hebrew for dramatic effect (21,3). There are also those who do not lead people to water but instead incant the formulae while pouring a mixture of oil and water on the initiate's head (21,4). Others reject all rites, considering them unworthy of the mysteries of an incorporeal reality, saying that γνῶσις itself is the redemption because it abolishes ignorance (21,4). Last, some celebrate a sacrament of extreme unction: they pour a mixture of water and oil on a dying person's head, saying invocations, in order to confer on that person the formulae necessary to traverse the heavenly realms and enter the Pleroma (21,5).

3.2.3.1
Irenaeus's main point in chapter 21, then, is the following: if the rite of redemption is so crucial to Valentinians, why can they not agree on how to perform it? In the midst of this discussion is section 21,2 which deals not with diversity, but with the Valentinian distinction between baptism and redemption. The passage is as follows:[42]

Λέγουσι δὲ αὐτὴν ἀναγκαίαν εἶναι τοῖς τὴν τελείαν γνῶσιν εἰληφόσιν, ἵνα εἰς τὴν ὑπὲρ πάντα Δύναμιν ὦσιν ἀναγεγεννημένοι· ἄλλως γὰρ ἀδύνατον ἐντὸς

---

[42] The text is from Rousseau and Doutreleau, SC 264, 296–99; the translation from Rousseau's *Irénée de Lyon,* 101 (which, aside from the omission of a few quotation marks, is identical to that in the SC edition).

Πληρώματος εἰσελθεῖν, ἐπειδὴ αὕτη ἐστὶν ἡ εἰς τὸ βάθος τοῦ βυθοῦ κατάγουσα κατ' αὐτούς. Τὸ μὲν γὰρ βάπτισμα τοῦ φαινομένου Ἰησοῦ < εἰς > ἄφεσιν < εἶναι > ἁμαρτιῶν, τὴν δὲ ἀπολύτρωσιν τοῦ ἐν αὐτῷ κατελθόντος Χριστοῦ εἰς τελείωσιν, καὶ τὸ μὲν ψυχικόν, τὴν δὲ πνευματικὴν εἶναι ὑφίστανται. Καὶ τὸ μὲν βάπτισμα ὑπὸ Ἰωάννου κατηγγέλθαι εἰς μετάνοιαν, τὴν δὲ ἀπολύτρωσιν ὑπὸ Χριστοῦ κεκομίσθαι εἰς τελείωσιν.

La «rédemption», disent-ils, est nécessaire à ceux qui ont reçu la gnose parfaite pour qu'ils soient régénérés dans la Puissance qui est au-dessus de tout. Faute de quoi il est impossible d'entrer au Plérôme, car c'est cette «rédemption», selon eux, qui fait descendre dans la profondeur de l'Abîme! Le baptême fut le fait du Jésus visible, en vue de la rémission des péchés, mais la «rédemption» fut le fait du Christ descendant en Jésus, en vue de la «perfection». Le baptême était psychique, mais la «rédemption» était pneumatique. Le baptême fut annoncé par Jean en vue de la pénitence, mais la «rédemption» fut apportée par le Christ en vue de la «perfection».

Καὶ τοῦτ' εἶναι περὶ οὗ λέγει· «Καὶ ἄλλο βάπτισμα ἔχω βαπτισθῆναι, καὶ πάνυ ἐπείγομαι εἰς αὐτό.» Ἀλλὰ καὶ τοῖς υἱοῖς Ζεβεδαίου, τῆς μητρὸς αὐτῶν αἰτουμένης τὸ καθίσαι αὐτοὺς ἐκ δεξιῶν καὶ ἐξ ἀριστερῶν μετ' αὐτοῦ εἰς τὴν βασιλείαν, ταύτην προσθεῖναι τὴν ἀπολύτρωσιν τὸν Κύριον λέγουσιν, εἰπόντα· «Δύνασθε τὸ βάπτισμα βαπτισθῆναι, ὃ ἐγὼ μέλλω βαπτίζεσθαι;» Καὶ τὸν Παῦλον ῥητῶς φάσκουσι τὴν ἐν Χριστῷ Ἰησοῦ ἀπολύτρωσιν πολλάκις μεμηνυκέναι, καὶ εἶναι ταύτην τὴν ὑπ' αὐτῶν ποικίλως καὶ ἀσυμφώνως παραδιδομένην.

C'est à cela qu'il faisait allusion, lorsqu'il disait: «Il est un autre baptême dont je dois être baptisé, et je me hâte vivement vers lui». De même, aux fils de Zébédée, tandis que leur mère demandait qu'ils fussent assis à sa droite et à sa gauche avec lui dans le royaume, le Seigneur présenta cette «rédemption», lorsqu'il leur dit: «Pouvez-vous être baptisés du baptême dont je dois être baptisé?» De même Paul, à les en croire, a indiqué expressément et à maintes reprises cette «rédemption» qui est dans le Christ Jésus: ce serait celle-là même qui est transmise par eux sous des formes variées et discordantes.

According to this passage, baptism is "psychic" (ψυχικόν) while the redemption is "pneumatic" (πνευματικόν). As well, baptism is said to have been proclaimed by John the Baptist with a view to repentance, and instituted by the visible Jesus (τὸ βάπτισμα τοῦ φαινομένου Ἰησοῦ) for the remission of sins. Redemption, on the other hand, was brought by Christ descending on Jesus, and with a view to perfection. Irenaeus informs us of the Valentinian tendency to gather gospel allusions to support the necessity of another baptism (e.g. Lk 12:50; Matt 20:20).

The need for the remission of sins, then, is not excluded. It is linked to baptism, which in turn is connected to penance, psychics, and the ministries of John and the visible Jesus. Redemption, on the other hand, is linked to pneumatics, perfection, and Christ descending on Jesus. On this side of the equation there is no room for the remission of sins. As well, although this discussion in 21,2 occurs within a chapter which focuses on Valentinian diversity over rites of redemption, Irenaeus's presentation of this particular Valentinian position suggests that when it came to distinguishing between baptism (for the remission of sins) and redemption (leading to perfection) the Valentinians spoke with one voice.

3.2.4

In summary, this pericope does not say that pneumatics themselves had no concern for sin. What it does say is that the remission of sins is connected to the baptism announced by John, brought by the visible Jesus, and concerned with the psychics. It does suggest, though, that the pneumatics require no such remission of sins. Moreover, even if one limits the remission of sins — and, by extension, perhaps even sin — to the psychic realm, previous discussion in the *Adversus haereses* (especially chaps. 6-7) makes it clear that the nature and fate of the psychics was of vital concern to (at least some of) the Valentinians. They thought that, while the best of the psychics can never hope to enter the Pleroma, they can indeed strive for the next best thing, i.e., to gain entry into the area immediately below it and to survive the destruction of the material realm at the end of time. Psychics were of concern to the Valentinians, and, according to Irenaeus (*Adv. haer.* I,21,2), it would seem that sin also was.

3.3 Clement of Alexandria

3.3.1.1

There is one reference to "sin" being used by a Valentinian in section 52 of the *Excerpta ex Theodoto*. An exegesis of this passage is facilitated by pausing first to appreciate the nature of the work as a whole and to set section 52 into its context.

The title introduces us to many facets of this work's nature: Ἐκ τῶν Θεοδότου καὶ τῆς ἀνατολικῆς καλουμένης διδασκαλίας κατὰ τοὺς Οὐαλεντίνου χρόνους ἐπιτομαί. This dates the material roughly to the second and third quarters of the second century, and it also brings to light two important issues: what are the implications of this work being a collection of "extracts" (ἐπιτομαί), and what can we say about their original author or authors ("Theodotus and the so-called Oriental school")?

3.3.1.2

Two questions emerge in turn from the observation that we are presented with Valentinian ἐπιτομαί : how much unity is there to this collection, and how intrusive was Clement's redactional hand? The first of these requires a qualified answer. Much points to a glaring lack of unity to this work. For one thing, as Robert Pierce Casey had observed, everything written by Clement which follows *Stromata* 7 (i.e., *Stromata* 8, the *Excerpta,* and the *Eclogae propheticae*) probably should be regarded as first-draft material. It is

> all of the nature of a note book or scrapbook, containing in part direct quotations from philosophical and Gnostic works, in part Clement's summaries of his reading in them, in part independent attempts at exegesis, criticism, or theological construction.[43]

Also, four clearly delimited and independent blocks of material stand out in this work: 1-28; 29-42; 43-65; 66-86.[44] The unfinished and disconnected elements of the *Excerpta,* then, are unquestionable.

The degree of unity present in this work also needs to be stressed. This point has been made most forcefully and convincingly by Sagnard. After extensive analysis of the contents of these four sections he concludes:

> La comparaison précise qui vient d'être instaurée fait ressortir, plus qu'on ne l'aurait pensé *a priori,* le solide fondement commun de ces quatres sections: et cela, malgré la différence des objets propres à chacune d'entre elles, et malgré les fâcheuses coupures de la présentation en Extraits. . . . En somme, les points de contact l'emportent de beaucoup sur les divergences.[45]

Our own analysis of the work supports this claim.

Clement's selection and arrangement of these Valentinian extracts already points to the need to recognize his redactional hand. Indeed, internal evidence reveals Clement's extensive role in these *Excerpta,* for roughly one quarter of the corpus represents Clement's own views. There are places where he states this explicitly (e.g., 1,3; 33,2), and others where the likelihood of a redactional comment is great. A scholarly consensus exists about which passages are Clementine. Using Sagnard's list, these include the following: 1,3; 4-5; 7,3c-4; 8-15; 17,2-4; 18-20; 23,4-5; 24,2; 27; 30,1-31,1 (partly); 33,2; 86 (perhaps).[46] What emerges from this list is that the redactional elements tend to come in extended sections (e.g., 4-5; 8-9; 10-15; 18-20; 27), to occur mainly in the first third of the work,

---

[43] Robert Pierce Casey, *The Excerpta ex Theodoto of Clement of Alexandria. Edited with Translation, Introduction and Notes* (London: Christophers, 1934) 4.

[44] Sagnard, *Extraits,* 28. Before him, cf. O. Dibelius, "Studien zur Geschichte der Valentinianer," *ZNW* 9 (1908) 240-42. Others have arrived at a slightly different division. E.g., Casey (*The Excerpta,* 8) includes extract 42 (and perhaps 6-7 as well) in the third part, while Foerster (*Von Valentin zu Herakleon,* 85) extends the third part to include extract 68.

[45] Sagnard, *Extraits,* 68.

[46] See Sagnard, *Extraits,* 8-9, for a discussion of these redactional sections and the criteria used to isolate them from the Valentinian base. Other scholars' lists vary only superficially; cf. Dibelius, "Studien," 242-47; Casey, *The Excerpta,* 25-33.

and to be relatively disentangled from the Valentinian base. We will now turn to this Valentinian element and ask what can be known about its specific origin.

3.3.1.3

The title is worth examining closely. It states that the extracts are ἐκ τῶν Θεοδότου καὶ τῆς ἀνατολικῆς καλουμένης διδασκαλίας. The problems here are that we know nothing about Theodotus and little about the Oriental school, so we are unable to decide whether Theodotus is to be included in this particular school or not. Occasionally elsewhere (e.g., in Hippolytus *Ref.* VI,35,4–7; Tertullian *Adv. val.* 11,2) a distinction is made between the Italian school (ἡ ἰταλιωτικὴ διδασκαλία), to which Heracleon and Ptolemy are said to belong, and the Oriental school, to which belonged Marcus and Theodotus. What separated them, according to Hippolytus, was principally their view of Jesus' body: the Italian school claimed that his body was born *psychic* while the Oriental school claimed that it was *pneumatic* (and that he travelled through Mary's body as one would through a pipe). The qualifier καλουμένης ("so-called") in our title suggests that Clement was aware of the distinction but did not consider it particularly useful.

From the title it is also unclear just how much of this work was culled from Theodotus's own teaching and writing and how much goes back to this "so-called Oriental school." As Sagnard summarizes:

Les notations de Clément attribuent les Extraits, soit à Théodote (5 fois seulement), soit à un «dit-il» anonyme (φησί, 6 fois), soit à un «disent-ils» très général (φασί, 13 fois; λέγουσι, 4 fois; noter aussi un ἀγνοοῦσι), soit enfin aux «Valentiniens» (οἱ Οὐαλεντινιανοί, οἱ ἀπὸ Οὐαλεντίνου, 10 fois). Au sujet de la répartition de ces notules, il faut remarquer: 1. Qu'elles se continuent assez régulièrement de 1 à 43,1,— soit 34 sur 39, comprenant toutes celles qui désignent explicitement Théodote, et souvent coupées, jusqu'à 33,2, par les développements de Clément; 2. Que la section C (43,2-65) n'en contient aucune; 3. Que la section D (66-86) ne renferme en tout et pour tout qu'un seul φησί [67,1], puis quatre φασί [only one—79—probably refers to Theodotus, and it simply reiterates 67,1].[47]

3.3.2.1

It is clear from the general discussion of the *Excerpta* that Extract 52, which falls within the third section of the work (Extracts 43-65), seems to contain no editorial additions from Clement, or any specific links to Theodotus himself. Meanwhile, it still exhibits considerable overlap with the other three sections. Actually, the distinctive feature of this section is the remarkable degree to which it parallels the Ptolemaic doctrine presented by Irenaeus in Book 1 of his

⁴⁷ Sagnard, *Extraits,* 30.

Adversus haereses. Clement and Irenaeus may have used a common source here.[48] If, as Irenaeus claims, such a source derives from Ptolemy, who, unlike Theodotus, supposedly was a member of the "Italian school," Clement's hesitation about using these "Italian/Oriental" categories may be explained. In many respects, then, the third and middle section stands on its own, and this provides added incentive to appraise its contents.

3.3.2.2

Sagnard has noted the internal fivefold division of this section: the foundational event, i.e., the sending of the Savior to Sophia outside the Pleroma (43,2–45,1); cosmogony (45,2–49); anthropology (50–57); Christology (58–62); and eschatology (63–65).[49] The first subsection is brief. Ἰησοῦς Χριστὸς Σωτήρ is sent outside the Pleroma to help Sophia, whose passion to know the origins of the Pleroma has resulted in her expulsion from the divine realm. The Savior bestows on her the "formation according to gnosis" and the "healing of the passions." The second subsection presents the emergence of the non-pneumatic world. The passions (τὰ πάθη) which have been separated from Sophia by the Savior are transformed by him into matter (ὕλη), then given bodies (45–46). Sophia, in turn, emits over all of this a (psychic) ruler who is ignorant of his limitations and through whom she creates Heaven and Earth. This Demiurge (who is considered to be the Hebrew "God") in turn emits a psychic Son, or Christ, then some angels and archangels.

The material part of this creation is composed of three elements. One of these is grief (λύπη), from which emerge the πνευματικὰ τῆς πονηρίας; another is fear (φόβος), and the last element is τὸ δὲ ἐκ τῆς <ἐκ>πλήξεως καὶ ἀπορίας ("stupeur et angoisse"). What is important to keep in mind is that the spirits of evil are one element of this *hylic* world.

The middle part of this section focuses on the creation and constitution of humans. In this system one begins with the hylic or "choical" human, the one made from matter or the dust of the earth. In some instances, another whole, or a human of psychic nature, can be superimposed onto it: Ἄνθρωπος γοῦν ἐστιν ἐν ἀνθρώπῳ, ψυχικὸς ἐν χοϊκῷ, οὐ μέρει μέρος, ἀλλὰ ὅλῳ ὅλος συνών (51). This psychic whole is consubstantial with its creator, the Demiurge.

The two "humans" do not merge. It is a mismatched marriage, where two unities come together, one being of lesser nature than the other. Yet it is this lower or hylic human who strives to dominate, and it is only with great effort that its partner can resist these advances and keep its individuality.[50] The psychic

---

[48] So Sagnard, *Extraits,* 153 n. 1: "La Grande Notice et les Extraits de Théodote viennent d'un même document. . . . Irénée l'abrège parfois. . . . Mais il arrive aussi, en sens contraire, qu'il donne des détails importants qui ne figurent pas dans les Extraits."

[49] Sagnard, *Extraits,* 35.

[50] The author tells us that Paul was referring specifically to this hylic human when he wrote about another "law warring against the law of my mind" (Rom 7:23).

human needs to be aware of, and to beware, the hylic component to which he has been fused, taking care not to strengthen it even more by partaking of evil. Into this odd couple is sometimes injected a third partner, τὸ σπέρμα τὸ πνευματικόν. It derives from Sophia and enters the scene not so much as a third whole, but as the marrow which fills the psychic bone: πρῶτον οὖν σπέρμα πνευματικὸν τὸ ἐν τῷ Ἀδὰμ προέβαλεν ἡ Σοφία, ἵνα ᾖ τὸ ὀστοῦν, ἡ λογικὴ καὶ οὐρανία ψυχή, μὴ κενή, ἀλλὰ μυελοῦ γέμουσα πνευματικοῦ (53,5). Adam has begotten these three "humans." All people on earth are hylic, created in the image (κατ' εἰκόνα) of God, or the Demiurge, and possess an irrational φύσις (symbolized by Cain). A few also have superimposed psychic wholes. These were created in God's (the Demiurge's) likeness (καθ' ὁμοίωσιν) and have a reasonable and just (λογικὴ καὶ δίκαια) nature (symbolized by Abel). Very few (σπάνιοι — 56,2) have a pneumatic human within the psychic one. These are created κατ' ἰδίαν and have a spiritual disposition (symbolized by Seth).

A fourth stage is added (55,1) when the hylics receive tangible, visible bodies (τοὺς δερματίνους χιτῶνας). This stage is mentioned only briefly, and probably is a reflection on Genesis 3:21: "And the Lord God made for Adam and for his wife garments of skins and clothed them."[51]

When the end of the Age arrives (56,3–57) the hylics (and their "bodies") will perish along with everything else that is hylic, while the pneumatic "marrow" will be collected and returned to its home in the Pleroma. As for the psychics, their destiny rests more in their own hands (κατὰ τὴν οἰκείαν). They too will perish if they choose to align themselves with the hylic evil and corruption, but their survival of the holocaust is assured if they align themselves with the incorruptible πνευματικά.

The last two parts of the middle section of the Excerpta (43–65) deal with Christology and eschatology. In the first (58–62) the Savior, ὁ μέγας ἀγουνιστὴς Ἰησοῦς Χριστός, descends from the Pleroma and takes up three coverings. First he puts on a pneumatic seed from Sophia; then, descending further, he clothes himself with the psychic Christ; and finally a special psychic body is spun in order that he might be seen. This psychic Christ is the one who was predicted in the Scriptures, the one seated at the right hand of God (the Demiurge). "The great agonistes" came to provide people with gnosis, to teach them about the end time, and to save those of like nature (ὁμοούσιοι — 51,1).

Four major stages are posited concerning the events which are to occur at the end of this age (63–65). The first finds the pneumatics dwelling with Sophia in the eighth heaven (the Ogdoad) where they will have gathered as they died, and they will be clothed with the psychic elements. Meanwhile, the dead psychics will have gathered in the seventh heaven with the Demiurge. In the second stage, at the end of the Age, all matter will be destroyed (including the psychic elements having close links to it), and the psychics who have striven to be good will pass to the Ogdoad and dwell together in harmony and knowledge. This will be the marriage feast. Third, at a certain moment the pneumatics will leave behind their psychic bodies, as well as the other psychics, and, joining with their bridegrooms (the angels), will enter the bridal chamber in the Pleroma to consummate their relationship. Finally, the Demiurge and the psychics who have been left behind in the Ogdoad (for only πνευματικά can enter the Pleroma) will also rejoice in their own way when they hear the joy emanating from the bridal chamber. Even for the psychics there remains τὸ πλήρωμα τῆς χαρᾶς καὶ τῆς ἀναπαύσεως (65,2).

3.3.3.1

This brings us to the core of the analysis, an examination of the reference to sin in section 52. The passage, in context, is as follows:[52]

51.

Ἄνθρωπος γοῦν ἐστιν ἐν ἀνθρώπῳ, ψυχικὸς ἐν χοϊκῷ, οὐ μέρει μέρος, ἀλλὰ ὅλῳ ὅλος συνών, ἀρρήτῳ δυνάμει θεοῦ. Ὅθεν ἐν τῷ Παραδίσῳ, τῷ τετάρτῳ οὐρανῷ, δημιουργεῖται, Ἐκεῖ γὰρ χοϊκὴ σὰρξ οὐκ ἀναβαίνει, ἀλλ' ἦν τῇ ψυχῇ < τῇ > θείᾳ οἷον σὰρξ ἡ ὑλική.

Il y a donc l'homme dans l'homme, le «psychique» dans le «terrestre», non comme une partie qui s'ajoute à une partie, mais comme un tout se joignant à un tout, par l'inexprimable puissance de Dieu [=du Démiurge]. De là vient que l'homme est façonné dans le Paradis, au quatrième Ciel. Car, la chair «terrestre» ne monte pas jusque-là: mais, pour l'âme «divine» [=psychique], l'âme «hylique» était comme une «chair».

Ταῦτα σημαίνει· «Τοῦτο νῦν ὀστοῦν ἐκ τῶν ὀστῶν μου» (τὴν θείαν ψυχὴν αἰνίσσεται τὴν ἐγκεκρυμμένην τῇ σαρκὶ καὶ στερεὰν καὶ δυσπαθῆ καὶ δυνατωτέραν), «καὶ σὰρξ ἐκ τῆς σαρκὸς μου» (τὴν ὑλικὴν ψυχὴν σῶμα οὖσαν τῆς θείας ψυχῆς). Περὶ τούτων τῶν δυεῖν καὶ ὁ Σωτὴρ λέγει «φοβεῖσθαι δεῖν τὸν δυνάμενον ταύτην τὴν ψυχὴν καὶ τοῦτο τὸ σῶμα» τὸ ψυχικὸν «ἐν γεέννῃ ἀπολέσαι».

C'est ce que signifie: «Voici maintenant l'os de mes os»,—allusion à l'âme «divine», cachée à l'intérieur de la «chair», âme «solide», difficilement «passible», suffisamment forte,—«et la chair de ma chair», l'âme «hylique», qui est le «corps» de l'âme «divine». C'est au sujet de ces deux âmes que le Sauveur dit: «Il faut craindre celui qui a le pouvoir de perdre dans la géhenne et notre âme et notre corps»,— le «corps psychique».

---

[52] Text and translation are taken from Sagnard, SC 23, 164–69.

52.

Τοῦτο τὸ σαρκίον «ἀντίδικον» ὁ Σωτὴρ εἶπεν καὶ ὁ Παῦλος «νόμον ἀντιστρατευόμενον τῷ νόμῳ τοῦ νοός μου»· καὶ «δῆσαι» παραινεῖ καὶ «ἁρπάσαι ὡς ἰσχυροῦ τὰ σκεύη», τοῦ ἀντιπολεμοῦντος τῇ οὐρανίῳ ψυχῇ, ὁ Σωτήρ· καὶ «ἀπηλλάχθαι αὐτοῦ» παραινεῖ «κατὰ τὴν ὁδόν, μὴ τῇ φυλακῇ» περιπέσωμεν καὶ τῇ κολάσει.

C'est cet élément charnel que le Sauveur a appelé «l'Adversaire», et Paul: «la loi qui lutte contre la loi de mon esprit». C'est lui que le Sauveur conseille de «lier» et de «dépouiller de ses biens» comme de ceux de «l'homme fort», de l'homme qui fait la guerre à l'âme «céleste». Il conseille de «se dégager de lui en chemin, de crainte que nous ne soyons jetés en prison» et soumis au châtiment.

ὁμοίως δὲ καὶ «εὐνοεῖν» αὐτῷ, μὴ τρέφοντας καὶ ῥωννύντας τῇ τῶν ἁμαρτημάτων ἐξουσίᾳ, ἀλλ' ἐντεῦθεν νεκροῦντας ἤδη καὶ ἐξίτηλον ἀποφαίνοντας ἀποχῇ τῆς πονηρίας, ἵνα ἐν τῇ διαλύσει ταύτῃ διαφορηθὲν καὶ διαπνεῦσαν λάθῃ, ἀλλὰ μὴ καθ' αὐτό τινος ὑποστάσεως λαβόμενον, τὴν ἰσχὺν ἔχῃ παράμονον ἐν τῇ διὰ πυρὸς διεξόδῳ.

Et de même: «d'avoir de bons sentiments» à son égard,—non pas de le nourrir et de le fortifier par le pouvoir de nos péchés,—mais déjà dès maintenant de le mettre à mort et de manifester son caractère caduc, en nous abstenant du mal: afin que, dans cette séparation, cet <élément charnel> soit secrètement dispersé et évaporé, et que, n'ayant reçu de lui-même aucune subsistance, il n'ait pas la force de persister dans l'être lors de son passage à travers le feu.

53.

Τοῦτο «ζιζάνιον» ὀνομάζεται συμφυὲς τῇ ψυχῇ, τῷ χρηστῷ σπέρματι· τοῦτο καὶ «σπέρμα τοῦ Διαβόλου», ὡς ὁμοούσιον ἐκείνῳ, καὶ «ὄφις» καὶ «διαπτερνιστὴς» καὶ «λῃστὴς» ἐπιτιθέμενος κεφαλῇ βασιλέως.

C'est lui que est appelé «l'ivraie» qui croît avec l'âme, avec «la bonne semence». C'est lui «la semence du diable», en tant qu'elle est consubstantielle à celui-ci: et aussi «le serpent», «celui qui s'en prend au talon», et «le brigand» qui s'attaque à la tête du roi.

In context, the reference to sin in this passage is fairly straightforward. Section 51 explains that many people tend to be made up of two wholes, a ψυχικὸς ἐν χοϊκῷ, and that the "choical," or fleshly, soul acts as a kind of body to the divine soul (ψυχὴ θεία). Then (51,2–53,1) the author points out that this choical part is frequently alluded to in Scripture. The "Savior," for instance, called it the "Adversary" (Matt 5:25), while for Paul (Rom 7:23) it was "the law which struggles against the law of my spirit." As well, the Savior through Scripture cautions us to "bind" it and strip it of its possessions as one would do to a "strong man" (Matt 12:29).

The author then proceeds to state that one must be "properly disposed"[53] (cf. Matt 5:25) to the fleshly part. This entails a refusal to nourish or fortify it by the power of sins (μὴ τρέφοντας καὶ ῥωννύντας τῇ τῶν ἁμαρτημάτων ἐξουσίᾳ). Sin feeds the hylic human; abstaining from sin leads to starvation. This reveals that the fleshly part can be destroyed—indeed, its reign is said to be on its way out (ἐξίτηλον).

To whom is this advice directed? Again, the context makes it clear. The two wholes, the hylic and psychic humans, are introduced in 50,1-53,1; the pneumatic human is added as the third aspect in 53,2-5; and sections 54-57 discuss how all three of these relate to one another. So sin and evil are part of the hylic-psychic discussion and do not seem to be of concern to the pneumatics.[54] Sin comes from the hylic power of evil, and it affects the psychic. It is the psychic who is encouraged to sin by the hylic partner, and it is up to the psychic to master that power—and to weaken and even shatter it.

Two questions remain unanswered concerning this pericope: from where does the evil come, and how can one overcome it? The first can quickly be dealt with: the spirits of evil (πνευματικὰ τῆς πονηρίας—48,2) are one of the three hylic elements, and this is the source of all evil and sin. The answer to the second question is surprising only for how "Christian" it is: baptism gives one the strength to overcome sin. The *Excerpta* end on this note, and this is a feature well worth exploring.

3.3.3.2

The author is as clear on this matter as Paul is: Ὁ γὰρ εἰς θεὸν βαπτισθεὶς εἰς θεὸν ἐχώρησεν καὶ εἴληθεν "ἐξουσίαν ἐπάνω σκορπίων καὶ ὄφεων περιπατεῖν" [Lk 10:19], τῶν Δυνάμεων τῶν πονηρῶν (76,2). Baptism results in a regeneration

---

[53] "Properly disposed" is my translation of εὐνοεῖν αὐτῷ in 52,2. This verb usually means "to be well-disposed towards," or "favorable to." Accordingly, Casey translates it as "be kind to" the sarkic man, and Sagnard as "d'avoir de bons sentiments à son égard." However, translating it as "properly" (rather than "well") disposed—i.e., knowing full well where you stand and what needs to be done—does more justice to the context, while not doing injustice to the meaning of the verb.

[54] Casey (*The Excerpta*, 144) is not certain whether the pneumatics are implicated in some way in this discussion of sin. His uncertainty arises from the occurrence of "divine soul" in section 51: "θεία ψυχή, ὑλικὴ ψυχή, and χοϊκη σάρξ appear to take the place here of the usual distinction between τὸ πνευματικόν, τὸ ψυχικόν, and τὸ ὑλικόν (Iren. i. 1, 9ff.)." Concerning section 52, then, he comments: "It seems that the πνευματικοί, though certain of ultimate salvation, did not escape the moral struggle nor a temporary punishment for their misdeeds. . . . The alternative to this view is that the whole discussion refers only to the ψυχικοί, whose fate is uncertain and whose future depends on their own moral conduct." Casey's final hunch is almost certainly the correct one. The θεία ψυχή in section 51 refers to the psychic (and not the pneumatic) soul (so also Sagnard, *Extraits*, 167 n. 3).

(ἀναγέννησις — 76,4) and a new birth (τί γέννησις, τί ἀναγέννησις — 78,2): ὃν δὲ ἀναγεννᾷ Χριστὸς εἰς ζωὴν μετατίθεται, εἰς Ὀγδόαδα (80,1).
Baptism consists of water immersion in which the initiate is "sealed" by the Father, the Son, and the Holy Spirit (80,3).[55] These three "names" are said to remove the triad of destruction (τῆς ἐν φθορᾷ τριάδος — 80,3). This triad almost certainly refers to the three elements (στοιχεία) making up the hylic human, which are mentioned in 48,2-3.[56]

The role of the Spirit in baptism is fundamental. The visible part of every baptism, the water immersion, is said to be coupled with the invisible presence of the Spirit (81,2) who transforms the water. This leads not only to separation of the inferior element but to sanctification: Οὕτως καὶ τὸ ὕδωρ, καὶ τὸ ἐξορκιζόμενον καὶ τὸ βάπτισμα γινόμενον, οὐ μόνον χωρίζει τὸ χεῖρον, ἀλλὰ καὶ ἁγιασμὸν προσλαμβάνει (82,2). Impure spirits sometimes enter the baptismal water, and extensive preparation is required to ward off their powers: Διὰ τοῦτο νηστεῖται, δεήσεις, εὐχαί, θέσεις χειρῶν, γονυκλισίαι (84).

The role that baptism as a whole plays in the *Excerpta* cannot be overstated. It is also another indication of unity in a sometimes disparate collection. This work begins with a mention of Jesus delivering his Spirit into his father's hands (1,1), and it ends with a description of baptism in the name of the Father, the Son, and the Holy Spirit (e.g., 76,1). The last section itself (86,2) emphasizes the importance of the σφραγίς. The focus throughout lies on the psychic and on the removal of the power of evil which is made possible only through baptism by the Spirit.

Sin is mentioned only once in the *Excerpta*, yet it is an integral part of the whole because of the part it plays in the important confrontation between the spirits of evil and the Spirit of God.[57] These πνευματικὰ τῆς πονηρίας encourage the psychic to act in a way that is contrary to the psychic inclination. This is sin. These spirits, which derive from the hylic human, lead the psychic to sin because they derive their nourishment from these sins. Previously these spirits were too powerful to oppose, but baptism in the Spirit has given the psychic enough power to begin to reduce evil-inspired actions. The less the psychic sins the weaker the spirits of evil become until they starve to death. Another way of stating this is

[55] The baptismal seal (σφράγις) of the Spirit plays a major role in the final section of the work (e.g., 83).

[56] Sagnard (*Extraits*, 205 n. 4) is being overly cautious when he declares: "On ne voit pas bien ce que peut être cette «triade de corruption»." It is important to note in this regard that the reference in 48,2 to πνευματικὰ τῆς πονηρίας is followed by the hortatory remark, καὶ μὴ λυπείτε τὸ πνεῦμα τὸ ἅγιον τοῦ θεοῦ, ἐν ᾧ ἐσφραγίσθητε. In other words, the antidote, baptism, is introduced as soon as the "spirits of evil" are mentioned.

[57] In this passage, Clement, like Irenaeus before him, offers no critique of the Valentinian position on sin. However, one does not expect one either. Section 43,2-65 seems to reproduce quite faithfully a source tapped by Clement, and he has kept his redactional remarks to the first part of the work.

that it is a battle to the death for both of these adversaries (who know each other so well); only now the one combatant has been given the arms necessary to defeat his opponent. Hence, according to the *Excerpta ex Theodoto,* the baptismal seal is the beginning of the end for the spirits of evil. It holds the promise of a sinless existence for the psychics and, consequently, entry into the joyful marriage feast in the Ogdoad at the end of this Age.

3.4 Hippolytus

3.4.1.1

Two parallel trajectories have emerged in the modern critical study of the *Refutatio omnium haeresium.* The first is the recognition, to use Vallée's words, that "everything concerning Hippolytus has indeed become enigmatic."[58] The authorship of the *Refutatio,* and indeed of all the works previously ascribed to Hippolytus, is now very much in question. The second direction of research on the *Refutatio,* well represented by Vallée's *A Study in Anti-Gnostic Polemics,* has focused on the author's redactional concerns. The remainder of this introductory section will highlight these trajectories to set the groundwork for a detailed examination of Book 6, and then of section 41,[59] where sin is introduced.

3.4.1.2

Johannes Quasten's overview of Hippolytus provides an indication of the *status quaestionis* in the previous generation.[60] He describes Hippolytus's career and his writings in broad strokes — and confidently, as though scholars finally had assembled all of the major pieces to the Hippolytean puzzle. Hippolytus is depicted as the first anti-pope, severing relations with Callistus, the bishop of Rome, allegedly as a result of the latter's overly lenient attitude towards sinners.[61] His list of writings is taken in part from a mutilated statue discovered in 1551 and thereafter reconstituted in the likeness of Hippolytus. The writings range from exegetical treatises to a chronicle of world history going back to Adam.[62]

---

[58] Vallée, *Anti-Gnostic Polemics,* 41.

[59] The section divisions in Book 6 follow Wendland's edition. J. H. MacMahon's translation which appeared in 1868 in the *Ante-Nicene Fathers* has different divisions. Legge's edition, though later than Wendland's, does not take that work into account. However, its section divisions are virtually identical: Wendland's sections 38 and 39 are combined in Legge's edition, resulting in a difference of one in the following sections.

[60] Johannes Quasten, *Patrology.* II. *The Ante-Nicene Literature after Irenaeus* (Westminster, MD: Neuman, 1953) 163-207.

[61] This information about Callistus is gleaned from *Refutatio* IX,12.

[62] The most notable extant works include the *Apostolic Tradition,* for the information it provides about early Church order and rites; the *Refutatio*; and the *Syntagma,* an anti-heretical work (covering 32 heresies) much copied by later Christians. The *Syntagma* is not extant. A reconstruction was attempted by Pierre Nautin in *Hippolyte contre les hérésies. Fragment,* ETHDT 2 (Paris: Les Éditions du Cerf, 1949).

According to Quasten, then, the information from and about Hippolytus is both abundant and relatively secure. Meanwhile much has happened in the study of Hippolytus. This has been due in part to the repercussions of Pierre Nautin's thesis. He argued in 1947 that two people were probably responsible for the works which now all tend to be attributed to Hippolytus: a Roman presbyter named "Josipus" ('Ιώσηπος) who became anti-pope in opposition to Callistus and who wrote, among other things, the *Refutatio;* and a bishop named Hippolytus who had an unknown oriental post in the mid-third century.[63]

At present, the best summary of the *status quaestionis* is the collection of articles presented at a conference held at the Institutum Patristicum Augustinianum in 1976.[64] This collection reveals how data previously considered "factual" are now being questioned. For instance, M. Guarducci's article argues that the now-famous statue found in the sixteenth century was originally that of a female figure and could not have been Hippolytus.[65] As well, the authorship of the Hippolytean corpus continues to be questioned, and a modified version of Nautin's thesis is thought to be the likeliest option.[66] This would still assume that Hippolytus composed the *Refutatio.*[67]

3.4.1.3.

The *Refutatio* itself, meanwhile, is understood better than before. Regardless of who wrote it, the author's purpose can be determined, and this is a task which has recently occupied several scholars.[68] Actually, one does not have to be a sleuth to uncover the author's major redactional concerns, for Hippolytus himself (to call him them) is quite forthright about his intention.

---

[63] Pierre Nautin, *Hippolyte et Josipe: Contribution à l'histoire de la littérature chrétienne du troisième siècle,* ETHDT 1 (Paris: Les Éditions du Cerf, 1947). Josipus is said (in *Ref.* IX,6) to be the one who opposes Callistus.

[64] These were subsequently published in *Ricerche su Ippolito,* ed. by V. Loi et al., SEphA 13 (Rome: Institutum Patristicum "Augustinianum," 1977).

[65] M. Guarducci, "La statua di «Sant' Ippolito»," *Ricerche,* 17–30.

[66] Cf. the summary article by Manlio Simonetti, "A modo di conclusione: une ipotesi di lavoro," *Ricerche,* 151–56.

[67] Depending on whom one follows today, the author of the *Refutatio* could be Josipus (1) or Hippolytus (2), and the same author may (3) or may not (4) be the writer of the *Contra Noetum,* which in turn may (5) or may not (6) be a fragment of the lost anti-heretical *Syntagma* written before the *Refutatio.* See (1) Nautin, *Hippolyte et Josipe;* (2) Simonetti, "A modo di conclusione"; (3) Simonetti, "A modo di conclusione"; (4) Nautin, *Hippolyte et Josipe;* J. Frickel, "Contraddizioni nelle opere e nella persona di Ippolito di Roma," *Ricerche,* 137–50; (5) Nautin, *Hippolyte et Josipe;* (6) Frickel, "Contraddizioni."

[68] The two most notable attempts to isolate a *Tendenz* in the *Refutatio* are Vallée, *A Study in Anti-Gnostic Polemics,* 41–62; and Klaus Koschorke, *Hippolyts Ketzerbekämpfung und Polemik gegen die Gnostiker,* GOH 4 (Wiesbaden: Harrassowitz, 1975).

Hippolytus sets out to refute all the heresies known to him and includes the theories of Callistus among them.[69] He proceeds in the following manner. First, he seeks to uncover (his ἔλεγχος) these "heretical" doctrines. His intention is not to argue against them directly, but simply to expose them. The introductory sections of the work make it clear that he intends to show how the heresies are in fact not Christian. They derive their support neither from Scripture nor from the tradition of a Christian saint (μηθὲν ἐξ ἁγίων γραφῶν λαβόντες ταῦτα ἐπεχείρησαν ἤ τινος ἁγίου διαδοχὴν φυλάξαντες; Prooem. 8),[70] but depend on—and indeed shamefully "plagiarize"—the pagan philosophical systems. They "have their source in the wisdom of the Greeks, in the systems of the philosophers, in would-be mysteries, and the vagaries of astrologers" (ἀλλὰ ἔστιν αὐτοῖς τὰ δοξαζόμενα ἀρχὴν μὲν ἐκ τῆς Ἑλλήνων σοφίας λαβόντα, ἐκ δογμάτων φιλοσοφουμένων καὶ μυστηρίων ἐπικεχειρημένων καὶ ἀστρολόγων ῥεμβομένων; Prooem. 8).

The groundwork for this is prepared in Books 1-4 (of which the middle two are no longer extant), where Hippolytus surveys the non-Christian philosophical systems. Then in Books 5-9 he "exposes" each heresy and links it to the non-Christian theories described earlier. For Hippolytus, to make the connection is to offer a refutation. Guilt is by association, and to be Greek is to be dead in the faith.[71] Let us now turn to how he puts this into practice in Book 6.

3.4.2.1

Book 6 is devoted to an examination of Simon Magus (sections 7-20); then of Valentinus (21-38) and some of his followers, notably Marcus (39-54). The

[69] Koschorke (*Hippolyts Ketzerbekämpfung,* 56-92) claims that the polemic against Callistus is the driving force behind the entire work. This is overstated, and Vallée's cautionary remarks in this regard are well taken: "It appears that Callistus remains only one among many heretics whom the *Elenchos* wishes to unmask" (*Anti-Gnostic Polemics,* 46).

[70] Irenaeus makes his polemical point quite differently, intending to show that the heretics used Scripture, but misrepresented it—that they end up with a picture of a "dog" instead of a "king" (*Adv. haer.* I,8,1; 9,4). Hippolytus wants to distance the heretics as much as possible from the "true faith," so chooses not to deal with them at all as Christians.

[71] Following Koschorke (*Hippolyts Ketzerbekämpfung*), Vallée has argued that Hippolytus also worked with a view of reality predicated on progressive corruption. "The first heretics are assumed to be closer to the truth than those nearer or contemporary to Hippolytus. In this theory of the degradation of truth, Christian truth (or what Hippolytus holds for such) is identical with the truth of the primeval revelation. Some of the original truth was already lost in Judaism, but clearly more was wasted among the pagans—both barbarian and Greek. The heretics borrowed from the pagans and so lost even more of the truth. And so, from one heresy to the other, the phenomenon is seen as a descending genealogy, in which truth kept being degraded and lost" (*Anti-Gnostic Polemics,* 55-56). However, the internal support for this theory is based only on a few passages (i.e., Prooem. 8-9; VII,36,2), and cannot be considered a major redactional feature in the *Refutatio.*

"exposure" of other Valentinians which is promised in the introductory remarks either occurs rapidly (Secundus and Ptolemy in section 38) or never materializes at all (in the case of Heracleon and Colarbasus[72]). A close reading of the Valentinian section (21-55) reveals Hippolytus's sources and his *Tendenz*. The information is said to derive both from Irenaeus and from firsthand experience. Hippolytus claims to have observed some of their practices closely himself.[73] As well, he does not hide his dependence on Irenaeus. Note, for instance, the following remarks:

ἤδη τοῦ μακαρίου πρεσβυτέρου Εἰρηναίου δεινῶς καὶ πεπονημένως [ὡς] τὰ δόγματα αὐτῶν διελέγξαντος, παρ' οὗ καὶ αὐτῶν ἐφευρήματα <παρειλήφα-μεν>.

Now the blessed presbyter Irenaeus has powerfully and elaborately refuted the opinions of these (heretics). And to him we are indebted for a knowledge of their inventions. (55,2; cf. also 42,1; MacMahon, ANF)

Hippolytus's purpose in this section is not to argue against his opponents' views or to treat them as deviant Christians, but simply to expose their doctrines and then show how they plagiarize Pythagorean and Platonic insights (Πυθαγορι-κὴν ἔχουσα καὶ Πλατωνικὴν τὴν ὑπόθεσιν; 21,1).[74] He states at the end of section 41 that he has deliberately refrained from arguing against these deviant views so as

---

[72] Heracleon may be the ἄλλος δέ τις ἐπιφανὴς διδάσκαλος αὐτῶν of 38,2. As for the absence of Colarbasus, the best explanation is that both Irenaeus and Hippolytus mistook the Supreme Tetrad of Marcus's vision for a Valentinian person. Legge's remark is *apropos* (*Philosophumena*, II, 57 n. 4): "The name which is repeated by Tertullian, Philaster and Theodoret can be traced back to a single passage in Irenaeus, where it appears in connection with the name Σιγή as 'the Sige of Colarbasus.' A German commentator [G. Volkmar] long since suggested that it was not the name of a brother heretic or follower of Marcus, but a corruption of the words קל־ארבע Qol-Arba, or the 'Voice of the Four,' and this seems now generally accepted. As most if not all of Marcus' pretended revelations are said to have been dictated to him by an apparition of the Supreme Tetrad, he may well have called the book in which they were written and which seems to have been known to Irenaeus, by some such name."

[73] Koschorke (*Hippolyts Ketzerbekämpfung*) claims that the burning controversies between gnostics and other Christians were for the most part dead by the time Hippolytus wrote: "Hipp.s Refutatio ist kein Dokument, das uns über den Vorgang der Auseinandersetzung zwischen kirchlichem und gnostischem Christentum Auskunft gibt, vielmehr setzt sie die erfolgreiche Abdrängung der Gnostiker durch die Kirche bereits voraus" (94). Vallée (*Anti-Gnostic Polemics*, 61) supports this position. It is overstated, and the least we can say is that Hippolytus certainly claimed to have partaken in certain Valentinian ceremonies in his day.

[74] This Pythagorean and Platonic foundation in turn is said to derive from Egyptian thought (21,3).

to prevent someone from accusing him of misrepresenting them. In his opinion, his refutation will be stronger simply by showing how their views derive from the pagans.[75] Hippolytus's conclusion is that the Valentinian ideas have nothing to do with the teachings of Jesus. Rather, they are a degenerated form of these earlier pagan ideas and are simply worthless opinions, φλύαρα δόγματα (55,3).

3.4.2.2.

The passage about Marcus in this sixth book falls into two unequal parts separated by a few transitional lines. The introductory sections, 39–41, present Marcus as a deceiver or trickster who leads his followers to believe that he can grant them more power than he actually has. Hippolytus claims that this is accomplished first by cheap conjuring acts which he performs with the eucharistic cup (39–40): sometimes he secretly adds one type of potion to the eucharistic mixture, resulting in a change of color; other times he adds another type of potion into a small cup held by a female assistant, causing a rapid increase in the volume of the liquid and allowing Marcus to fill his larger cup to overflowing with the liquid. In both instances, his followers are led to assume that the eucharistic mixture has received a special power or grace of which they can partake. The deceit is also said to occur (41) when Marcus claims that his followers can acquire even more powers than other Christians through under-going a second baptism of repentance—and being given the promise of still higher levels of initiation. Hippolytus insists that it is the promise of these powers which keeps Marcus's followers returning to him. It is striking how all three of these introductory sections are united thematically and how they are bound by key words, e.g., πλάνη (39,3), πλάνος (41,1), πανοῦργος (39,2), and πανοῦργημα (41,3,5).[76]

The transition in the Marcosian section occurs in 42,1-2, where Irenaeus's contribution to the discussion is acknowledged, especially concerning the second baptism of redemption. Following this is an extended account of Marcus's theories of numerology and grammatology (42,2–55), coupled with the link with the Pythagoreans. This for Hippolytus is his most important section, since the Pythagorean connection allows him to belittle and dismiss Marcus and the other Valentinians (55).

One intriguing aspect of this passage is the comparison that is possible with the parallel section in Irenaeus. Not only does Hippolytus himself claim to have used Irenaeus, but we are able to observe a word-for-word overlap in many of

[75] This could be a reaction to criticisms already directed at Irenaeus's *evertio* in Book 2 of his *Adversus haereses*. Hippolytus's position would be even more understandable if he were trying to prevent others from undermining his results by accusing him of mis-representing his opponents' views as Irenaeus had done.

[76] These words drop out of usage in the following sections. Their absence from the parallel text from Irenaeus supports the view that Hippolytus either reworked the passage from Irenaeus significantly or had access to another written source. Given the similarities, the former is more likely.

the sections (e.g., from 43-55). In his use of Irenaeus, Hippolytus appears to reveal as much creative energy as Matthew, for instance, in his use of the Marcan *Vorlage*. The passage in Irenaeus has its own internal logic. Four aspects of the Marcosian teachings are introduced: their thaumaturgy (*Adv. haer.* 13,2-7), grammatology and arithmology (14,1-18,4), (false) biblical exegeses (19,1- 20,3), and the diversity of redemptive rites (21,1-5). This is followed by Irenaeus's account of the Church's *regulam veritatis* (22,1).

Hippolytus has omitted the third section in the *Adversus haereses*, in keeping with his tendency to deny the heretics any connection with the Church. He has also placed the fourth section after the first and combined the two. Furthermore, Irenaeus's first section focused on Marcus's womanizing tendencies and accepted the magical power of his feats, attributing their source to the demons and other Satanic spirits who helped him (13,4). According to Irenaeus, Marcus was a rogue, but one to be reckoned with because of his demonic cohorts. Hippolytus focused his discussion on showing how Marcus was simply a clever trickster, a πανοῦργος (a word which is absent from Irenaeus's passage). Gone is his link with the evil powers. Gone also is the attention to the diversity of rites of redemption which Irenaeus used as proof of his error. Instead, the rites of redemption are lumped together with the wine tricks and are treated as simply another way of keeping Marcus's followers dependent on him. Finally, Hippolytus has modified Irenaeus's second section by linking the grammatology and arithmology to the Pythagoreans. So, while Irenaeus ended his discussion on the point which he considered to be their Achilles' heel, i.e., their diversity of rites, Hippolytus does the same by linking the Marcosian speculations with Greek philosophy. The result is the same in each author's mind, but the means are different.

3.4.3.1

The passage which refers to sin occurs in section 41. It is part of the general discussion of baptism, as it was in the parallel passage in Irenaeus. Yet just as we saw how that passage in Irenaeus occurred in a very different context than the one in Hippolytus, it will become clear how the discussion in these passages also is somewhat different.

The passage is as follows:[77]

πολλὰ τοίνυν ἐξαφανίσας [καὶ] πολλοὺς τοιούτους < εἶναι, > μαθητὰς αὐτοῦ γενομένους προεβίβασεν, εὐκόλους μὲν εἶναι διδάξας πρὸς τὸ ἁμαρτάνειν, ἀκινδύνους δὲ διὰ τὸ εἶναι < αὐτοὺς > τῆς τελείας δυνάμεως καὶ μετέχειν τῆς ἀνεννοήτου ἐξουσίας.

---

[77] The text is from Marcovich, *Hippolytus*, 258-59; the translation is by Legge (*Philosophumena*, II, 42-43).

Further he utterly ruined many, and led on many of them to become his disciples (by) teaching them to be indifferent to sin as free from danger (to them) through their belonging to the Perfect Power and partakers of the Inconceivable Authority.

οἷς μετὰ τὸ <πρῶτον> βάπτισμα καὶ ἕτερον ἐπαγγέλλονται, ὃ καλοῦσιν ἀπολύτρωσιν, καὶ ἐν τούτῳ ἀναστρέφοντες κακῶς τοὺς αὐτοῖς παραμένοντας ἐπ᾿ ἐλπίδι τῆς ἀπολυτρώσεως, <ὡς> δυναμένους μετὰ τὸ ἅπαξ βαπτισθῆν<αι ἁμαρτάνον>τας πάλιν τυχεῖν ἀφέσεως.

To whom also after baptism they promise another which they call Redemption, and thereby turn again to evil who remain with them in the hope of deliverance, (as if) those who had been once baptized might again meet with acquittal.

<οἳ> καὶ διὰ τοῦ τοιούτου πανουργήματος συνέχειν δοκο[ῦ]σι τοὺς ἀκροατάς, οὓς ἐπὰν <οὖν> νομίσωσι δεδοκιμάσθαι καὶ δύνασθαι φυλάσσειν αὐτοῖς τὰ πιστά, τότε ἐπὶ <τὸ πρῶτον> λουτρὸν ἄγουσι, μηδὲ τούτῳ μόνῳ ἀρκούμενοι, ἀλλὰ καὶ ἕτερον [τι] ἐπαγγελ<λ>όμενοι, πρὸς τὸ συγκρατεῖν αὐτοὺς τῇ ἐλπίδι, ὅπως ἀχώριστοι ὦσι.

Through such jugglery, they seem to retain their hearers, whom, when they consider that they have been (duly) indoctrinated and are able to keep fast the things entrusted to them, they then lead to this (second baptism), not contenting themselves with this alone, but promising them still something else, for the purpose of keeping control over them by hope, lest they should separate from them.

λέγουσι γοῦν τι φωνῇ ἀρρήτῳ, ἐπιτιθέντες χεῖρα τῷ τὴν ἀπολύτρωσιν λαβόντι, ὃ φάσκουσιν ἐξειπεῖν εὐκόλως μὴ δύνασθαι εἰ μή τις εἴη ὑπερδόκιμος, ἢ ὅτε τελευτῶν<τι> πρὸς τὸ οὖς ἐλθὼν λέγει ὁ ἐπίσκοπος.

For they mutter something in an inaudible voice, laying hands on them for the receiving of Redemption which they pretend cannot be spoken openly unless one were highly instructed, or when the bishop would come to speak it into the ears of one departing this life.

καὶ τοῦτο δὲ <ἐστι> πανούργημα πρὸς τὸ ἀεὶ παραμένειν τοὺς μαθητὰς τῷ ἐπισκόπῳ, γλιχομένους μαθεῖν τὸ τί ποτε εἴη <ἐ>x<εῖν>ο τὸ ἐπ᾿ ἐσχάτων λεγόμενον, δι᾿ οὗ <τῶν> τελείων ἔσται ὁ μανθάνων.

And this jugglery is practised so that they may remain the bishop's disciples, eagerly desirous to learn what has been said about the last thing whereby the learner would become perfect.

3.4.3.2
    The general intent of the passage is clear. Hippolytus claims that the postbaptismal rites offered by Marcus to his followers, allegedly granting them

access to certain powers, is not only a knavish trick (πανούργημα—41,3,5) to keep his followers attached to him, but has also led many to ruin (πολλοὺς ἐξαφανίσας—41,1) because now they believe that sin need no longer concern them. It would seem that after his followers underwent the second baptism, ὃ καλοῦσιν ἀπολύτρωσιν, they belonged to the perfect power and shared in the inconceivable authority. This rendered them free from danger, ἀκινδύνοι, allowing them to be "at ease" (εὐκόλους) about sin.[78] Hippolytus hints at another degree of initiation available beyond the rite of redemption, but nothing is said about this except that it is seen as another way of keeping Marcus's followers coming back for more. In Hippolytus's view, then, the Marcosian claim to the existence of another level of redemption for sin is folly and is nothing but a clever marketing technique to reinforce the leader's powers and the group's (temporary) success.

This section is not in keeping with Hippolytus's claim throughout the book to be disinterested in engaging the heretics on their own ground and arguing with them. Here he does precisely that, and no doubt his troubles with Callistus played a part in this. We encounter this other πανοῦργος in sections 11 and 12 of Book 9:[79] according to Hippolytus, Callistus is "artful in evil and versatile in falsehood" (ἐν κακίᾳ πανοῦργος καὶ ποικίλος πρὸς πλάνην). Like Marcus—and unlike Hippolytus—he is willing to remit the sins of those who have transgressed after baptism (λέγων πᾶσιν ὑπ' αὐτοῦ ἀφίεσθαι ἁμαρτίας), and he too allowed the practice of second baptism (δεύτερον αὐτοῖς βάπτισμα—12,26). It is not surprising, then, given Hippolytus's troubles with Callistus, that Marcus's rite of redemption and

[78] MacMahon (ANF) has translated εὐκόλους as "prone" to sin, while Legge has "indifferent." Lampe's Patristic Lexicon supports MacMahon's reading. Both translations are possible, yet result in quite different interpretations. It is not easy to determine which translation is better. Εὔκολος has a standard range of meanings (so both Liddell and Scott, and Lampe): easily satisfied, contented (after a meal), good-natured; (used negatively) easily led, prone; (for things) easy, easy to understand. An examination of the occurrences of εὔκολος, εὐκόλως listed in Wendland's Wortregister (εὔκολος: IV,4,4; 14,6; 34,1; V,17,13; εὐκόλως: IV,45,2; 46,4; V,15,1; VI,41,4; VII,13,3; 14; IX,18,2) is of little use because in every one of these instances—including an adverbial use in our pericope (VI,41,4)—the author meant "easy, easy to understand."

The reading "prone to sin," however, does not seem to make as much sense in context as "indifferent." In this passage Hippolytus is not accusing the Marcosians of sinning excessively, but of undergoing a rite which allows them to feel "at ease" about their past sins, and perhaps also about those which they continue to commit.

[79] Πανοῦργος is listed five times in Wendland's Wortregister to the Refutatio: twice of Callistus (IX,11,1; 12,5); once of Marcus (VI,39,2); once of some magicians (IV,42,2); and once of sirens (VII,13,1). Similarly, one of the four occurrences of πανουργία concerns Callistus (IX,11,2). Furthermore, two of the occurrences of πανούργημα concern Marcus (VI,41,3,5), and another the Elchesaites (IX,13,4) in the context of their view of baptism and sins (which resembled that of Marcus). It is notable that seven out of thirteen uses of these words refer directly to a "heretical" view of baptism and remission of sins. Indeed, for Hippolytus, "knavery" goes hand in hand with a mistaken view of baptism and the remission of sins.

its corresponding freedom from sin should have required a rebuttal by Hippolytus.

3.4.3.3

Reconstructing the Marcosian view of sin and baptism from this passage is no easy matter, but the following synthesis seems to be the likeliest. Marcus taught that a second washing or baptism, called redemption (ἀπολύτρωσιν), was available to Christians and could be administered by him. It normally required special and extensive instructions beforehand, but Marcus himself could also administer it to those who were on their deathbed. All who passed through this rite belonged to ἡ τελεία δύναμις καὶ ἡ ἀνεννόητος ἐξουσία, and for them sin was no longer a concern. The rite of redemption had removed their sins. This meant that the sins they had committed after their baptism would not be counted against them, and perhaps also (though there is no direct evidence for this) that they would no longer sin. One assumes that those Marcosian Christians who had not yet received the second baptism were bound by sin in the same manner as the Hippolytean Christians. They seemed to have differed not over their definition or understanding of sin, but over Marcus's teaching that another step was possible for some (the pneumatics? the psychics?), granting them access to enormous powers, including the power over sin.

3.5 Origen

3.5.1.1

Heracleon introduces sin on three occasions in what remains of his commentary on John's gospel, which Origen has imbedded in his own. Before turning our attention to these passages we summarize what can be said about Heracleon, his commentary, Origen's commentary on the same gospel, and their inclusion of sin.

3.5.1.2

The information which the second and third century Fathers provide about Heracleon's life can be listed in a paragraph. Irenaeus mentions him once, in conjunction with Ptolemy, whose theories he explores in detail;[80] Clement calls him the most illustrious member of the Valentinian school (ὁ τῆς Οὐαλεντίνου σχολῆς δοκιμώτατος);[81] Origen, with more reserve, states that Heracleon is considered to be Valentinus's disciple — or perhaps his acquaintance (τὸν Οὐαλεντίνου λεγόμενον εἶναι γνώριμον);[82] Tertullian mentions him once, and places him on the

---

[80] Irenaeus, *Adversus haereses* I,2,4.

[81] Clement, *Stromata* IV,71.

[82] Origen, *In Joannem* II,14,100. Cf. also A. E. Brooke's remark: "The exact meaning of Origen's description of him ... is uncertain, but the phrase used (γνώριμος) would hardly be neutral, unless Heracleon has been a prominent member of the school during the lifetime of Valentinus." In *The Fragments of Heracleon,* TextsS 1,4 (Cambridge:

Ptolemaic trajectory;[83] and Hippolytus assumes he is a Valentinian who, along with Ptolemy, falls into the Italian school (i.e., those who claimed that Jesus' body was psychic rather than pneumatic).[84] Actually, Hippolytus's remark is the closest one gets to an interpretation of what Heracleon thought. In a composite sketch, one would include Heracleon within the Valentinian movement, perhaps in the Western camp, and deduce that he was respected yet not particularly well-known.

3.5.1.3

Fortunately, Origen has preserved parts of Heracleon's commentary on John's gospel.[85] To be sure, the sections are few, and they are set in a polemical context (one also thinks of Celsus's remarks preserved in another of Origen's works). Yet before the Nag Hammadi find they provided the most extensive primary source for Valentinianism.

As far as we can tell, Heracleon's work was the earliest full commentary on this gospel. It seems to have been a running commentary on the entire gospel, with the odd verse left out.[86] Heracleon sometimes interpreted the Johannine text literally (in his words, κατὰ τὸ ἁπλοῦν), and sometimes allegorically or spiritually (κατὰ τὸ νοούμενον). Origen did the same, and it is fascinating to witness how at times he accuses Heracleon of not looking for a deeper meaning in a passage, and conversely at times of being too fanciful.[87] All that remains from Heracleon's commentary are remarks on sixty-four gospel verses from the following sections: 1:3-29; 2:12-20; 4:13-53; and 8:21-50.[88]

3.5.1.4

Origen's commentary on John also is no longer complete. Actually, even Eusebius had access to only about half of the *In Joannem*,[89] and he wrote merely

---

University Press, 1891) 33. Origen's phrase (λεγόμενον εἶναι γνώριμον) is more ambiguous than Brooke suggests.

[83] Tertullian, *Adversus valentinianos* 4.

[84] Hippolytus, *Refutatio* VI,29,36.

[85] These are now commonly listed as a series of 48 fragments. So Völker, *Quellen,* 63-85; and Foerster, *Gnosis,* 162-81. Three other fragments, two from Clement and one from Photius, are preserved from Heracleon's work. The first two probably are not from his commentary on John's gospel; the last one is an indirect remark about John 1:17.

[86] Cf. Origen's comment on John 4:32: οὐδὲν δὲ εἰς τὴν λέξιν εἶπεν ὁ Ἡρακλέων (Frag. 29).

[87] For Origen's critique of Heracleon's method see *In Joannem* VI,35,174; 39,198; XIX,19,124.

[88] The specific gospel verses extant from Heracleon's commentary are 1:3-4, 17-19, 21, 23-29; 2:12-15, 17, 19-20; 4:13-42, 46-53; 8:21-22, 37b, 43-44, 50.

[89] The complete Greek title of the work, which occurs in several manuscripts, is Ὠριγένους τῶν εἰς τὸ κατὰ Ἰωάννην εὐαγγέλιον ἐξηγητικῶν (τόμος α', β', . . .), which sometimes (e.g., in Brooke's edition) is simply rendered into Latin: Origenis commentariorum in evangelium Joannis.

a century later than the Alexandrian.[90] Aside from additional fragments of the work scattered in the Fathers,[91] what remains now (of the *ca.* 40 volume work) are the following books: 1 (covering Jn 1:1), 2 (re: 1:1-7), 4-5 (in fragmentary form, and dealing with general exegetical issues), 6 (re: 1:19-29), 10 (re: 2:12-25), 13 (re: 4:13-54), 19 (re: 8:19-25), 20 (re: 8:37-53), 28 (re: 11:39-57), and 32 (re: 13:2-33).

It is clear from this extant collection that the commentary was both massive in length and unequal in focus. Book 1 takes us no further than the first five words of the gospel (Ἐν ἀρχῇ ἦν ὁ λόγος), and Book 6 reaches only the midway point of Chapter 1; yet twelve books later we are in the eighth chapter. It is remarkable that in the 480 pages of Greek text which remain (in Preuschen's edition), Origen has managed to cover only one sixth of the gospel.[92]

Two Valentinians also had important roles to play in the genesis and development of the *In Joannem*. One was Heracleon, whose commentary on John's gospel helped to instigate Origen's version. The other was Ambrose, whom Origen claims to have turned away from Valentinianism, and who backed the enterprise with his enthusiasm and financial support.[93] Ambrose would have been familiar with Valentinian exegesis, and perhaps eager for Origen to distance himself from it. Origen himself makes it clear that he decided to write a Scriptural commentary in order to counter those already in existence which had been written by heretics:[94]

> Voilà pourquoi il me paraît nécessaire que, si quelqu'un peut défendre sans la falsifier la pensée de l'Église et confondre les partisans de la prétendue gnose, il se dresse pour opposer aux inventions des hérétiques la sublimité de la prédication évangélique (*In Jo.* V,8).

Ironically, a work which emerged partly as a rebuttal of the Valentinian interpretation of John's gospel has preserved the most extensive Valentinian discussion of this gospel.

3.5.1.5

Heracleon does not have a great deal to say about sin. In fact, on the surface, sin seems to play a role in only three of the forty-eight fragments. The detailed exegeses of these pericopes which follow determine what can be said about Heracleon's view of sin.

---

[90] Eusebius (*Eccl. hist.* VI,24) acknowledges having access to only 22 books. Moreover, he claims in VI,21,3-4 that this was one of Origen's first works.

[91] Dozens of fragments, even those of dubious authenticity, are conveniently listed in Preuschen's edition of the *In Joannem,* pages 483-574.

[92] 149 verses out of a total of 878 in the Gospel of John are treated in the *In Joannem.*

[93] We read of Ambrose's influence and support in Eusebius (*Eccl. hist.* VI,18,23,1-2), and in the *In Joannem* I,21; V,1; VI,6.9.

[94] Blanc, SC 120, 388-89.

What needs to be stressed at this point is that, given the nature of Heracleon's work, its location in Origen's commentary, and the poor textual transmission of the *In Joannem,* the infrequent mention of sin is to be expected and by itself says nothing about the importance of sin to Heracleon. First, it happens that we have access to only one of Heracleon's works, and this is a commentary on a gospel in which sin does not play a major role. How different the situation would be if this were a commentary on Romans! Second, Heracleon's comments have been placed in another work where roughly half of the energy has been devoted to explaining John 1–7. These are chapters in which sin is mentioned only twice in the gospel (1:29; 5:14). Finally, Origen's commentary on most of the sections in John's gospel which do mention sin is no longer extant. Of the twenty-four instances where sin is introduced directly into the Johannine discussion,[95] Origen's surviving text covers only five (1:29; 8:21, 24[bis], 46), and in only two of these (1:29, 8:21) has he provided Heracleon's views. Actually, Heracleon introduced sin into his discussion of 4:46–47 (Fr. 40) where it was absent from the Johannine text itself. It is surprising that under these conditions any Valentinian reference to sin has survived in the *In Joannem.*

3.5.2.1
The first mention of sin by Heracleon is in Fragment 10, a comment on John 1:29 which occurs at the end of Book 6. In fact, the very end of this book is lost, and Origen's rebuttal which follows Heracleon's commentary is now incomplete. Our analysis of this passage will proceed as follows. The pericope will be quoted in full; then the exegesis will focus on the passage itself and on setting it into context.

3.5.2.2
The passage in question (VI,60,306) is as follows:[96]

Πάλιν ἐν τῷ τόπῳ [Jn 1:29b: ὁ ἀμνὸς τοῦ θεοῦ ὁ αἴρων τὴν ἁμαρτίαν τοῦ κόσμου] ὁ Ἡρακλέων γενόμενος χωρὶς πάσης κατασκευῆς καὶ παραθέσεως μαρτυριῶν ἀποφαίνεται ὅτι τὸ μὲν «Ἀμνὸς τοῦ θεοῦ» ὡς προφήτης φησὶν ὁ Ἰωάννης, τὸ δὲ «Ὁ αἴρων τὴν ἁμαρτίαν τοῦ κόσμου» ὡς περισσότερον προφήτου.

Arrivé à ce passage, Héracléon déclare de nouveau, sans construire ni apporter aucune preuve, que, en tant que prophète, Jean dit «l'Agneau de Dieu» et, en tant que plus que prophète, «celui qui ôte le péché du monde».

---

[95] I.e., ἁμαρτία—1:29; 8:21, 24(bis), 34(bis), 46; 9:34, 41(bis); 15:22(bis), 24; 16:8, 9; 19:11; 20:23; ἁμαρτάνω—5:14; 9:2, 3; ἁμαρτωλός—9:16, 24, 25, 31.
[96] Text and translation are taken from Blanc, SC 157, 364–67. Cf. also Preuschen, *Origenes,* 168–69; Foerster, *Gnosis,* 165–66; and Völker, *Quellen,* 68.

Καὶ οἴεται τὸ μὲν πρότερον περὶ τοῦ σώματος αὐτοῦ λέγεσθαι, τὸ δὲ δεύτερον περὶ τοῦ ἐν τῷ σώματι, τῷ τὸν ἀμνὸν ἀτελῆ εἶναι ἐν τῷ τῶν προβάτων γένει, οὕτω δὲ καὶ τὸ σῶμα παραθέσει τοῦ ἐνοικοῦντος αὐτῷ.

Il pense que la première affirmation concerne son corps, parce que l'agneau est un être imparfait dans la race des ovins et de même le corps, comparé à celui qui l'habite.

Τὸ δὲ τέλειον εἰ ἐβούλετο, φησί, τῷ σώματι μαρτυρῆσαι, κριόν εἶπεν ἂν τὸ μέλλον θύεσθαι.

Car, dit il, s'il avait voulu attribuer la perfection au corps, il aurait appelé bélier ce qui était sur le point d'être sacrifié.

Οὐχ ἡγοῦμαι δὲ εἶναι ἀναγκαῖον μετὰ τηλικαύτας γεγενημένας ἐξετάσεις τευτάζειν περὶ τὸν τόπον, ἀγωνιζομένους πρὸς τὰ εὐτελῶς ὑπὸ τοῦ Ἡρακλέωνος εἰρημένα.

Je ne pense pas qu'après l'avoir si longuement étudié il soit nécessaire de nous attarder à ce sujet pour réfuter les allégations qu'Héracléon avance à la légère.

Μόνον δὲ τοῦτο ἐπισημειωτέον, ὅτι ὥσπερ μόγις ἐχώρησεν ὁ κόσμος τὸν κενώσαντα ἑαυτόν, οὕτως ἀμνοῦ καὶ οὐ κριοῦ ἐδεήθη, ἵνα ἀρθῇ αὐτοῦ ἡ ἁμαρτία . . . [texts breaks off].

Remarquons seulement ceci: de même que le monde pouvait à peine contenir celui qui s'est anéanti lui-même, de même avait-il besoin, pour ôter son péché, d'un agneau et non d'un bélier. . . .

3.5.2.3

The "simple" meaning of this pericope — or, as Heracleon would say, the one κατὰ τὸ ἀπλοῦν — is straightforward. It revolves around John and Jesus, the world and sin. Heracleon begins by separating the first part of the phrase, "Behold, the Lamb of God," from the second, "who takes away the sin of the world." He relegates the former to a lower level of awareness, and focuses on something which troubled Origen as well (but which now strikes us as curious): the lamb is imperfect in the genus of sheep (the mature ram, one learns from Origen's concluding remark, is the perfect one), so calling Jesus "the Lamb of God" attributes imperfection to him.[97] This could not reflect the true nature of Jesus,

---

[97] In beginning his commentary on this verse (51,264–52,272), Origen has attempted to determine why John depicts Jesus as a lamb. He too has trouble with attributing this seemingly imperfect animal to something perfect. It is the daily offering of the two lambs at the temple (required in Exod 29:38–44) which allows him to appreciate its attribution to Jesus, for Origen can then claim that John applied the term symbolically to Jesus to represent his sacrifice offered in perpetuity.

according to Heracleon, so it throws doubt on the quality of John's statement. Heracleon then exonerates John the Baptist, tapping into the insights of the Evangelist to claim that the Baptist had two roles or natures (the vocabulary here is imprecise). Following the one he is a prophet and has access to a limited reality. As such he can call Jesus "Lamb of God." His other nature is to be "more than a prophet," and this provides access to a deeper truth. In this instance, it is the insight that Jesus removes the sin of the world. In turn, these two natures of John allow him to discern Jesus' two natures: his external body and that which dwells within this body. John's lower nature, then, permits him to bear witness to Jesus' lower reality, while his higher nature allows him to see beyond this to Jesus' internal nature.[98]

John's insight is that Jesus came into the world to take away sin. This implies that sin was in the world, that Jesus' mission was to remove it, and that it was a secret mission — or, at any rate, one which was not evident to anyone, even to a prophet. It also implies that the task of removing the world's sin was important enough to warrant Jesus' descent.

3.5.2.4

The deeper meaning of this pericope is not as easy to discern, especially for those of us who are not even prophets! We would like to know more about sin, for instance, and in particular its role before and after Jesus' descent. It is best to postpone that inquiry pending the exegesis of fragments 40 and 41. Meanwhile, examining other fragments will provide more information about Heracleon's understanding of the "world" (κόσμος) and the two natures of John, allowing us to say more about Fragment 10.

3.5.2.5

Three features about the "world" recur in the fragments. The first is that it is a realm which physically occupies a middle position between the aeon (or the Pleroma) and matter. It is the "Middle" (Μεσότης — Frag. 40). The aeon was created before the Logos, and the world was created by the Demiurge through the agency of the Logos (Frag. 1). Fragments 8 and 17 contrast the greatness of the aeon with the limited nature of the world.[99] The second feature is an extension of the first: the world is described in negative terms. Actually, this is consistent with what one finds in the Gospel of John itself. "Worldly" (Κοσμική) life

---

[98] This two-nature distinction drawn by Heracleon concerning Jesus accords with Hippolytus's claim that Heracleon belonged to the "Italian school" which argued that Jesus' body was psychic, not pneumatic.

[99] This use of αἰών in contrast to κόσμος recalls Valentinus's usage of the word in one of the fragments remaining from his work (Frag. 5 — Clement, *Strom.* IV,89,6–90,1): ὁπόσον ἐλάττων ἡ εἰκὼν τοῦ ζῶντος προσώπου, τοσοῦτον ἥσσων ὁ κόσμος τοῦ ζῶντος αἰῶνος ("the world is as much inferior to the living aeon as the picture is inferior to the living figure" — Foerster).

for Heracleon is "insipid, temporary and unsatisfactory" (Frag. 17). Third, the world is the place to which the Savior was sent to begin a new dispensation (οἰκονομία — Frag. 11). It is compared to the "sandal" which Jesus wears (Frag. 8 — re: Jn 1:26-27), or "Samaria," the place to which he was sent (Frag. 31 — re: Jn 4:34).

3.5.2.6

Fragments 3-10 deal with John 1:18-29 and focus on John the Baptist.[100] Heracleon's intent is clear and consistent: he wants to pinpoint John's position in relation to the Christ and the prophets, and concludes that John definitely is inferior to the Christ, but is also partly more than a prophet. In Fragment 8 John claims to be unable even to describe the lower, "fleshly" aspect of Christ (an aspect symbolized by his sandal), while in Fragment 4 he acknowledges that he is neither a prophet nor the Christ.[101] Heracleon, though, is familiar with the pericope in Matthew's gospel where Jesus calls John Elijah (Matt 11:9-14), and deduces from that passage that John must be a prophet. How, then, can he be both a prophet (following Matthew) and not a prophet (following John)? His solution to this problem is that John functions sometimes as a prophet, and sometimes as more than a prophet (but still not on a par with Christ).[102] There is then an overlap between John and the old dispensation, but John remains only a precursor of the new.

Fragment 5 effectively summarizes this portrayal of John. In explaining John 1:23 Heracleon finds a triple distinction implied in the text and says that the Word (Λόγος) is the Savior, the voice in the desert is John, and the cry, or echo, is the entire prophetic order. These are three distinct levels of being, although the lowest can move up to the second, and the second to the highest. He characterizes "John himself" as the voice (τότε αὐτὸν τὸν 'Ιωάννην χαρακτηρίζει), and assigns his "attributes" (οὐκ αὐτὸν ἀλλὰ τὰ περὶ αὐτόν) to the echo, or the prophetic order.

---

[100] For discussions of John the Baptist in these fragments, see Blanc, SC 157, 27-38; and J. Mouson, "Jean-Baptiste dans le fragments d'Héracléon," EThL 30 (1954) 301-22.

[101] Origen takes Heracleon to task in Fragment 4 for not paying attention to the definite article in front of "prophet" ("Are you Elijah . . .? Are you *the* prophet?"), but it is likely that Heracleon deliberately placed an indefinite article there, for it would then accord well with his understanding of John.

[102] A. Orbe claims that when John was "more than a prophet," he was in fact seen to be a disciple. He supports this from Fragment 3 ("Heracleon says that the words 'No one has ever seen God, etc.' were said 'not by the Baptist, but by the disciple'."): "Orígenes no ha percibido el significado inherente al término μαθητής; cree que Heracleón atribuye simplemente Io 1, 15-17 al Bautista, y Io 1, 18 al Evangelista. Y le combate desde este punto de vista." In "El primer testimonio del Bautista sobre el Salvador, según Heracleón y Orígenes," EstE 30 (1956) 35. This is possible, but one then has to assume that Origen failed to see the distinction anywhere else too, for no other fragment suggests such an interpretation.

This depiction of John the Baptist is often assimilated to the "classical" account of Valentinianism in Irenaeus. Foerster's comment is typical: "For Heracleon, John the Baptist is at one moment a symbol for the psychics, or for the Demiurge; at another, a symbol for the pneumatics."[103] This interpretation does not do full justice to Heracleon's remarks. For one thing, in the Fragments John remains devoid of absolute knowledge. When Heracleon insists in Fragment 3 that the perceptive statement about God in 1:18 was not said by the Baptist, it is probably because it could not have been, given John's level of perception. Also, it is important to recognize in Fragment 5 that while the top level (Logos–Savior) indeed is pneumatic, the bottom one (Echo–Prophecy) is not sarkic. Judged from Irenaeus's perspective, Heracleon has added another psychic level and has attributed it to John's inner self. In other words, in these fragments John the Baptist seems to be entirely limited to the psychic realm, but to an expanded one![104]

The only passage which could suggest an overlap between the Christ and John is the reference to baptism in Fragment 6. This concerns the question raised by the priests and the levites in John 1:25: "Why do you baptize if you are neither the Christ nor Elijah nor the Prophet?" Heracleon comments on this Jewish question by accepting their restriction (only the Christ, Elijah, or the Prophet can baptize), removing the definite article in front of "prophet," and including John among them![105] Elaine Pagels interprets this to mean that in "discussing the baptist, Heracleon explains that only the representatives of the lowest, 'prophetic order' have the duty of baptizing. . . . John, in his 'external' and historical role, does baptize. Yet inwardly, 'he himself' does not baptize."[106] She is correct in

---

[103] Foerster, *Gnosis,* 164. So also Sagnard, *La gnose,* 492–93; 513–14.

[104] Mouson has arrived at a similar conclusion and has formulated a distinctive explanation: "Rien dans la science de Jean-Baptiste ne trahissant une nature pneumatique, le Précurseur est et demeure, pour Héracléon, tout entier psychique. Reste qu'il peut être considéré successivement comme «prophète» et comme «supérieur aux prophètes». S'il n'est pas un psychique doublé d'un pneumatique, comment expliquer cette dualité en lui? La solution découle encore de ce qui précède. Elle n'est pas à chercher sur le plan *ontologique* d'une dualité de nature en Jean-Baptiste, mais, au niveau de la *sotériologie* valentinienne, dans la distinction de deux états successifs de l'unique nature psychique, l'un antérieur, l'autre postérieur à la venue du Sauveur" ("Jean-Baptiste," 313).

Elaine Pagels also finds that the fragments do not support the view that John, as "more than a prophet," spoke as a pneumatic. However, her claim that Heracleon is depicting a "process of *transformation in gnosis*" in which John has progressed from the sarkic ("as a prophet") to the psychic ("as more than a prophet") level is less convincing. See *The Johannine Gospel in Gnostic Exegesis: Heracleon's Commentary on John,* SBLMS 17 (Nashville: Abingdon, 1973) 55–57. Her position in this regard is consistent with the classic Valentinian thought, yet what is problematic is assigning the prophets to the sarkic level. Mouson's position does more justice to the Fragments.

[105] Origen interprets this verse differently and puts into question the validity of the Jewish claim. He insists on keeping the definite article in front of "prophet," says that the Christ is in fact "the prophet," and then points out that neither he nor Elijah baptized.

[106] Pagels, *The Johannine Gospel,* 59.

saying that John, as a prophet, would be baptizing in his "external role." It is not certain, however, whether this excludes baptism by him in his role "as more than a prophet," especially since "Christ" is also mentioned in this list of baptizers, a list which Heracleon seems to accept. If Christ can baptize, surely the "enhanced John" can do as much. Baptism, then, may be something which Heracleon considered applicable both to Christ and to John.

3.5.2.7

In Fragment 10, Jesus' mission to remove the sin of the world is consistent with the description of κόσμος elsewhere in Heracleon's commentary. Jesus came from the aeon and was sent to the world. This world was not evil since it was created through the agency of the Logos. But it was inferior and "unsatisfying." Jesus was sent to begin a new dispensation or age of salvation, and this included (or entailed?) baptism in the spirit and the removal of sin from the world. When John the Baptist announced that the Christ came to "take away the sin of the world," he spoke as "more than a prophet," and provided a deeper understanding of Christ's role. However, this was an understanding of Christ which still emanated from the psychic level, for Heracleon seems not to have set John among the pneumatics.

3.5.3.1

Fragments 40, a commentary on the Capernaum official whose son was ill (Jn 4:46–53; *In Jo.* XIII,60, 416–26), is the longest of the 48 fragments. Although sin is not part of the Johannine text, it does play a significant role in Heracleon's commentary. In seeking to understand his view of sin, we proceed as we did above, determining what the text is, what it says and what can be added to the explanation by setting it in context.

3.5.3.2

The entire fragment is as follows (due to the length of this passage, the Greek is quoted only after the appropriate sections):[107]

> LX. 416. Héracléon semble dire que le *basilikos,* c'est le démiurge, car il régnait, lui aussi, sur ses subordonnés, mais parce que, toujours selon les dires d'Héracléon, son royaume était petit et éphémère, il fut appelé *basilikos,* comme qui dirait «petit roi» établi sur un petit royaume par un roi universel.

> Quant à son fils de Capharnaüm, il raconte que c'est celui de la partie inférieure du milieu, proche de la mer, c'est-à-dire attenant à la

---

[107] For the text and translation of Fragment 40, see Blanc, SC 222, 262–67. Cf. also Völker, *Quellen,* 80–82; Foerster, *Gnosis,* 177–79; Preuschen, *Origenes,* 291–93. For discussion of this fragment, see Foerster, *Von Valentin,* 25–28; and Blanc, "Le commentaire d'Héracléon sur Jean 4 et 8," *Aug* 15 (1975) 109–16.

matière, et il dit que l'homme personnellement attaché au démiurge, étant malade, c'est-à-dire dans un état contraire à sa nature, était dans l'ignorance et les péchés.

τὸν δὲ ἐν Καφαρναοὺμ υἱὸν αὐτοῦ διηγεῖται τὸν ἐν τῷ ὑποβεβηκότι μέρει τῆς μεσότητος τῷ πρὸς θάλασσαν, τουτέστιν τῷ συνημμένῳ τῇ ὕλῃ, καὶ λέγει ὅτι ὁ ἴδιος αὐτοῦ ἄνθρωπος ἀσθενῶν, τουτέστιν οὐ κατὰ φύσιν ἔχων, ἐν ἀγνοίᾳ καὶ ἁμαρτήμασιν ἦν.

417. Ensuite les mots «de Judée en Galilée» seraient mis pour «de la Judée d'en haut». . . . A propos de l'expression «Il était sur le point de mourir», il imagine, je ne sais sous quelle impulsion, que par là sont réfutées les opinions de ceux qui admettent l'immortalité de l'âme: à la même conclusion aboutit, d'après lui, le texte «L'âme et le corps périssent dans la géhenne».

418. Héracléon pense donc que l'âme n'est pas immortelle, mais capable de salut, et affirme que c'est elle l'être corruptible qui revêt l'incorruptibilité, l'être mortel qui revêt l'immortalité, lorsque sa mort est engloutie dans la victoire. 419. Il affirme, en outre, que ces mots «Si vous ne voyez des signes et des prodiges, vous ne croirez pas» s'adressent, comme il convient, à un tel personnage (le démiurge), pour qui il est naturel de se laisser persuader par des événements sensibles et non de croire un parole.

420. Quant à la demande «Descends avant que mon enfant ne meure», elle aurait été formulée, pense-t-il, parce que la mort est l'aboutissement de la loi qui, par les péchés, cause la ruine. Donc, dit-il, avant qu'il n'ait été complètement mis à mort selon ses péchés, le père supplie l'unique Sauveur de porter secours à son fils, c'est-à-dire à une telle nature.

420. Τὸ δὲ «Κατάβηθι πρὶν ἀποθανεῖν τὸ παιδίον μου» διὰ τὸ τέλος εἶναι τοῦ νόμου τὸν θάνατον εἰρῆσθαι νομίζει, ἀναιροῦντος διὰ τῶν ἁμαρτιῶν· πρὶν τελέως οὖν, φησί, θανατωθῆναι κατὰ τὰς ἁμαρτίας δεῖται ὁ πατὴρ τοῦ μόνου σωτῆρος, ἵνα βοηθήσῃ τῷ υἱῷ, τουτέστιν τῇ τοιᾷδε φύσει.

421. Il a expliqué, en outre, que c'est par modestie que le Sauveur a dit: «Ton fils vit», vu qu'il n'a pas dit «Qu'il vive» et qu'il n'a pas montré que c'est lui qui a procuré la vie. C'est, affirme-t-il, après être descendu vers le malade, l'avoir guéri de sa maladie, c'est-à-dire de ses péchés, et l'avoir vivifié par cette rémission, qu'il a dit: «Ton fils vit».

Πρὸς τούτοις τὸ «Ὁ υἱός σου ζῇ» κατὰ ἀτυφίαν εἰρῆσθαι τῷ σωτῆρι ἐξείληφεν, ἐπεὶ οὐκ εἶπεν· «ζήτω», οὐδὲ ἐνέφηνεν αὐτὸς παρεσχῆσθαι τὴν ζωήν. Λέγει δὲ ὅτι καταβὰς πρὸς τὸν κάμνοντα καὶ ἰασάμενος αὐτὸν τῆς νόσου, τουτέστιν τῶν ἁμαρτιῶν, καὶ διὰ τῆς ἀφέσως ζωοποιήσας εἶπεν· «Ὁ υἱός σου ζῇ».

422. Après les mots «Cet homme crut», il ajoute: car le démiurge croit facilement que le Sauveur peut guérir, même sans être présent.

Καὶ ἐπιλέγει πρὸς τὸ «Ἐπίστευσεν» ὁ ἄνθρωπος· ὅτι εὔπιστος καὶ ὁ δημιουργός ἐστιν, ὅτι δύναται ὁ σωτὴρ καὶ μὴ παρὼν θεραπεύειν.

423. Les serviteurs du *basilikos* seraient, d'après son interprétation, les anges du démiurge qui, en disant «Ton enfant vit», annoncent qu'il se comporte convenablement selon son caractère et qu'il ne fait plus ce qui ne convient pas. Il pense que le motif pour lequel les serviteurs portent au *basilikos* l'annonce du salut de son fils, c'est que les anges sont, à ce qu'il croit, les premiers à voir les actions des hommes en ce monde et à voir si, à partir de la venue du Sauveur, ils manifestent vigueur et pureté dans leur manière de vivre.

424. A propos de la septième heure, il dit encore que cette heure caractérise la nature de l'enfant guéri. Enfin, la phrase «Il crut lui-même ainsi que toute sa maison», il l'a rapportée à l'ordre angélique et aux hommes apparentés au démiurge. 425. On se demande, dit-il, à propos de certains anges, ceux qui sont descendus vers les filles des hommes, s'ils seront sauvés. A son avis, la perte des hommes du démiurge est manifestée dans le passage: «Les fils du royaume iront dans les ténèbres extérieures». 426. A leur sujet, Isaïe aurait prophétisé ceci: «J'ai engendré des fils, je les ai élevés et ce sont eux qui m'ont repoussé»: il les appellerait «fils étrangers», «race perfide et sans loi» et «vigne produisant des épines».

3.5.3.3

This is a pericope which Heracleon interprets κατὰ τὸ νοούμενον, since he assumes that the evangelist did not simply wish to describe an isolated healing and conversion experience. So, when Jesus is said to come down to Cana ἐκ τῆς Ἰουδαίας εἰς τὴν Γαλιλαίαν (4:47), Heracleon claims that he really came ἐκ τῆς ἄνωθεν Ἰουδαίας (417), i.e., from the upper, spiritual realm to the one below. Meanwhile the official in the story is a βασιλικός, or petty king set up by one who is greater to rule a small and ephemeral kingdom. This, according to Heracleon, symbolizes the Demiurge (416), the ruler of the lower realm, who is well-meaning but limited in understanding and power. It enables him to believe easily that the Savior can heal, but necessitates belief through works alone, καὶ οὐχὶ λόγῳ (419).

The Demiurge is concerned for the health of his son who is ill and living in Capernaum. This son symbolizes his offspring, humankind, who is of his (psychic) nature: ὁ ἴδιος αὐτοῦ [τοῦ δημιουργοῦ] ἄνθρωπος (416). This offspring lives close to matter (τῇ ὕλῃ — 416) and is on the verge of dying. Capernaum, as the area near the sea, symbolizes the region closest to matter, "the lowest part of the middle by the sea."[108] The combination in the gospel of the request for Jesus to heal the psychics and the presence of a psychic who is near death is a sign for Heracleon that the *psychē*/soul is not immortal, yet is capable of salvation (ἐπιτηδείως ἔχουσαν πρὸς σωτηρίαν — 418). The soul is mortal and corruptible (otherwise it could not die), but it can become immortal and incorruptible (or it could not be saved). Furthermore, the healing which Jesus is asked to perform on the "son" will not result in salvation for all. His remission of sins is for all and life is offered to all, but not all will choose to accept the offer (425-26).

The official's servants in the Johannine pericope are said to be the Demiurge's angels. Their function is to watch over people and to decide whether, once the Savior has gone, the psychics continue to lead their lives ἐρρωμένως καὶ εἰλικρινῶς (423). These terms are apt. The first means "vigorously, manfully, in good health"; the second, "without mixture, pure." The French translation ("vigueur et pureté") is better than the bland English in Foerster ("well and sincerely"), yet it still does not bring out the full force of these terms in context. One must remember that the Savior has just healed some of the psychics, removing their sins and ignorance, pulling them away from the material realm. What the angels must ascertain afterwards is whether these psychics stay "in good health" (i.e., sinless) and "pure" (i.e., away from the hylic realm and in keeping with their own nature). Determinism is downplayed: the psychics have been pulled away from the brink of death and given a new lease on life, but the choice of what they do with that life is theirs alone.

The crucial factor is to what degree the psychic is able to keep away from sins. According to Heracleon the psychic is under the dominion of the Law which the Demiurge has provided. The result is death (τὸ τέλος εἶναι τοῦ νόμου τὸν θάνατον — 420). Alluding to Paul's argument in Romans 7:9-13, Heracleon seems to be saying that the Law itself is not the cause of death. Rather, it destroys διὰ τῶν ἁμαρτιῶν (420). The removal of sins means the removal of death and the gift of life (διὰ τῆς ἀφέσεως ζωοποιήσας — 421). Furthermore, removing sins goes hand in hand with the removal of ignorance (or, conversely, the provision of knowledge), and it restores the person to the full psychic state (416). This is the Savior's role. In this account he does not raise the psychics to a pneumatic state, but allows them instead to fulfill their potential as psychics.

The closer psychics get to matter, the more they move to a state contrary to their nature, a state of sin and ignorance. This need not imply that sin *is* ignorance. The text only goes as far as to state that ignorance and sins go hand in hand and that both are on the lower end of the psychic realm.

Origen presents Heracleon's commentary on this verse in order to refute its

[108] Cf. Heracleon's remarks in Fragment 11 (Book X,11): "Capernaum means the uttermost ends of the world" (τὰ ἔσχατα τοῦ κόσμου). Cf. also Blanc's remark (SC 157, 415-16 n. 4) that the sea signified the power of death and sin for Origen as well.

major premises (61,427-33). The absence of objections to Heracleon's comments on sin is striking.

3.5.3.4

Setting Fragment 40 in context in Heracleon's commentary is instructive. While this particular fragment represents the psychic's reception of the Savior's message, Fragments 17-39 present the pneumatic's response. The two are complementary. [109]

Fragments 17-39 offer a running commentary on the Johannine story of Jesus' encounter with the Samaritan woman at the well. For Heracleon she appears to represent the pneumatic elect. His interpretation is extensive, but the details need not concern us! [110] Only the following points are relevant to our inquiry. Challenged by the Savior's offer of living water, the Samaritan woman responds in a manner suited to her nature (ὡς πρεπόντως τῇ αὐτῆς φύσει — Frag. 19), and accepts his call without hesitation or the need for signs. Ignorance of God (ἄγνοια θεοῦ — Frag. 19) is part of her present state. She has lived in the depth of matter (ἐν βαθείᾳ ὕλῃ), yet there is no mention of sin, which accompanied ignorance and proximity to matter in Fragment 40. It may be that the omission of sin is accidental, or that sin is understood when Heracleon mentioned ignorance and matter. It is more likely, though, that he assumes that a fallen pneumatic has no need of the forgiveness of sins in order to have life! [111]

3.5.3.5

According to Fragment 40, then, sin concerns the psychics. As well (in the context of the preceding fragments), it is not a concern for pneumatics. Where there are sins there is ignorance and proximity to matter. Death also awaits the sinner's ψυχή, as a consequence of living under the Law. Only the removal of sins by the Savior can wipe away the specter of death and provide new life. The continuation of this new life is possible only if the person keeps away from matter and sins no more, and it is up to the Demiurge's angels to verify how well everyone is doing in this regard.

3.5.4.1

Fragment 41 is brief. It is a comment on the last phrase of John 8:21: "And again he said to them, 'I go away, and you will seek me and die in your sin; where

---

[109] Pagels (*The Johannine Gospel*, 83-97) is the one who has pointed out most clearly the "two types of conversion" which emerge when one compares Heracleon's comments about the Samaritan woman in Fragments 17-39 with those about the official's son in Fragment 40.

[110] For an excellent summary of these fragments, see Pagels, *The Johannine Gospel*, 86-92.

[111] This is what Pagels claims unequivocally (*The Johannine Gospel*, 88). Foerster is justifiably more cautious: "Für die Samaritanerin war offenbar die Sünde nicht tödlich. Wohl aber ist sie für den Psychiker" (*Von Valentin*, 26).

I am going you cannot come'." The passage is as follows (XIX,14,89):[112]
3.5.4.2

Εἰς δὲ τὸ «"Οπου ἐγὼ ὑπάγω ὑμεῖς οὐ δύνασθε ἐλθεῖν» φησί· πῶς ἐν ἀγνοίᾳ καὶ ἀπιστίᾳ καὶ ἁμαρτήμασιν ὄντες ἐν ἀφθαρσίᾳ δύνανται γενέσθαι;

Au sujet de la déclaration «Là où je vais, vous, vous ne pouvez pas venir», il demande: Comment, alors qu'ils sont dans l'ignorance, l'incrédulité et les péchés, peuvent-ils parvenir à l'incorruptibilité?

3.5.4.3
In this passage Jesus is addressing the Pharisees. After declaring that he is about to leave them to go to an area of incorruptibility (ἀφθαρσία), he announces that they will not be able to follow because they are ἐν ἀγνοίᾳ καὶ ἀπιστίᾳ καὶ ἁμαρτήμασιν. The combination of ignorance and sins is not surprising, but the addition of ἀπιστία is new. Origen assumes that Heracleon is saying that they will *never* be able to follow him, and he disagrees with this determinism. He claims that change and accessibility to the incorruptible sphere is always possible: Δύνανται οὖν οἱ ἐν ἀγνοίᾳ καὶ ἀπιστίᾳ καὶ ἐν ἁμαρτήμασιν γενόμενοι γενέσθαι ἐν ἀφθαρσίᾳ εἰ μεταβάλλοιεν, δυνατὸν αὐτοὺς μεταβαλεῖν (90).

Foerster perceptively calls this "ein wichtiges, leider zu kurzes Fragment,"[113] for many tantalizing questions remain unanswered. For instance, is Heracleon's comment as deterministic as Origen claims, or does the ὄντες imply the possibility of change—as Fragment 40 does? We would also like to know (quoting Foerster again) "ob Her.[akleon] dabei eine bestimmte Klasse von Menschen im Auge hat, etwa die Choiker, oder Teile der Psychiker."[114] The passage itself does not allow us to answer these questions.

3.5.4.4
Heracleon's comments on the following Johannine passage allow us to say somewhat more about Fragment 41. The key pericope in this regard is Fragment 46, which is a comment on John 8:44: "You are of your father the devil." The text is important enough to quote in full:[115]

Héracléon dit que cela ne s'addressait pas aux fils du diable par nature [φύσει], les terrestres [τοὺς χοϊκούς], mais aux psychiques, devenus fils du diable par adoption [θέσει][116]—d'où il résulte qu'on peut être

---

[112] For the text and translation of Fragment 41 see Blanc, SC 290, 100-03. Cf. also Völker, *Quellen,* 82; Foerster, *Gnosis,* 179; and Preuschen, *Origenes,* 314.

[113] Foerster, *Von Valentin,* 41.

[114] Foerster, *Von Valentin,* 41.

[115] *In Joannem* XX,24,211-16 — Blanc, SC 290, 260-63.

[116] Foerster, (*Gnosis*) translates θέσις as "intent," but Blanc's "adoption" is more consistent with the usual meaning of that word and also balances nicely with φύσις in the pericope.

appelé fils de Dieu par nature et par adoption. Il dit que c'est parce qu'ils ont aimé les désirs du diable et qu'ils les accomplissent que ceux-ci deviennent enfants du diable, alors qu'ils ne sont pas tels par nature. Il distingue trois sens selon lesquels il faut entendre l'appellation d'«enfants», d'abord par nature [φύσει], puis par libre décision [γνώμη], en troisème lieu par mérite [ἀξίᾳ]. . . .

Heracleon distinguishes between those who are "of the same substance as the devil" and those who are called psychics or pneumatics in Fragment 41. The triple Valentinian division between choics, psychics, and pneumatics is clearly expressed. What is notable is how Heracleon claims that some psychics can become choics by adoption, because they have "loved the desires of the devil." Once they do become choics — or, to use the metaphor from Fragment 40, once they fall into the sea — they lose the possibility of salvation. The choice remains theirs, and the implications for them are staggering.

If Fragment 41 is to be read in this context, it would seem that the Pharisees' sins are not capable of being remitted by the Savior, nor can their ignorance be removed, because they have become choics. Indeed, given the fragments we have surveyed, it is tempting to attribute ignorance to the pneumatics, ignorance and sins to the psychics, and ignorance, sins, and unbelief to the choics and their "adopted" psychic brethren. This neat division, though, probably reflects the chance survival of texts more than Heracleon's own view.

3.5.5

What emerges from an examination of the fragments of Heracleon is that sin played an important role in his understanding of reality. Furthermore, it is an understanding of sin which did not cause Origen grief, although much else about Heracleon's remarks did.

Sin affected each of the three human natures differently. The absence of any remission of sins in the salvation of the Samaritan woman, especially when compared with the account of the official's son which follows, strongly suggests that sin was of no concern to the pneumatics in Heracleon's schema. The pneumatic woman became enmeshed in the evil of the material world. One assumes that she acted "sinfully," yet she is saved through a recognition of her nature and not through the remission of sins. Evil and sin are a problem for her only insofar as they prevent her from recognizing her true pneumatic nature.

Swinging the pendulum to the other side, we meet the choics who by nature are "the children of the devil." Living in "ignorance, unbelief, and sins" they have no chance of salvation or of rising to the incorruptible level.

The psychics, the middle group, are of particular concern to Heracleon. Some of them live close to the influence of the choics — by the sea, as Heracleon states symbolically — and they are threatened by the ignorance and sins which are part of this lower realm. The official's son of Fragment 40 is one of these, and Jesus's descent into the world redeems the psychics and allows them to be saved in the end if they then avoid contact with the "sea." Others, either through lapsing after this redemption of sins or being overly attracted to the lower realm, have become children of the devil by choice and are lost. On the other hand, John the Baptist has risen to a higher level of psychic awareness and become "more than a prophet." All the psychics, however, are in need of the Savior descending to remove their sins and to offer them eternal life. Choice plays an important role for psychics, and the sea is never far away.

4. SUMMARY

4.1

In the Fathers the mention of sin is rarely attributed to a Valentinian. In fact, we have found this clearly to be the case in only six instances. Three come from the fragments of Heracleon's commentary on the Gospel of John,[117] two concern Marcus,[118] and one is an excerpt of Theodotus — or perhaps one of the other Valentinians from the "so-called Oriental school."[119] The small number of occurrences has enabled us to examine each of the relevant pericopes in considerable detail.

Our intent all along has been to determine, with as much precision as the texts allow, what each of these Valentinians had in mind when he used the expression "sin." An effort has been made to keep these passages separate and not to interpret one by another. It now remains to summarize the results, first by proceeding from Church Father to Church Father, and then by highlighting a few common threads running through the Valentinian understanding of sin seen through patristic eyes.

4.2.1

Irenaeus set out in *Adversus haereses* I,10–22 to contrast the diversity of Valentinian thought and practice with the "true Church's" unity. In this context he turned his attention to their rite of redemption, or second baptism, and proceeded to give examples of how varied this rite was among Valentinians. For Irenaeus, error followed on the heels of diversity, so this Valentinian rite of redemption was clearly wrong. Nothing else needed to be said about it.

Buried in this polemical discussion about redemption is a mention of sin, and the Marcosian use of that term emerges faintly from the passage. This discussion revolves around the two baptisms available to the psychics and pneumatics. The first baptism (the "only baptism" according to Irenaeus) is directed to the ψυχικοί. Its purpose is to encourage repentance (this was John's role) and to offer remission of sins (which was provided by the "visible Jesus"). The second baptism is for the πνευματικοί. It was brought by "Christ" and allows entry into the Pleroma. Remission of sins, then, does not lead directly to perfection

---

[117] *In Joannem* VI,60,306 (Frag. 10); XIII,60,416–26 (Frag. 40); and XIX,14,89 (Frag. 41).

[118] *Adversus haereses* I,21,2; *Refutatio* VI,41.

[119] *Excerpta ex Theodoto* 52.

according to this view; nor is it a priority for pneumatics. However, it does remain crucial for the psychics.

Much of course remains unanswered in this pericope. For instance, it is unclear what role sin played in the lives of the psychics after their baptism — or in the lives of the pneumatics, for that matter. Since the rite of redemption was their second baptism, presumably they too would have had their sins removed in the first baptism. The additional rite for them seems to supplement the first.

4.2.2

Hippolytus incorporated much of Irenaeus's narrative about Marcus into his *Refutatio,* including the discussion about the rite of redemption and the mention of sin. His redactional changes are striking, though, not least of which is a complete change of focus: the Marcosians are wrong, not because of their diversity but because they have plagiarized Pythagorean doctrine. Setting the stage for this major charge of plagiarism (VI,42–55) is a short section (39–41) intended to depict Marcus as a second-rate trickster who does everything he can to keep his followers devoted to him. We hear about the crowd-pleasing potions he mixes into the eucharistic wine, and then about the rite of redemption whose powers he is said to dangle deceptively before his followers.

At this point in his narrative, what is probably a fortunate historical accident has encouraged Hippolytus to supplement the reference to sin. This was his intense struggle with Callistus over their views of sin. Since Marcus's views in this regard seem to have overlapped with those of Callistus, Hippolytus insists on making his point in section 41 quite clear.

What are we told? Hippolytus believed that there was only one baptism available to Christians for the remission of their sins, and probably that any serious transgression afterwards meant that redemption was no longer possible. Marcus's view differed. He claimed that a second baptism existed for Christians in which the sins they had committed subsequent to their first baptism could be removed. In addition, this rite gave them tremendous powers, and allowed them to be "at ease about sins."

In this account, the rite of redemption once again is depicted as a second and superior baptism. As well, it is only available to some Christians, although the determining factor no longer seems to be whether one is a pneumatic or not. It is based instead on who masters the preparatory training sessions organized by Marcus. What is also different from the Irenaean passage is that the remission of sins is a feature of this second baptism. It would seem that only those who had undergone this rite could no longer feel oppressed by sins.

4.2.3

Sin is mentioned in Extract 52 of Clement's *Excerpta ex Theodoto.* This occurs in the middle part (50–57) of the middle section (43–65) of a work which, in spite of its genre, has a considerable amount of structural unity. There is no extract attributed to Theodotus in this section, nor is Clement's redactional hand particularly noticeable. What is striking are the similarities with Irenaeus's Ptolemaic section.

The focus of 50–57 is on the creation and constitution of humans. The familiar distinctions between the hylic, psychic, and pneumatic "humans" are presented in detail: all people have a "hylic component" (with an "irrational" nature); some also have a superimposed "psychic component" (with a "reasonable and just" nature); and a few have had their "psychic bones" filled with pneumatic "marrow" (the "spiritual" essence).

Extract 52 discusses how the psychics are expected to cohabit effectively with their hylic partners, who are stronger (today we might use the male-hylic/female-psychic analogy). The Achilles' heel for the hylics is their inability to nourish themselves. To survive, they must be fed by the psychics' sins. So, abstaining from sins starves the hylic partner. It might seem easy for the psychics to rid themselves of their adversaries in this manner. But one of the three constitutive elements of the hylics are the powerful "spirits of evil," whose role is to encourage the psychics to sin. Only one thing will reduce their power and give the psychic the opportunity to lead a sinless life: baptism in the Spirit.

According to this unknown Valentinian, then, to sin is to succumb to these hylic spirits of evil and to act in a way that is contrary to the psychic's "reasonable and just" nature. What is striking in the *Excerpta* is the importance of baptism, and also the focus on the psychics, who are encouraged, with the help of their baptism in the Spirit, to struggle against their hylic natures and to save themselves.

4.2.4

Origen's *In Joannem* preserves 48 fragments of Heracleon's commentary on John's gospel. This is a gospel in which sin does not play a major role, and the particular fragmentary nature of Origen's commentary, and Heracleon's especially, has provided little opportunity to appreciate Heracleon's understanding of sin. Nonetheless, three highly instructive fragments do remain which comment on sin (10,40,41).

As we have seen, the *Excerpta* explain the Valentinian notion of three natures by dealing with them as "humans," viewing their interaction on the psychological level. In the Fragments of Heracleon the metaphor becomes spatial, and each of these natures is given a "realm" to inhabit. The hylic realm is the lowest, and once one enters that "sea" of sin and ignorance one joins the "children of the devil" and loses the possibility of salvation, i.e., of rising to the incorruptible region. Some have always lived in this realm, but others have slipped down into it. These are the psychics, who inhabit the middle realm which has "upper" and "lower" borders to it. The more one moves down in this realm, the more one falls under the influence of sin and ignorance. The entire middle realm is controlled by the Demiurge, who governs it with his Law, which punishes transgressions by death. The upper realm, meanwhile, is for the pneumatics. They need not worry about coming into contact with the hylic realm and sin since their natures will be their salvation once they become aware of them.

Jesus descended into the world to remove sins and ignorance and to inaugurate a new age where salvation would be available to psychics as well. John the

Baptist's insight in his (super-psychic) role as "more than a prophet" was to perceive Jesus' redeeming role and to declare it publicly. After Jesus' act, the psychics are encouraged to move "up" in their realm and to live sinless lives according to their true psychic nature. If they choose to do so, they will gain eternal life; if not, they will slide down into the devil's realm and can only expect death. For psychics, Jesus' remission of their sins and their constant struggle to lead a sinless life are their promise of salvation.

4.3

Some areas of overlap stand out in these four individual summaries. The first is that the view of sin which emerges is consistent, yet not without variations. Actually, the degree of consistency far exceeds what we expected, and the variations often highlight the independence of these accounts. A second notable point concerns something which did not emerge in the discussions: sin in these texts is not tied to the Valentinian mythological construct of the Pleroma. For instance, the extensive speculation concerning Sophia's "sin" in the *Pistis Sophia* is absent from these patristic accounts. Rather, the focus is on how sin affects people and the "realm" which they inhabit. A third point concerns the lack of polemic directed by the Church Fathers against the Valentinian understanding of sin. The only contentious issue to emerge was Hippolytus's insistence that the rite of redemption did not provide a second general remission of sins.

The fourth common point is perhaps the most significant: sin is of great concern to the psychics, and the Valentinian authors take great pains to explain how these psychics can help themselves. It is clear, even from an examination of these few texts, that Valentinianism was not a movement directed exclusively at the pneumatic elect. These passages reveal that salvation for the psychics depends on their ability to lead sinless lives. Jesus has helped by descending into the world, giving them a fresh start (in Heracleon's Fragments), and the baptism of the Spirit can also provide the strength needed to avoid sin (in the *Excerpta*). The psychics will not sin if they are true to their nature. Hippolytus may also imply that the rite of redemption was open to the psychics (if so, Irenaeus would disagree). The hylics are those for whom the Valentinians have no concern. They live in sin and ignorance and are doomed to destruction. The pneumatics are surely not forgotten, but it is clear that they have no need of having their sins forgiven. Salvation for them comes instead through a recognition of their true nature (especially in Heracleon's Fragments), and can be hastened by other aids such as the rite of redemption mentioned by Irenaeus.

The most striking feature to emerge from the examination of these passages has been the close and frequent connection between sin and baptism. Only in the Fragments of Heracleon does baptism not play a central role in the discussion, yet even there it is John the Baptist, who, while baptizing, perceives Jesus' inner nature and mission to take away the sin of the world. Whether this point of similarity, and the others as well, will emerge in the Valentinian texts from Nag Hammadi is a matter to which we must now turn our attention.

3

The Evidence from
the Nag Hammadi Library

1. INTRODUCTION

This chapter examines the Valentinian works from Nag Hammadi. The purpose is to isolate the works in which sin is mentioned, and then to determine what each author meant by sin. The pattern in the previous chapter is repeated: a detailed analysis of each relevant text follows a survey of the primary sources. Each work continues to be examined on its own, exclusive of the others.

All of the Valentinian works from Nag Hammadi, it would seem, were written in Greek, but they are now extant only in Coptic translation. This requires a few remarks concerning terminology. Sin is a concept for which there are many possible terms in Greek and Coptic Christian literature. In Greek, ἁμαρτία/ ἁμαρτάνειν/ἁμαρτωλός dominate to such an extent as to render the other terms insignificant. In the New Testament, for instance, this word group occurs 265 times. [1] "Sin" for the early Greek-speaking Christians was ἁμαρτία, and this is principally what we examined in the patristic literature covered in the previous chapter. In Coptic one finds the same situation, for NOBε/P̄-NOBε/PεϤP̄-NOBε has taken over the role of the Greek word group. In fact, in the Coptic New Testament even ἁμάρτημα is translated as NOBε, and παράπτωμα sometimes as well. The other Coptic words (and loan words) for sin are relatively rare. [2] When examining the texts from Nag Hammadi, then, our attention is directed mainly to NOBε, but not to the exclusion of other related expressions such as ΠΑΡΑΠΤΩΜΑ, ΠΑΡΑΒΑCΙC/ΠΑΡΑΒΑ, and 2ε. We are concerned with tracing the use of a concept, not merely a word group.

[1] Contrast the relatively infrequent use of the following words for "sin" in the NT: παράπτωμα—23 times; ἁμάρτημα—6; παράβασις / παραβαίνειν / παραβάτης—16; ἀσέβεια / ἀσεβής—16; παρακοή / παρακούειν—6; ἀνομία / ἄνομος /ἀνόμως—28; ἥττημα / ἡττᾶσθαι—5; ἀγνόημα—1; and παρανομία—1.

[2] In the Coptic (Sahidic) NT, compare the following statistics: ΜΝΤϢΑϤΤε (ἀσέβεια)—6 times; ΑСεΒΗС (ἀσεβής)—10; ΜΝⲦ̄ΑⲦСΟΟΥΝ (ἀγνόημα)—1; ΠΑΡΑΠΤΩΜΑ (παράπτωμα)—9; 2ε (παράπτωμα / ἥττημα / ἡττᾶσθαι)—7; ΠΑΡΑΝΟΜΙΑ (παρανομία)—1; ΠΑΡΑΒΑСΙC / ΠΑΡΑΒΑ / ΠΑΡΑΒΑΤΗС (παράβασις / παραβαίνειν / παραβάτης)—16; ΑΧΝ ΝΟΜΟС / ΑΝΟΜΙΑ / ΑΝΟΜΟС (ἀνόμως / ἀνομία / ἄνομος)—28; 6ΟⲚС (ἀνομία)—1; and ΜΝⲦ̄ΑⲦСΩⲦⲘ̄ (παρακοή)—3.

2. A SURVEY OF THE VALENTINIAN SOURCES
FROM NAG HAMMADI

2.1

The Valentinian core of the Nag Hammadi collection was isolated in chapter 1. It includes a primary group of seven: *The Prayer of the Apostle Paul* (*Pr. Paul*—I,1), *The Gospel of Truth* (*Gos. Truth*—I,3/XII,2), *The Treatise on the Resurrection* (*Treat. Res.*—I,4), *The Tripartite Tractate* (*Tri. Trac.*—I,5), *The Gospel of Philip* (*Gos. Phil.*—II,3), *The Interpretation of Knowledge* (*Interp. Know.*—XI,1), and *A Valentinian Exposition* with accompanying fragments (*Val. Exp.*—XI,2). Three other works are possible candidates: *The First Apocalypse of James* (*1 Apoc. Jas.*—V,3), *The Second Apocalypse of James* (*2 Apoc. Jas.*—V,4), and *The Letter of Peter to Philip* (*Ep. Pet. Phil.*—VIII,2). It is time to examine each of these in turn.[3]

2.2.1 *The Prayer of the Apostle Paul* (I,1)

The Prayer of the Apostle Paul is a short prayer (46 lines) ascribed to the Apostle Paul, which the scribe of this codex seems to have copied on the front flyleaf after he completed the transcription of the other works. *Oratio Pauli Apostoli* (1975) is the *editio princeps* (and includes commentary and translations); Dieter Mueller's critical edition was published in 1985 in *Nag Hammadi Codex I*.[4]

Among his many petitions, the author asks his Redeemer to heal his body (ⲘⲀϯ Ⲛ̅ⲚⲞⲨ [ⲦⲀⲗ]ϬⲞ Ⲙ̅ⲠⲀⲤⲰⲘⲀ—A. 20), and save his light soul and spirit ([ⲚⲄ]ⲤⲰⲦⲈ Ⲛ̅ⲦⲀⲯⲨⲬⲎ Ⲛ̅ⲞⲨⲀⲈⲒⲚ [Ⲱⲗ Ⲉ]ⲚⲎⲨⲈ ⲘⲚ̅ ⲠⲀⲠⲚⲈⲨⲘⲀ—A. 21-22). Sin is absent from the discussion.

2.2.2 *The Gospel of Truth* (I,3/XII,2)

The Gospel of Truth is a reflection on Jesus' role in bringing truth or salvation to people, and discusses their place in this divine plan. It is probably the "Gospel of Truth" mentioned by Irenaeus (*Adv. haer.* III,11,9)—or, less likely, a

---

[3] Unless otherwise noted, translations are taken from James M. Robinson, *The Nag Hammadi Library in English* (New York: Harper and Row, 1977). The translators are as follows: I,1 (D. Mueller); I,3 (G. MacRae); I,4 (M. Peel); I,5 (H. Attridge and D. Mueller); II,3 (W. Isenberg); XI,1-2 (J. Turner); V,3 (W. Schoedel); V,4 (C. Hedrick); VIII,2 (F. Wisse).

[4] *Oratio Pauli Apostoli. Codex Jung f. LXXII (?) (p. 143?-144?)*, ed. by Rodolphe Kasser, Michel Malinine, Henri-Charles Puech, Gilles Quispel, Jan Zandee, Werner Vycichl, and Robert McL. Wilson (Bern: Francke Verlag, 1975); *Nag Hammadi Codex I (The Jung Codex). Introduction, Texts, Translations, Indices*, ed. by Harold W. Attridge, NHS 22 (Leiden: Brill, 1985), 5-11. The Coptic text is taken from this edition.

commentary on it. Many have thought that the author was Valentinus himself,[5] but this intriguing hypothesis is unprovable. *The Gospel of Truth* was the first tractate of the Nag Hammadi collection to be published. The *editio princeps* (1956) long offered the best critical text; now one must consult Attridge and MacRae's edition (1985).[6] Several commentaries and major studies have appeared.[7]

Sin is mentioned twice in this work. In the first passage (32,37) the author speaks of the Savior passing on "the Truth to those who search for it, and knowledge to those who have committed sin in their error" (ⲁⲩⲱ ⲡⲥⲁⲩⲛⲉ ⲛ̄ⲛⲉⲉⲓ ⲛ̄ⲧⲁⲩⲣ̄ ⲛⲁⲃⲓ ⲛ̄ϩⲣⲏⲓ̄ ϩⲛ̄ ⲧⲟⲩⲡⲗⲁⲛⲏ). In the second (35,25–26), incorruptibility (ⲁϯⲙ̄ⲛ̄ⲧ̄ⲁⲧⲧⲉⲕⲟ) pursues the one who committed sins, pardons him and provides rest (ⲁⲥⲟⲩⲁϩ̄ⲥ̄ ⲛ̄ⲥⲁ ⲡⲉⲧⲁϥⲣ̄ ⲛⲁⲃⲓ· ϫⲉⲕⲁⲥⲉ ⲉϥⲉⲙ̄ⲧⲁⲛ ⲙ̄ⲙⲁϥ). These passages require closer examination.

2.2.3 *The Treatise on the Resurrection* (I,4)

This is a ⲗⲟⲅⲟⲥ ⲉⲧⲃⲉ ⲧⲁⲛⲁⲥⲧⲁⲥⲓⲥ (50,18), written in the form of a letter, by an anonymous teacher to his "son" Rheginos. The first critical edition

[5]For the argument that Valentinus was the author of *The Gospel of Truth,* cf. especially Michel Malinine, Henri-Charles Puech and Gilles Quispel, *Evangelium Veritatis. Codex Jung f.* VIII^{v}–XVI^{v} (p. 16–*32) / f. XIX^{r}–XXII^{r} (p. 37–43),* SJI 6 (Zürich: Rascher Verlag, 1956), xiv. They attribute this hypothesis to W.-C. van Unnik's thesis (1954), published in 1955: "The 'Gospel of Truth' and the New Testament," in *The Jung Codex,* ed. by F. L. Cross (London: Mowbray and Company, 1955), 79–129. So also Kendrick Grobel, *The Gospel of Truth. A Valentinian Meditation on the Gospel* (New York/ Nashville: Abingdon Press, 1960), 26.

[6] *Evangelium Veritatis.* Two leaves of this gospel were not at first available to the editors. These (pages 33–36) were published in 1961: *Evangelium Veritatis. Codex Jung f. XVII^{r}–f. XVIII^{v} (p. 33–36),* ed. by Michel Malinine, Henri-Charles Puech, Gilles Quispel and Walter Till, SJI 6 (Zürich: Rascher Verlag). The edition prepared by Harold Attridge and George MacRae (*Nag Hammadi Codex I,* 55–117) appeared too late to be incorporated fully in this study.

The text in Codex I is in Subachmimic. The Sahidic fragments of *The Gospel of Truth* from Codex XII were published in *The Facsimile Edition of the Nag Hammadi Codices. Codices XI, XII, and XIII,* ed. by J. M. Robinson (Leiden: Brill, 1973), 95–100. Very little remains of this version, but there is enough to suggest that more than one recension of the Greek original existed. These fragments so far have not been analyzed. The text (without translation) has been edited by Frederick Wisse in *Nag Hammadi Codex I,* 119–22.

[7] The most important studies are the following: Grobel, *The Gospel of Truth;* Jacques-É. Ménard, *L'Évangile de Vérité,* NHS 2 (Leiden: Brill, 1972); Sasagu Arai, *Die Christologie des Evangelium Veritatis. Eine religionsgeschichtliche Untersuchung* (Leiden: Brill, 1964); and Harold W. Attridge and George MacRae, "The Gospel of Truth," in *Nag Hammadi Codex I (The Jung Codex). Notes,* ed. by Harold W. Attridge, NHS 23 (Leiden: Brill, 1985), 39–135.

was published in 1963, and since then several others have appeared, most notably those of Malcolm Peel (1969; 1985), Bentley Layton (1971–publ. 1979), and Jacques Ménard (1983).[8] This treatise aims to show how, because of Christ's resurrection, the elect themselves are assured of a resurrection when they die. They will be raised with spiritual bodies, but in the meantime ought to live as though they had already been raised (49,9-35). Rheginos is discouraged from living "in conformity to the flesh" (ΟΥΤΕ ΜΠΡΠΟΛΙΤΕΥΕϹΘΑΙ ΚΑΤΑ ΤΕϹΙϹΑΡΞ – 49,13-14), yet there is no ethical discussion and no mention of sin.

2.2.4 The Tripartite Tractate (I,5)

This actually is a *Schrift ohne Titel* which the editors of the first edition have called *Tractatus Tripartitus* because the content is divisible into three sections. It is one of the longest works from the Nag Hammadi collection (89 pages in Codex I). The *editio princeps* (1973–75) has recently been complemented by Attridge and Pagels's edition in *Nag Hammadi Codex I* (1985).[9]

Part 1 (*De supernis*–51,1-104,3) concerns the Pleroma. It discusses the three primary members (the Father, the Son and the Church–51-58), the Fall (with Logos mentioned rather than Sophia–75-98), and the Demiurge and his angels (99-104). Part 2 (*De creatione hominis*–104, 4-108,12) analyzes the creation of the human race and its division into three races or natures (pneumatic, psychic and hylic). Part 3 (*De generibus tribus*–108,13-140) focuses on these three types, their response to the Savior who descends into the world, and

---

[8] *De resurrectione (Epistula ad Rheginum). Codex Jung* f. XXII[r]–f. XXV[v] p.43–50), ed. by Michel Malinine, Henri-Charles Puech, Gilles Quispel, Walter Till, Robert McL. Wilson, and Jan Zandee (Zürich/Stuttgart: Rascher Verlag, 1963); *The Epistle to Rheginos. A Valentinian Letter on the Resurrection,* ed. by Malcolm Peel, NTL (London/ Philadelphia: SCM/The Westminster Press, 1969)–A revised German translation (by W.-P. Funk) appeared in 1974: *Gnosis und Auferstehung. Die Brief an Rheginus von Nag Hammadi* (Neukirchen-Vluyn: Neukirchener Verlag, 1974); *The Gnostic Treatise on the Resurrection from Nag Hammadi,* ed. by Bentley Layton, HDR 12 (Missoula, MT: Scholars Press, 1979); *Le traité sur la résurrection,* ed. by Jacques-É. Ménard, BCNHST 12 (Québec: Les Presses de l'Université Laval, 1983); and Peel's recent edition in *Nag Hammadi Codex I,* 123-157.

[9] *Tractatus Tripartitus.* I. *De supernis. Codex Jung f. XXVI[r]–f. LII[v] (p. 51-104).* II. *De creatione hominis.* III. *De generibus tribus. Codex Jung f. LII[v]–f. LXX[v] (p. 104-140),* ed. by Rodolphe Kasser, Michel Malinine, Henri-Charles Puech, Gilles Quispel, Jan Zandee, Werner Vycichl, and Robert McL. Wilson (Bern: Francke Verlag, 1973-75); Harold W. Attridge and Elaine H. Pagels, *Nag Hammadi Codex I,* 159-337. Their edition appeared too late to be used effectively in this study. An excellent commentary on this work has been prepared by Einar Thomassen ("The Tripartite Tractate from Nag Hammadi. A New Translation with Introduction and Commentary," Ph.D. diss., St. Andrews, 1982). It is to be published in French translation (with the assistance of Louis Painchaud) in the Laval series.

their anticipated salvation or destruction. Sin is mentioned twice in the third part (115,15;117,4).

2.2.5 The Gospel of Philip (II,3)

A flurry of publications appeared in the decade following the photographic edition of The Gospel of Philip in 1956. [10] This included German and English translations (Schenke, 1959; de Catanzaro, 1962), [11] and a commentary and translation by Robert McL. Wilson (1962) [12] followed by the first critical edition by Walter Till in 1963. [13] Jacques Ménard's edition of the Gospel of Philip in 1967 (text, translation and commentary) has remained the standard one for the last twenty years. [14]

This gospel is a didactic and hortatory treatise in which ethics and sacraments play an important role. Sacraments especially are emphasized, and five seem to be stated in 67,27-30: "The Lord did everything in a mystery, [i.e.] a baptism and a chrism [OYⲬⲢICMⲀ] and a eucharist and a redemption [OYCⲱTⲈ] and a bridal chamber [OYNYMϤⲱN]." Sin appears to play an important role in the discussion and is mentioned eight times in two sections (66,23-29; 77,15-78,11). [15]

---

[10] Coptic Gnostic Papyri in the Coptic Museum at Old Cairo, ed. by Pahor Labib (Cairo: Cairo Government Press, 1956).

[11] Hans-Martin Schenke, "Das Evangelium nach Philippus. Ein Evangelium der Valentinianer aus dem Funde von Nag-Hamadi," TLZ 84 (1959) 1-26; C.-J. de Catanzaro, "The Gospel of Philip," JTS 13 (1962) 35-71.

[12] The Gospel of Philip, ed. by Robert McL. Wilson (London: A. R. Mowbray & Co. Limited, 1962).

[13] Das Evangelium nach Philippos, hrsg. von Walter Till, PTS 2 (Berlin: Walter de Gruyter, 1963).

[14] L'Évangile selon Philippe. Introduction, text, traduction, commentaire, par Jacques-É. Ménard (Paris: Letouzey & Ané, 1967).

[15] We follow Isenberg's numbering of the pages. The Gospel of Philip has been paginated in three ways. Initially, scholars such as Wilson and Till followed the order of plates in Labib's Coptic Gnostic Papyri, in which The Gospel of Philip comprised plates 99-134. Then scholars turned to the order of the pages in the codex itself (which originally did not have page numbers). At first they did not notice that four of the fragments could be set in pairs and required only two pages instead of four. This resulted in a numbering system two numerals too high for the rest of the codex. This "inflated" reading, running from pages 53-88, was used by Ménard. The combination of these fragments was confirmed in The Facsimile Edition of the Nag Hammadi Codices. Codex II (Leiden: Brill, 1974), xv-xvii (discussion) and plates pp. 13-14. This adjusted numbering system (from pages 51-86) accordingly has been adopted by Isenberg in The Nag Hammadi Library in English.

2.2.6 The Interpretation of Knowledge (XI,1)

A critical edition of this work is in preparation. [16] The text has been published only in *The Facsimile Edition*,[17] and there is an English translation in *The Nag Hammadi Library in English*. In addition, secondary literature is not extensive. [18]

The situation appears to be similar to that addressed by Paul in 1 Cor 12–14; that is, the misuse of charismata has led to dissension in his church. Like Paul, the author encourages unity and an appreciation for all the spiritual gifts. Sin is mentioned several times throughout the work (i.e. 9,38; 12,26; 14,38; 21,21.29.30–31), and one of the challenges is to determine its meaning in such a badly-preserved manuscript.

2.2.7 A Valentinian Exposition (XI,2)

Jacques Ménard recently has prepared the first critical edition of *A Valentinian Exposition*.[19] Moreover, he has connected this work convincingly with the

---

[16] *Nag Hammadi Codices XI, XII and XIII*, ed. by C. W. Hedrick, NHS 28 (Leiden: Brill, forthcoming). Charles Hedrick has graciously passed on to me (with permission) John Turner's transcription of *The Interpretation of Knowledge*. This is the text I have used for this work.

[17] *The Facsimile Edition of the Nag Hammadi Codices. Codices XI, XII, and XIII*, 7–27.

[18] Besides the short introduction to Turner's translation by Elaine Pagels in *The Nag Hammadi Library* (427), there is the article by Klaus Koschorke: "Eine neugefundene gnostische Gemeindeordnung. Zum Thema Geist und Amt im frühen Christentum," *ZTK* 76 (1979) 30–60. This article is a development of his book, *Die Polemik der Gnostiker gegen das kirchliche Christentum, unter besonder Berücksichtigung der Nag-Hammadi-Traktate "Apokalypse des Petrus" (NHC VII,3) und "Testimonium Veritatis" (NHC IX,3)*, NHS 12 (Leiden: Brill, 1978), esp. 69–71. It is also the culmination of several papers he presented. In his own words, it is an "ausgearbeitete Fassung eines in Bethel (Kollegium der Kirchlichen Hochschule, April 1977), Yale (International Conference on Gnosticism, Marz 1978), Oxford (Sixth International Congress on Biblical Studies, April 1978) und Heidelberg (Kirchengeschichtliche Sozietät, Mai 1978) gehaltenen Vortrags" (30). His Yale paper was published: "Gnostic Instructions on the Organization of the Congregation. The Tractate Interpretation of Knowledge from CG XI," in *The Rediscovery of Gnosticism*, II, ed. by B. Layton (Leiden: Brill, 1981), 757–69. This English paper is not as detailed in its analysis of the gnostic attitude to ecclesiastical office, but its analysis of *The Interpretation of Knowledge* is virtually identical. As the titles of Koschorke's studies reveal, his intent is not to provide an extensive commentary on this work, but to examine how a congregation is organized on gnostic premises. The last part of *The Interpretation of Knowledge*, then (15–21), interests him in particular.

[19] *L'Exposé valentinien. Les fragments sur le baptême et sur l'eucharistie (NH XI,2)*, par Jacques-É. Ménard, BCNHST 14 (Québec: Les Presses de l'Université Laval, 1985).

three fragments "on baptism"[20] and the two "on the eucharist" which follow in Codex XI (40,1-44,37). Like the preceding work in this codex, it is not well-preserved. This work is a summary of Valentinian theology and anthropology. It opens with the composition of the Pleroma (22-30), turns to the Fall of Sophia and the descent of the Logos (31-36), and then describes the Demiurge's creation of the lower world (37-39). The baptismal and eucharistic prayers which follow perhaps point to the work's *Sitz*. Sin is mentioned twice in the second baptismal fragment (41,12.15).

2.2.8 The First Apocalypse of James (V,3)

William Schoedel's edition of this work (1979) has now superseded Alexander Böhlig and Pahor Labib's *editio princeps*.[21] This apocalypse, now called "the first" to distinguish it from the next tractate in Codex V which bears the same name, presents a series of responses by "the Lord" to the questions posed by his brother James over an extended period of time. Before Jesus' crucifixion, the Lord addresses issues concerning the heavenly realm and his own mission on earth (24,10-30,11). After his death, the discussion with James turns to suffering (31,2-44,10). The Lord explains how his inner self never suffered, and that James must undergo the same process of physical suffering until his body is destroyed. To make the ascent of his soul safe and sure, the Lord tells him what he must do to move past the archons and powers. Sin is absent from the discussion.

2.2.9 The Second Apocalypse of James (V,4)

This apocalypse, like its predecessor in Codex V, was edited by Böhlig and Labib in 1963.[22] Not many have examined this work. Yet Wolf-Peter Funk's *Die zweite Apokalypse des Jakobus aus Nag-Hammadi-Codex V* is one of the most complete and impressive editions to date of any of the Nag Hammadi works.[23]

---

[20] The editors of this work in *The Nag Hammadi Library* (E. Pagels and J. Turner) have called the second and third fragment "On Baptism A and B," and the first one "On Anointing." This understanding of the first fragment does more justice to the context.

[21] Alexander Böhlig and Pahor Labib, *Koptisch-gnostische Apokalypsen aus Codex V von Nag Hammadi im Koptischen Museum zu Alt-Kairo* (Halle-Wittenberg: Wissenschafliche Zeitschrift der Martin-Luther-Universität, 1963), 29-54; William R. Schoedel, "The (First) Apocalypse of James, V,3: 24,10-44,10," in *Nag Hammadi Codices V,2-5 and VI with Papyrus Berolinensis 8502,1 and 4*, ed. by D. M. Parrott (Leiden: Brill, 1979), 65-103.

[22] *Koptisch-gnostische Apokalypsen*, 56-85.

[23] Wolf-Peter Funk, *Die zweite Apokalypse des Jakobus aus Nag-Hammadi-Codex V*, TU 119 (Berlin: Akademie-Verlag, 1976). The important short studies are as follows: Böhlig, *Koptisch-gnostische Apokalypsen*, 56-65; and his *Mysterion und Wahrheit. Gesammelte Beiträge zur spätantiken Religionsgeschichte*, AGSU 6 (Leiden: Brill, 1968),

Besides establishing a critical edition of the text (with the help of Hans-Martin Schenke), Funk has provided textual notes, full word indices, excurses, three translations (one more literal than the other,[24] and one in English), and an extensive commentary (87-192). Charles Hedrick has since published (1979) and outstanding critical edition with an English translation.[25]

This work contains two parts of unequal length. In the first (46,1-60,29), James relates the insights which he received from the risen Jesus, while the second (61,1-63,32) recounts James's death. Both are narrated to Theuda, James's father, by a priest called Mareim. Before James is put to death he has time for a long prayer (62,12-63,29), and sin is mentioned in this part of the work. James prays to Jesus that he not linger in his "sinful flesh" (ⲤⲀⲢⲜ ⲚⲚⲞⲂⲈ – 63,11) or be handed over to a "judge who is severe with sin" (ⲚⲢⲈϤϤ)ⲱ)ⲱⲦ ⲈⲂⲞⲖ ⲂⲘ̄ ⲠⲚⲞⲂⲈ – 63,16-17), but that he have all his debts forgiven (Ⲕ)ⲱ ⲚⲀⲒ̈ ⲈⲂⲞⲖ ⲚⲚⲎ ⲈⲦⲈⲢⲞⲒ̈ ⲦⲎⲢⲞⲨ ⲚⲦⲈ ⲚⲈⲂⲞⲞⲨ – 63,17-18). Earlier in the work James is called "an illuminator and a "redeemer" (ⲚⲦⲔ̄ ⲞⲨⲈϤⲦⲞⲞⲦⲈ ⲈⲂ2ⲞⲨⲚ ⲘⲚ̄ ⲞⲨⲢⲈϤⲤ)ⲱⲦⲈ – 55,17-18), so his open recognition of being a sinner is striking.

2.2.10 The Letter of Peter to Philip (VIII,2)

The Letter of Peter to Philip did not receive serious scholarly attention until the late 1960's,[26] and only a decade later did the critical editions emerge from Jacques Ménard (1977), Hans-Gebhard Bethge (1978) and Marvin Meyer (1979 – publ. 1981). [27]

The title of this work comes from the brief introductory section (132,10-133,8) which is a letter addressed from the apostle Peter to his fellow apostle Philip, asking Philip to rejoin him and the others to teach and preach. When Philip arrives, the apostles all go to the Mount of Olives where Jesus appears to them in the form of a great light (133,8-134,18). There ensues a series of questions by the apostles and answers by the heavenly Christ (134,18-138,3), after which the apostles return to Jerusalem (138,3-139,9). Peter then preaches a sermon in the Temple, and they all set off to preach and heal (139,9-140,27).

112-18; S. Kent Brown, "Jewish and Gnostic Elements in The Second Apocalypse of James (CG V,4)," *NovT* 17 (1975) 225-37; and Charles W. Hedrick, "The (Second) Apocalypse of James," in *Nag Hammadi Codices, V,2-5 and VI*, 105-9.

[24] As Funk explains, one of his translations is "so wörtlich wie erträglich, so idiomatisch wie nötig," while the other is "so idiomatisch wie möglich, so wörtlich wie nötig" (*Die zweite Apokalypse*, 7).

[25] Hedrick, *Nag Hammadi Codices V,2-5 and VI*, 105-49.

[26] For a review of scholarship, see Marvin W. Meyer, *The Letter of Peter to Philip. Text, Translation and Commentary*, SBLDS 53 (Chico, CA: Scholars Press, 1981), 6-9.

[27] Jacques-É. Ménard, *La lettre de Pierre à Philippe*, BCNHST 1 (Québec: Les Presses de l'Université Laval, 1977); H.-G. Bethge, "Der sogenannte 'Brief des Petrus an Philippus': Die zweite 'Schrift' aus Nag-Hammadi-Codex VIII," *TLZ* 103 (1978) 161-70; and Meyer, *The Letter of Peter to Philip*.

Peter's sermon focuses on the need to suffer in this world. People suffer, he states, because of "the transgression of the mother" (ⲀⲚⲞⲚ ⲠⲈⲦⲈ Ⲁ[Ⲛ]ⲬⲒ ⲘⲔⲀⲒ ⲒⲚ ⲦⲠⲀⲢⲀⲂⲀⲤⲒⲤ ⲚⲦⲘⲀⲀⲨ—139,23). The nature of the transgression is explained somewhat in one of Jesus' earlier revelations (135,8-16). The "Mother" is the one who caused the deficiency of the aeons by attempting to set up aeons "without the command of the majesty of the Father" (135,13-14). This came about through her "disobedience" (ⲘⲚⲦⲀⲦⲤⲰⲦⲘ) and "foolishness" (ⲘⲚⲦⲀⲦⲰⲞⲬⲚⲈ). This is as close as we get to a mention of sin in the work. What is at issue here is the Mother's transgression (perhaps of the ⲚⲞⲘⲞⲤ of the Pleroma).[28]

2.3 Conclusion

Two different hypotheses are tenable after this survey of the Valentinian works from Nag Hammadi, for what emerges is both the importance and unimportance of sin in this corpus. On the one hand, sin is not mentioned often. In fact, ⲚⲞⲂⲈ, Ⲣ̄-ⲚⲞⲂⲈ and ⲠⲈϤⲠ̄-ⲚⲞⲂⲈ occur only twenty-one times in the core group of seven[29] and twice again in one of the three works which are possibly Valentinian.[30] In addition, there is no extended discussion of sin in any of these ten works. With the exception of *The Gospel of Philip* and *The Interpretation of Knowledge,* sin is mentioned no more than twice in any one work. On the other hand, it is striking that sin is actually mentioned as often as it is. The statistics are challenging: ⲚⲞⲂⲈ and its derivatives occur only seventy times in the entire Nag Hammadi collection,[31] and nearly 30% of these occurrences (21/75) are in the 15% of the works which are probably Valentinian (7/46). Indeed, *The Gospel of Philip* and *The Interpretation of Knowledge* themselves contain 20% of the entire number (15/75). These figures merit further examination.

---

[28] Those who threaten the apostle and are enemies of the Pleroma are called "lawless ones" (ⲀⲚⲞⲘⲞⲤ) in 139,30.

[29] The 21 occurrences are as follows: *Gos. Truth* (2)—I,32,37; 35,25-26; *Tri. Trac.* (2)— I,115,15; 117,4; *Gos. Phil.* (8)—II,66,23-29; 77,15-21; 78,11; *Interp. Know.* (7)—XI, 9,38; 12,26; 14,38; 21,21.29.30.31; *Val. Exp.* (2)—XI,41,12-15.

[30] These are in *2 Apoc. Jas.* V,63,11.17.

[31] This number is not certain given the fragmentary nature of some of the works. The following references to sin do not include the Valentinian works mentioned in the preceding two notes: *Ap. Jas* (4)—I,9,28; 11,39; 12,5.10; *Ap. John* (2)—II,28,25.30; *Gos. Thom.* (2)—II,14,104; *Hyp. Arch.* (3)—II,86,31; 91,26; 94,23; *Orig. World* (2)—II,103,13; 121,33; *Exeg. Soul* (2)—II,135,10.32; *Apoc. Paul* (2)—V,20,14; 21,14; *Acts Pet. 12 Apost.* (1)—VI,12,6; *Thund.* (3)—VI,19,16.17; 21,22; *Asclepius* (1)— VI,77,32; *Paraph. Shem* (2)— VII,24,30; 37,25; *Treat. Seth* (8)—VII,62,34; 63,4.11.17.26; 64,17.24.29; *Teach. Silv.* (10)— VII,86,23; 101,27; 103,28; 104,13; 105,25; 108,4; 109,9.11; 110,6; 114,30; *Zost.* (4)— VIII,25,6; 27,23.28; 28,5 [1,30?; 130,20?]; *Marsanes* (4)—X,27,23; 40,7.25; *Testim. Truth* (2)—IX,33,2; 48,6.

3. AN EXAMINATION OF THE RELEVANT SOURCES

3.1 Introduction

Six of the Valentinian works from Nag Hammadi mention sin: *The Gospel of Truth, The Tripartite Tractate, The Gospel of Philip, The Interpretation of Knowledge, A Valentinian Exposition,* and *The Second Apocalypse of James.* We now turn our attention to determining the meaning and function of sin in the relevant passages.

3.2 The Gospel of Truth

3.2.1

The Gospel of Truth is "a Valentinian meditation on the gospel." On this point there is wide agreement.[32] The lack of definite structure to this work makes it difficult to analyze one pericope in isolation from the others. Like a river, the thoughts flow into one another from beginning to end. This can also create an advantage, for the work in many respects is essentially the same wherever one steps into it. This meditation proceeds from topic to topic, sometimes repeating a point and other times introducing a new one. This is not to say that one cannot break it down into sections. In fact, most commentators have introduced divisions for the sake of discussion, and the degree of overlap in these choices is substantial.[33]

Twice in this work the author mentions sin. Using Cullen Story's subdivisions, the first time is in the "Exhortation to the Gnostics concerning their life in the world" (32,31–33,32);[34] the second is in the discussion concerning "The

---

[32] This particular expression comes from Grobel's subtitle to his book, *The Gospel of Truth.* Cf. also Ménard: "L'ouvrage est une suite de méditations plus ou moins bien soudées les unes aux autres" (*L'Évangile de Vérité,* 40); Malinine, Puech and Quispel: "De toute façon, il paraît être, bien plutôt qu'un 'évangile' à proprement parler, une méditation, une 'élévation' sur l'Évangile" (*Evangelium Veritatis,* xv); Arai, who calls this work "eine Homilie" with a baptismal *Sitz* (*Die Christologie,* 13–14); MacRae, who claims that the "*Gospel of Truth* . . .discusses, in the manner of a meditation, the person and work of Christ" (*The Nag Hammadi Library,* 37); and Cullen I. K. Story's remark: "*Ev Ver.* is a meditation or homily on the gospel" (*The Nature of Truth in "The Gospel of Truth" and in the Writings of Justin Martyr. A Study of the Pattern of Orthodoxy in the Middle of the Second Christian Century,* NovTSup 25 [Leiden: Brill, 1970], 1).

[33] Ménard, for instance (*L'Évangile de Vérité,* 38–39), has taken over the text divisions established by Hans-Martin Schenke in his *Die Herkunft des sogenannten Evangelium Veritatis* (Göttingen: Vandenhoeck & Ruprecht, 1959). Story's divisions are almost the same (*The Nature of Truth,* 1–42).

[34] Ménard (following Schenke) calls this section "Exhortations parénétiques," and he begins and ends it at the same place as Story; so also Arai (*Die Christologie,* 16).

Father's fullness (=forgiveness) for the one who lacks" (35,24–36,17).[35] In the following analysis we examine each of these sections in depth, and then set them in the context of the work as a whole.

3.2.2.1

Sin is mentioned first in 32,37. The relevant passage is as follows (32,31–33,32):[36]

ϣⲉϫⲉ ϭⲉ ⲁⲃⲁⲗ ϩⲙ̄ ⲫⲏⲧ ϫⲉ (32,31)	Say, then, from the heart that
ⲛ̄ⲧⲱⲧⲛ̄ⲛⲉ ⲡⲉ ⲡⲓϩⲱⲟⲩ ⲉⲧϫⲏⲕ	you are the perfect day
ⲁⲃⲁⲗ ⲁⲩⲱ ⲉϥⲟⲩⲏϩ ϩⲛ̄ ⲧⲏⲛⲉ	and in you dwells
ⲛ̄ϭⲓ ⲡⲟⲩⲁⲉⲓⲛ ⲉⲧⲉⲙⲁϥⲱϫⲛ̄	the light that does not fail.
ϣⲉϫⲉ ⲁⲧⲙⲏⲉ ⲙⲛ̄ ⲛⲉⲉⲓ ⲉⲧϣⲓ (35)	Speak of the truth with those who
ⲛⲉ ⲛ̄ⲥⲱⲥ ⲁⲩⲱ ⲡⲥⲁⲩⲛⲉ ⲛ̄ⲛⲉⲉⲓ	search for it, and (of) knowledge
ⲛ̄ⲧⲁⲩⲣ̄ ⲛⲁⲃⲓ ⲛ̄ϩⲣⲏⲓ̄ ϩⲛ̄ ⲧⲟⲩⲡⲗⲁⲛⲏ	to those who have committed
	sin in their error.
ⲧⲁϫⲣⲟ ⲛ̄ⲧⲟⲩⲣⲓⲧⲉ ⲛ̄ⲛⲉⲉⲓ ⲛ̄(33,1)	Make firm the foot of those
ⲧⲁϩⲥⲗⲁⲁⲧⲉ ⲟⲩⲁϩⲁ ⲥⲱⲧ ⲛ̄ⲛⲉ	who have stumbled and stretch out
ⲧⲛ̄ϭⲓϫ ⲁⲛⲉⲉⲓ ⲉⲧϣⲱⲛⲉ ⲥⲁⲛϣ̄	your hands to those who are ill. Feed
ⲛ̄ⲛⲉⲉⲓ ⲉⲧϩⲕⲉⲉⲓⲧ ⲁⲩⲱ ⲛⲉⲧϩⲁ	those who are hungry and
ⲥⲓ ⲛ̄ⲧⲉⲧⲛ̄ϯ ⲙ̄ⲧⲁⲛ ⲛ̄ⲛⲉⲩ ⲛ̄ⲧⲉ (5)	give repose to those who are weary,
ⲧⲛ̄ⲧⲟⲩⲛⲉⲥ ⲛⲉⲉⲓ ⲉⲧⲟⲩⲱϣⲉ ⲁ	and raise up those who wish to
ⲧⲱⲱⲛ ⲛ̄ⲧⲉⲧⲛ̄ⲛⲉϩⲥⲉ ⲛ̄ⲛⲉⲧⲛ̄	rise, and awaken those who
ⲕⲁⲧⲕⲉ ⲛ̄ⲧⲱⲧⲛ ⲛ̄ⲅⲁⲣ ⲧⲉ ⲧⲙⲛ̄ⲧ	sleep. For you are the
ⲣⲙ̄ⲛ̄ϩⲏⲧ ⲉⲧⲧⲁⲕⲙ̄ ⲉϣⲱⲡⲉ ⲉⲣⲉ	understanding that is drawn forth. If
ϣⲁⲛⲡⲧⲱⲕ ⲣ̄ ϯϩⲉ ϣⲁϥⲧⲱⲕ (10)	strength acts thus, it becomes even
ⲛ̄ϩⲟⲩⲟ ϫⲓ ϩⲣⲏⲧⲛ̄ ⲁⲣⲱⲧⲛ̄ ⲙ̄ⲙⲓⲛ	stronger. Be concerned with your-
ⲙⲓⲛ ⲙ̄ⲙⲱⲧⲛ̄ ⲙ̄ⲡⲣ̄ϫⲓ ϩⲣⲏⲧⲛ̄ ⲁϩⲛ̄	selves; do not be concerned with
ⲕⲁⲩⲉ ⲉⲧⲉ ⲛⲉⲉⲓ ⲛⲉ ⲛ̄ⲧⲁⲧⲉⲧⲛ̄	other things which you have
ⲛⲁϫⲟⲩ ⲁⲃⲁⲗ ⲙ̄ⲙⲱⲧⲛ̄ ⲛⲉⲛⲧⲁⲧⲉ	rejected from yourselves. Do not
ⲧⲛ̄ⲕⲁⲃⲁⲗ ⲙ̄ⲙⲁⲩ ⲙ̄ⲡⲣ̄ⲥⲱⲧⲉ (15)	return to what you have vomited
ⲁⲣⲁⲩ ⲁⲟⲩⲁⲙⲟⲩ ⲙ̄ⲡⲣ̄ⲣ̄ ϫⲁⲗⲉⲥ	to eat it. Do not be moths.

[35] Ménard (again following Schenke) divides the section as Story does, and calls it "Le perfectionnement est le pardon." Arai stops it at 36,9 (the "39,9" in the text is a misprint) and calls it "Die Vergebung, die Vollendung und der Mangel."

[36] The text and translation are from *Nag Hammadi Codex I,* 102–04. The last two lines on page 32 (32,38–39) have been excluded since they almost certainly are out of place. Cf. Grobel's remarks: "Here [32,23a] a whole line plus one word (32:38–39) dropped out of the text by homoioteleuton (ⲛ̄ϩⲏⲧ to ⲛ̄ϩⲏⲧ) as the scribe realized before he finished the page. So he drew a sign that looks like a closed pair of shears under line 37, copied the missing words, and placed matching references and footnote signs in the margin to indicate where they belong" (*The Gospel of Truth,* 137). The emendation was first suggested by the editors of *Evangelium Veritatis* (58). It has subsequently been accepted by Ménard (*L'Évangile de Vérité,* 154); MacRae (*The Nag Hammadi Library,* 44); and Attridge and MacRae (*Nag Hammadi Codex I,* 102).

ⲘⲠⲢⲢ ϤⲚⲦ ϫⲉ ⲀⲦⲉⲦⲚ̄ⲞⲨⲱ .... Do not be worms, for you have
ⲉⲢⲉⲦⲚ̄ⲚⲞⲨⲌⲉ ⲘⲘⲀϤ ⲀⲂⲀⲖ .... already cast it off.
ⲘⲠⲢⲱϢⲱⲠⲉ ⲉⲢⲉⲦⲚⲞⲉⲒ Ⲛ̄ⲦⲞ .... Do not become a
ⲠⲞⲤ ⲘⲠⲆⲒⲀⲂⲞⲖⲞⲤ ϫⲉ ⲀⲦⲉ (20) .... (dwelling) place for the devil, for
ⲦⲚ̄ⲞⲨⲱ ⲉⲢⲉⲦⲚ̄ⲞⲨⲱⲤϤ ⲘⲘⲀϤ .... you have already destroyed him.
ⲘⲠⲢⲦⲀϫⲢⲞ Ⲛ̄ⲚⲉⲦⲚ̄ϫⲢⲞⲠ Ⲛⲉ .... Do not strengthen (those who are)
.... obstacles to you
ⲉⲒ ⲉⲦⲌⲀⲉⲒⲉ ⲌⲱⲤ ⲞⲨⲤⲞⲌⲉ Ⲡⲉ .... who are collapsing, as though
.... (you were) a support (for them).
ⲞⲨⲖⲀⲨⲉ ⲄⲀⲢ Ⲡⲉ ⲠⲒⲀⲦⲌⲉⲠ ⲀϪⲒ .... For the lawless one is one to treat
ⲦϤ Ⲛ̄ⲂⲀⲚⲤ̄ Ⲛ̄ⲌⲞⲨⲞ ⲀⲠⲒⲌⲉⲠ (25) .... ill rather than the just one.
ϫⲉ Ⲛ̄ⲦⲀϤ ⲄⲀⲢ ⲠⲉⲦⲘ̄ⲘⲉⲨ .... For the former
ϤⲒⲢⲉ Ⲛ̄ⲚⲉϤⲌⲂⲎⲨⲉ ⲌⲱⲤ ⲞⲨ .... does his works as a
ⲀⲦⲌⲉⲠ Ⲡⲉ ⲠⲉⲉⲒ Ⲛ̄ⲦⲀϤ ⲌⲱⲤ .... lawless person; the latter as
ⲞⲨⲆⲒⲔⲀⲒⲞⲤ Ⲡⲉ ϤⲒⲢⲉ Ⲛ̄ⲚⲉϤ .... a righteous person does his
ⲌⲂⲎⲨⲉ Ⲍ̄Ⲛ Ⲍ̄Ⲛ̄ⲔⲉⲔⲀⲨⲉ ⲉⲒⲢⲉ (30) .... works among others. So
Ⲍⲉ Ⲛ̄ⲦⲱⲦⲚ̄ ⲘⲠⲞⲨⲱϣ ⲘⲠⲒⲱⲦ .... you, do the will of the Father,
ϫⲉ Ⲛ̄ⲦⲱⲦⲚ̄ ⲌⲚ̄ⲀⲂⲀⲖ ⲘⲘⲀϤ .... for you are from him.

3.2.2.2

This passage is a tightly constructed ethical discourse which could well be
a meditation on Matthew's Sermon on the Mount, and Matthew 7:21 in particular: "Not everyone who says to me, 'Lord, Lord,' shall enter the kingdom of
heaven, but he who does the will of my Father who is in heaven."

The structure helps to reveal the author's intent. The first part (32,35–
33,11) contains an unbroken string of seven imperatives (ϢⲉϪⲉ ... ⲦⲀϫⲢⲞ
... ⲤⲱⲦ ... ⲤⲀⲚⲱ ... Ⲛ̄ⲦⲉⲦⲚ̄† Ⲙ̄ⲦⲀⲚ ... Ⲛ̄ⲦⲉⲦⲚ̄ⲞⲨⲚⲉⲤ ...
Ⲛ̄ⲦⲉⲦⲚ̄ⲚⲉⲌⲤⲉ),[37] with a concluding phrase introduced by ⲄⲀⲢ. The second part
(33,11–30) also has seven imperatives, the last six of which are negative (ϫⲒ
ⲌⲢⲎⲦⲚ̄ ... ⲘⲠⲢϫⲒ ⲌⲢⲎⲦⲚ̄ ... ⲘⲠⲢⲤⲱⲦⲉ ... ⲘⲠⲢⲢ ... ⲘⲠⲢⲢ ...
ⲘⲠⲢⲱϢⲱⲠⲉ ... ⲘⲠⲢⲦⲀϫⲢⲞ). Another concluding phrase (with a ⲄⲀⲢ)
follows. These two parts are introduced by an imperative sentence (ϢⲉϪⲉ Ⲍⲉ
ⲀⲂⲀⲖ Ⲍ̄Ⲙ ⲪⲎⲦ ... 32,31–34), and are concluded by one (ⲉⲒⲢⲉ Ⲍⲉ Ⲛ̄ⲦⲱⲦⲚ̄
ⲘⲠⲞⲨⲱϣ ⲘⲠⲒⲱⲦ ... 33,30–32). What is striking are the sixteen imperatives,
the two distinct parts, and the opening and concluding "caps" to the argument.[38]

---

[37] The last three verbs are conjunctives in form, but this is the way of expressing a series
of imperatives in Coptic.

[38] The care with which the author has constructed this section has not yet been appreciated, even by those who have delimited 32,31–33,32 as a subsection. Story comes the
closest when he highlights the two sets of imperatives (*The Nature of Truth*, 24–25). Meanwhile, the content surprised Grobel: "33:1–8 is full of *ethical* imperatives, astonishing in
a Gnostic work, for the Gnostics are generally held to have been devoid of ethical concern"
(*The Gospel of Truth*, 139–140).

3.2.2.3

The main argument is contained in the opening and closing sentences and in the concluding phrases to each of the two parts. The parallels to Matthew 5–7 can easily be seen, as the following paraphrase shows. You are from the Father, and his light dwells within you. ("You are the light of the world . . . . Let your light so shine before men that they may see your good works and give glory to your Father" — Matt 5:14–16.) The Father's light makes you perfect. ("You, therefore, must be perfect, as your heavenly Father is perfect" — 5:48.) Perfection not only involves attaining a particular state, but it also requires that you act accordingly. If you are really from the Father, you will do his will. This actually makes you stronger. ("Not everyone who says to me, 'Lord, Lord,' shall enter the Kingdom of Heaven, but he who does the will of my Father who is in heaven" — 7:21.[39]) Lawlessness leads away from the Father. Abide by the Father's Law and perform your actions as righteous individuals among others.[40] ("Think not that I have come to abolish the law and the prophets; I have come not to abolish them but to fulfil them" — 5:17.)

Precisely what "doing the Father's will" entails is described in the series of ethical injunctions in the first two parts. Some of these are meant to be taken literally. The opening statements reflect this: "Speak of the truth with those who search for it" (32,35–36), and "Be concerned with yourselves" (33,11). Other commands surely were intended metaphorically, as the phrase "Wake those who are sleeping" helps us to appreciate. Part 1 has a missionary flavor (cf. Matt 5:13: "You are the salt of the earth"). It states that doing the Father's will entails helping others by spreading the message of salvation far and wide. The focus is on teaching. The author's audience is encouraged to teach those who are already seeking salvation ("the hungry," "those who wish to rise"), those who are oblivious to their state (the sleeping — who can be wakened!), and also those who have identified the narrow road leading to the Father but who have difficulty staying on it (the "weary and sick," those who have "stumbled"). Part 2 turns the spotlight on the audience itself. It is not enough to help others, the author claims. Be concerned yourselves and do not slide back into your former materialistic ways. "Do not return to what you have vomited to eat it. Do not be moths, do not become worm-eaten" (33,15–17).[41] ("Do not lay up for yourselves treasures on earth, where moth and worm consume" — Matt 6:19; cf. also

[39] Note the opening and closing imperatives: "say" (ϣⲉϫⲉ — 32,31) . . . and "do" (ⲉⲓⲣⲉ — 33,30).

[40] The second concluding phrase (33,24–30) is difficult to understand in its present form. Literally, the passage reads as follows: "For the one without the Law [ⲡⲓⲁⲧⲍⲉⲛ] is one to do violence to, rather than the law-abiding one [ⲁⲛⲓⲍⲉⲛ], since that one [the former] does his work as a lawless person but the latter is a righteous person [ⲟⲩⲇⲓⲕⲁⲓⲟⲥ] and does his work among others." Among the evangelists, Matthew is the one who focuses on righteousness.

[41] Ⲙ̄ⲠⲢ ϤⲚⲦ literally means "do not produce worms, be worm-eaten."

6:25–33.) Doing the Father's will, then, involves keeping the spiritual level which the audience has attained and teaching others how to reach it.

3.2.2.4

Sin is mentioned in the first part of the pericope: "speak. . . . (of) knowledge to those who have committed sin in their error." The main difficulty in understanding this passage is whether to take the reference literally (as one does, for instance, with the phrase which precedes it), or metaphorically (as one does with those that follow). Ménard opts for the latter: "Le péché est l'erreur elle-même. Il n'y a que celle-ci qui soit considérée comme le mal, et le terme 'péché' est vidé de son sens moral."[42] According to Ménard, "those who have committed sins" are those who lack *gnosis* and truth, and sin has no connection with actual wrong actions and moral concerns. Similarly, when the author mentions the devil in 33,20, Ménard states: "Le diable, comme d'ailleurs Jésus, n'a que valeur de mythe: si la terminologie de l'auteur est d'inspiration nettement chrétienne, elle est vidée de son sens authentique [sic]."[43] These remarks are consistent with Ménard's attempt to set *The Gospel of Truth* firmly on the gnostic trajectory.

The evidence can be interpreted differently. We have seen how the author's remarks reflect not only a knowledge of Matthew's Gospel, but also an appreciation of the major tenets of the Sermon on the Mount. The argument in 32,31–33,32 is far more "Christian" than "gnostic." Furthermore, the author does not say that sin is error, but that people commit sins because they live in error. This is not necessarily the same. According to this passage, one can live either in a state of ignorance and error, or in a state of knowledge and truth. Knowing the truth means recognizing one's roots in the Father and sharing his perfection. It also includes the responsibility to live according to his will, which entails shunning the material aspects of the world and preaching the good news to others. This is a state which seems to be sinless. On the other hand, living in ignorance means acting improperly and "unlawfully," probably under the direction of the devil. One sins due to ignorance of the Father, but sin itself remains a wrong action, i.e., an action not in accord with the Father's will. With truth comes freedom over the devil and a recognition of what the Father expects.

3.2.3.1

Sin is mentioned a second time in 35,25–26. The relevant passage is as follows (35,24–36,13):[44]

ⲉⲧⲃⲉ ⲡⲉⲉⲓ ⲁϯⲙⲛ̄ⲧⲁⲧⲧⲉⲕⲟ (35,24)	. . . . For this reason incorruptibility
ⲛⲓϥⲉ ⲁⲃⲁⲗ ⲁⲥⲟⲩⲁϩⲥ̄ ⲛ̄ⲥⲁ ⲡⲉ(ⲛ)	. . . . breathed forth; it pursued the one
ⲧⲁϥⲣ̄ ⲛⲁⲃⲓ ϫⲉⲕⲁⲥⲉ ⲉϥⲉⲙ̄	. . . . who had sinned in order that he might
ⲧⲁⲛ ⲙ̄ⲙⲁϥ ⲡⲕⲱϭ ⲅⲁⲣ ⲁⲃⲁⲗ ⲡⲉ	. . . . rest. For forgiveness is what

---

[42] Ménard, *L'Évangile de Vérité*, 154.

[43] Ménard, *L'Évangile de Vérité*, 157. This is the only occurrence of "devil" in this work.

[44] The text and translation are from *Nag Hammadi Codex I*, 106–08.

ⲡ ⲱ ϣ ⲭ ⲡ ⲁ ⲡ ⲟ ⲩ ⲁ ⲉ ⲓ ⲛ 2ⲛ ⲡ ⲓ ⲱ ⲧ ⲁ ..... remains for the light in the deficiency,
ⲡ ⲓ ⲱ ϫ ⲉ ⲛⲧⲉ ⲡ ⲓ ⲡ ⲗ ⲏ ⲣ ⲱ ⲙ ⲁ .... the word of the pleroma.
ⲡ ⲥ ⲁ ⲉ ⲓ ⲛ ⲅ ⲁ ⲣ ⲱ ⲁ ϥ ⲡ ⲱ ⲧ ⲁ ⲡ ⲙ ⲁ ⲉ (30) ..... For the physician runs to the place
ⲧⲉ ⲟ ⲩ ⲛ̅ ⲱ ⲱ ⲛ ⲉ ⲛ 2ⲏ ⲧ ϥ̅ ϫ ⲉ ⲡ ⲓ ⲟ ⲩ .... where a sickness is, because
ⲱ ⲱ ϣ ⲉ ⲛ̅ⲧ ⲁ ϥ ⲡ ⲉ ⲉ ⲧ ⲱ ⲟ ⲟ ⲡ .... that is the will that is in him.
ⲛ 2ⲏ ⲧ ϥ̅ ⲡ ⲉ ⲧ ⲡ̅ ⲱ ⲧ ⲁ 6ⲉ ⲙ ⲁ ϥ ⲁ 2 ⲁ ...... He who has a deficiency, then, does not
ⲡ ϥ̅ ϫ ⲉ ⲟ ⲩ ⲛ̅ⲧ ⲉ ϥ ⲙ̅ⲙ ⲉ ⲩ ⲙ̅ⲡ ⲉ .... hide it, because one has what
ⲧ ϥ ⲱ ⲁ ⲁ ⲧ ⲙ̅ⲙ ⲁ ⲩ ⲡ ⲓ ⲣ ⲏ ⲧⲉ ⲡ ⲓ ⲡ ⲗ ⲏ (35) .... the other lacks. So the pleroma,
ⲣ ⲱ ⲙ ⲁ ⲉ ⲧⲉ ⲛ ϥ̅ⲡ̅ ⲱ ⲧ ⲁ ⲉ ⲛ ⲡ ⲓ ⲱ ⲧ ⲁ .... which has no deficiency,
ⲛ̅ⲧ ⲁ ϥ ϥ ⲙ ⲟ ⲩ 2 ⲙ̅ⲙ ⲁ ϥ ⲡ ⲉ ⲛ ⲧ ⲁ ϥ .... but fills up the deficiency,
ⲧⲉ ⲉ ⲓ ϥ ⲁ ⲃ ⲁ ⲗ 2ⲓ̈ⲧ ⲟ ⲟ ⲧ ϥ̅ ⲁ ⲙ ⲁ 2 (36,1) .... is what he provided for himself
.... for filling up
ⲡ ⲉ ⲧ ϥ ⲱ ⲁ ⲁ ⲧ ⲙ̅ⲙ ⲁ ϥ ϫ ⲉ ⲕ ⲁ ⲥ ⲉ ...... what he lacks, in order that therefore he
6ⲉ ⲡ ⲓ 2ⲙ ⲁ ⲧ ⲉ ϥ ⲁ ϫ ⲓ ⲧ ϥ̅ ϫ ‹ⲉ› ⲙ̅ⲡ ⲥ ⲁ ⲡ .... might receive the grace. For when
ⲉ ⲧⲉ ⲛ ⲉ ϥ ⲱ ⲁ ⲁ ⲧ ⲛ ⲉ ⲙ ⲛ ⲧⲉ ϥ ⲙ̅ .... he was deficient, he did not have
ⲙ ⲉ ⲩ ⲙ̅ⲡ ⲉ 2ⲙ ⲁ ⲧ ⲉ ⲧ ⲃ ⲉ ⲡ ⲉ ⲉ ⲓ (5) .... the grace. That is why
ⲛ ⲉ ⲟ ⲩ ⲧ ⲥ ⲃ̅ⲕ ⲟ ⲡ ⲉ ⲉ ⲧ ⲱ ⲟ ⲟ ⲡ 2ⲛ̅ .... there was diminution existing in
ⲡ ⲙ ⲁ ⲉ ⲧⲉ ⲣ ⲉ ⲡ ⲉ 2ⲙ ⲁ ⲧ ⲙ̅ⲙ ⲉ ⲩ .... the place where there is no grace.
ⲉ ⲛ ⲡ ⲥ ⲁ ⲡ ⲉ ⲛ ⲧ ⲁ ⲩ ϫ ⲓ ⲙ̅ⲡ ⲉ ⲉ ⲓ ⲉ .... When that which was diminished
ⲧ ⲥ ⲁ ⲃ ⲕ̅ ⲡ ⲉ ⲧ ϥ ⲱ ⲁ ⲁ ⲧ ⲙ̅ⲙ ⲁ ϥ ⲁ ϥ .... was received, he revealed what he
ⲟ ⲩ ⲁ ⲛ 2̅ϥ ⲉ ϥ ⲟ ⲉ ⲓ ⲛ̅ⲛ ⲟ ⲩ ⲡ ⲗ ⲏ ⲣ ⲱ ⲙ ⲁ (10) .... lacked, being (now) a pleroma;
ⲉ ⲧⲉ ⲡ ⲉ ⲉ ⲓ ⲡ ⲉ ⲡ 6ⲓ ⲛ ⲉ ⲙ̅ⲡ ⲟ ⲩ ⲁ ⲉ ⲓ ⲛ .... that is the discovery of the light
ⲛ̅ⲧ ⲙ ⲏ ⲉ ⲉ ⲛ ⲧ ⲁ 2ⲱ ⲁ ⲉ ⲓ ⲉ ⲁ ⲣ ⲁ ϥ ϫ ⲉ ..... of truth which rose upon him because
ⲟ ⲩ ⲁ ⲧ ⲱ ⲃ̅ⲧ ϥ̅ ⲡ ⲉ .... it is immutable. ...

3.2.3.2

The Father's role is presented in the first six lines of this pericope: people have sinned, the Father (†ⲙ̅ⲛ̅ⲧ ⲁ ⲧⲧⲉ ⲕ ⲟ) goes out of his way (ⲁ ⲥ ⲟ ⲩ ⲁ 2ⲥ̅ ⲛ̅ⲥ ⲁ) to offer forgiveness, and this provides salvation (ϫ ⲉ ⲕ ⲁ ⲥ ⲉ ⲉ ϥ ⲉ ⲙ̅ⲧ ⲁ ⲛ ⲙ̅ⲙ ⲁ ϥ). Why he acts in this manner and how he does it are the author's next concerns. To answer these questions he introduces a physician-patient metaphor (35,30), probably because healing and the forgiveness of sins were interconnected in his mind. The physician's nature, he says, is to go where sickness is present and to cure it. He has the skills and the desire to heal (ⲡ ⲥ ⲁ ⲉ ⲓ ⲛ ⲅ ⲁ ⲣ ⲱ ⲁ ϥ ⲡ ⲱ ⲧ ⲁ ⲡ ⲙ ⲁ ⲉ ⲧⲉ ⲟ ⲩ ⲛ̅ ⲱ ⲱ ⲛ ⲉ ⲛ 2ⲏ ⲧ ϥ̅ ϫ ⲉ ⲡ ⲓ ⲟ ⲩ ⲱ ⲱ ϣ ⲉ ⲛ̅ⲧ ⲁ ϥ ⲡ ⲉ ⲉ ⲧ ⲱ ⲟ ⲟ ⲡ ⲛ 2ⲏ ⲧ ϥ̅ — 35,30-33). The sick person's nature is to recognize the need for assistance and to allow the physician to intervene (ⲡ ⲉ ⲧ ⲡ̅ ⲱ ⲧ ⲁ 6ⲉ ⲙ ⲁ ϥ ⲁ 2ⲁ ⲡ ϥ̅ ϫ ⲉ ⲟ ⲩ ⲛ̅ⲧ ⲉ ϥ ⲙ̅ⲙ ⲉ ⲩ ⲙ̅ⲡ ⲉ ⲧ ϥ ⲱ ⲁ ⲁ ⲧ ⲙ̅ⲙ ⲁ ϥ[45] —35,33-35). So it is with the Father. He recognizes human illness, wants to help, and has the requisite skills. The "patients" will not get better on their own. Only "interventionist medicine" can save them. Grace (2ⲙ ⲁ ⲧ) provides the healing power. The Father is part of the "fullness" (ⲡ ⲓ ⲡ ⲗ ⲏ ⲣ ⲱ ⲙ ⲁ) while humans live in deficiency (ⲱ ⲧ ⲁ). Grace is the transfer of some of that fullness to fill the deficiency.

[45] Reading ⲙ̅ⲙ ⲁ ϥ for ⲙ̅ⲙ ⲁ ⲩ, which makes no sense here.

3.2.3.3

Sin is not used clearly in this passage. The author claims that people are "sick"; that is, they sin and know it, because they live in this deficient world. Sinning is connected with a deficient ecological state. The Father forgives these sins, and provides grace, enabling people to sin no more. Grace and the forgiveness of sins lead to salvation ("rest"). According to Ménard's interpretation of this passage,

le "péché" y a perdu son sens moral. Le ἁμαρτάνειν de la mystique hellénistique, c'est la fatalité, la εἱμαρμένη, où la volonté de l'homme n'est pas mis en jeu, mais où elle est l'enjeu de ces deux forces métaphysiques opposées, la γνῶσις et l'ἄγνοια.[46]

He is correct that the vocabulary resembles that found in the *Corpus Hermeticum*, but Paul for one would not have disagreed much with the content. The most we can say about this passage on its own is that we do not know whether sin has lost its "sens moral."

3.2.4.1

We now must set these two pericopes in their context in *The Gospel of Truth*. The first passage to approach is the one which lies sandwiched between 32,31– 33,32 and 35,24–36,13, and which Story calls "The Fortune of the Father's Aroma." Its introductory words (ϪⲈ ⲠⲒⲰⲦ ⲄⲀⲢ) make it clear that the author did not draw a solid line after 33,32; similarly, the ⲈⲦⲂⲈ ⲠⲈⲈⲒ at 35,24 links the second and third pericopes solidly. According to 33,33–35,23 people come from the Father. Their time on earth has separated them from their source, yet the Father responds to those who seek salvation by drawing them to him. The author expresses this point effectively with a gentle metaphor. The Father's children are his fragrance (ⲤⲦⲀⲈⲒ) who are beloved and come from his grace. This fragrance has become heavy and cold in the world, and the warmth of the Father's breath will revive it and draw it upwards once again to be united with the Father. This ties in with the presentation of the Father in the adjoining pericopes. The Father wills that people recognize their need for salvation and unity with him, and he is eager to help them. In their present state they live in "error," "illness," and "cold" and need redemption. Their sins do not alienate them from the Father; rather, they seem to reflect this alienation.

3.2.4.2

The rest of this work reinforces the points which emerge in 32,31–36,13, as a quick overview will show.

People live in a world created by Error (ⲠⲖⲀⲚⲎ), which is a mere imitation of the heavenly realities. All appear to be the same, but in fact there are two distinct classes: those who come from the Father and those who are merely hylics (the psychics play no discernible role). These hylics originate in the lower

---

[46] Ménard, *L'Évangile de Vérité*, 167.

world and will be destroyed (with this world) in the end times. They can never hope to understand the Father, nor can they accept his son's message. The other humans have their origin with the Father, and will return to join him, although they now dwell in the lower realm. Oblivion (†ⲃⲱⲉ) has come over them, causing them to forget their roots. This class of humans has several categories: those (like the writer) who have already realized their ascent and dwell "with the Father," those who openly are seeking the Father, and those who recognize the Father when they hear the proper message. The Father is eager to be reunited with these "children," so he sends his son, Jesus, to impart saving knowledge to those who are receptive. Jesus' role, then, is to descend into the world of Error, to teach and anoint (36,13–35) those who receive his word, and to leave behind a "living book" of disciples (19,35 – cf. 2 Cor 3:2-3) to continue the spread of his message.

As the final words of this gospel state, those upon whom "the love of the Father is poured out" are expected to spread the message ("speak of the light which is perfect") and appear as children worthy of the Father's name (43,9-23). Ethics surely is not absent from this discussion.

3.2.5

Sin probably played a more significant role in the author's community than the two occurrences in *The Gospel of Truth* suggest. Furthermore, contrary to Ménard's claims, it would seem that sin was closely tied to morality, and meant "doing something contrary to the Father's will." Such improper actions were done often (always?) by the hylics; and sometimes also by the "Father's children," both those who did not yet know any better and those who ought to have known better. The paraenetical sections encourage those with knowledge not to return to what they "have vomited to eat it" (33,16).

Sin, then, was a constant reality and a threat for this community of Christians. The author also encouraged his audience to struggle to lead their lives in accordance with the Father's will; that is, to lead sinless lives. Being "perfect" meant acting correctly, which included "speaking the truth to those who search for it" (32,35-36) and being "concerned with yourself" (33,11).

3.3 *The Tripartite Tractate*

3.3.1

Structurally, *The Tripartite Tractate* resembles the understanding of people which emerges from this work: there are two basic divisions, but the whole is organized in three parts. The first division (and part), which comprises roughly sixty percent of the whole (51,1–104,3), covers "the things which are exalted" (ⲛⲉⲧϪⲁⲥⲓ – 51,1-2).[47] It offers several distinctive variants on the "classical"

---

[47] The title given to the first part by the editors of the *editio princeps* is somewhat deceptive. The second section of this part (75,17-104,3) concerns the Fall of the Logos and the

Valentinian description of the Pleroma and the Fall. Notably, the Father has no female companion, and it is the divine Logos who replaces Sophia as the agent of devolution and creation.[48] In the second division the author turns his attention to people. One part (104,4–108,12) focuses on the creation account and the fall from the Garden of Eden, the other (108,13–140) on the different types of people and their responses to the Savior.[49] Sin is mentioned twice in this final part (115,15; 117,4). Given the unity of the narrative, it is helpful to begin by summarizing the author's argument in 108,13–140. Then we can turn to a detailed analysis of the pericopes in question.

A cautionary note is in order since this work is both easy and frustratingly difficult to summarize. The author has a basic message to impart to his audience, and has chosen to use a variety of metaphors with which to do it. Elements in some of these metaphors at times are contradictory, and many of the metaphors themselves are incomprehensible to a twentieth century audience. We do most justice to this work, then, by focusing on the underlying message—and not by asking, for instance, whether the three human parts were called "races" (ΓΕΝΟС—118,22), "essences" (ΟΥСΙⲀ—106,6–15) or "orders" (ΤⲀⲌΙС—108,32).

3.3.2.1

The title De generibus tribus chosen for the final part of this work by the editors of the editio princeps is fitting,[50] for the 31 pages of text focus on humanity's three natures, or essences, and their possibilities of salvation through the intervention of Christ the Savior. The overlap between the author's presentation and Irenaeus's summary of the Ptolemaic system is significant. Yet there are major differences.[51] This section of The Tripartite Tractate outlines the optimistic depiction of human destiny, within a modified dualistic framework, and grounded in certain Christian myths and rituals.

---

ensuing cosmogony, not only life in the Pleroma (De supernis).

[48] For brief discussions of Part 1, see the following: J. Zandee (with H.-C. Puech), Tractatus Tripartitus, I, 37–64; Antonio Orbe, "En torno a un tratado gnóstico," Greg 56 (1975) 558–66; Domenico Devoti, "Una Summa di teologia gnostica: il 'Tractatus Tripartitus'," RSLR 13 (1977) 326–39; Ulrich Luz, "Der dreiteilige Traktat von Nag Hammadi," TZ 33 (1977) 385–87; and (notably) Einar Thomassen, "The Structure of the Transcendent World in the Tripartite Tractate (NHC I,5)," VC 34 (1980) 358–75.

[49] For brief discussions of Parts 2–3, see J. Zandee, Tractatus Tripartitus, II, 9–30; Devoti, "Una Summa," 340–53; and Luz, "Der dreiteilige Traktat," 388–91.

[50] The editors of the editio princeps initially wanted to call the entire work De generibus tribus because of the importance of "the three natures" in the work, and its striking resemblance to Irenaeus's description of Valentinianism (Zandee, Tractatus Tripartitus, II, 17).

[51] These differences do not emerge clearly if one reads Zandee's harmonizing preface (in Tractatus Tripartitus, II). He has woven several accounts of Valentinianism (e.g. from Irenaeus, Heracleon, and this work) into a consistent whole, thereby obscuring each author's redactional concerns.

3.3.2.2

Optimism reigns even within a cosmological construct where people need assistance to remove themselves from the material sphere. In fact, the author believes that any being in the world needs outside redemption, including the redeemer who descends from above (124,32–125,11). Yet most will be saved. The "litmus test" is how people react to the Savior. The pneumatics accept him at once, the psychics believe in him and adore him, and the hylics reject him (118,28–119,10). Only the last group is doomed, and the author pays little attention to them. In this discussion, the striking aspect is the positive portrayal of the psychic race. It is not inclined to evil (ϹΡΑΚΕ ΕΝ ΑΠΕΤΘΑΟΥ—106,14). Similarly, the rancor against the Jews which one finds in many early Christian works (e.g. Matt 23; Barnabas) is absent,[52] as is the negative depiction of the Demiurge. According to *The Tripartite Tractate*, then, people are not oppressed by the forces of evil. They have lived for some time under their control, not knowing any better, but now that the Savior has come they can, and will, take their rightful place close to the Father.

This optimism derives in great part from the author's mitigated dualism which borders on monism. In this tractate God (the Father) is in complete control.[53] The forces of evil are not pitted against the forces of good. When God chooses to act to save his children, he does not even struggle with the lower powers. His plan of salvation includes placing people temporarily in ignorance so that they might experience the evils of the lower world and then appreciate the world of the Pleroma all the more (126,20–127,8). This includes sending his Son to save humanity at the appropriate time. There are two worlds, then, but only one guiding force in control of both the upper and lower realms.[54]

Similarly, people are divided into three groups, but the fundamental separation is between "those on the left" (the hylics) and "those on the right" (the others—132,9–10). Furthermore, the hylics, the "bad order" (ϯΤΑΞΙϹ ΕΘΑΥ—108,25), are destined to destruction and function only to help purify the psychics and pneumatics (136,32–139,15). The attention is placed on "those on the right," the pyschics (those who are called) and the pneumatics (the elect). The pneumatics, or "hidden order" (ϯΤΑΞΙϹ ΕΤ2ΗΠ—108,34–35), "will receive complete salvation in every way" (ϤΝΑΞΙ ΜΠΝΟΥ2ΜΕ ΤΗΡϤ ΚΑΤΑ ΡΗΤΕ ΝΙΜ—119,17–18). Nonetheless, there seem to be different categories of pneumatics, each of which has a distinct role to play (116,13–17). Differences also exist within the

---

[52] In 111,6–29 the psychics are symbolized as the Hebrews, and the author accepts the legitimacy of the claims made by the Hebrew prophets of old.

[53] In this work, "God" is not the "Hebrew God" or the inferior Demiurge of "classical" Valentinian thought. Throughout the tractate (e.g. 112,24–28; 120,36; 126,13; 128,16; 133,19–22) God is equated with the Father.

[54] Cf. Luz's remarks: "Der klassische Dualismus des Gnostizismus wird zu einem Typ des Monismus, der im Gedanken der göttlichen oikonomia seinen prägnantesten Ausdruck findet. Die Welt ist nicht mehr abgründig böse, sondern unwissend durchdrungen vom guten Gott" ("Der dreiteilige Traktat," 391).

psychics, or "intelligent order" (†TAᶻIC ṀMṄT2HT −108,32). Psychics gain salvation through their good works (130,23–24). All can be saved, and indeed they tend towards what is superior. But within this order some are lower by nature,[55] and often "mix with matter" (131,22−132,3). Others have a good disposition (120,6–8) and are virtually guaranteed salvation (119,32–33) in "the aeon of the images [=the Ogdoad?], where Logos has not yet joined with the Pleroma" (122,25–27). The author minimizes the distinctions between the pneumatics and the psychics. He is concerned with the salvation of "all those on the right" (ⲠⲒⲞⲨ𝕏Ⲁ𝟼ⲒⲦ𝟼 ⲚⲀ𝟼 ⲚⲒⲞⲨⲚ𝟼Ⲙ ⲦⲎ𝗣ⲞⲨ −132,8–9).[56]

Ⲧ𝟼ⲔⲔⲀ𝗛ⲤⲒⲀ represents ⲚⲒⲞⲨⲚ𝟼Ⲙ. "We are the Lord's Church," exclaims the author in 125,5.[57] He envisions the moment of salvation when "all the members of the body of the church are in a single place and receive the restoration at one time" (123,17–20). More striking yet is the importance placed on baptism:

> There is no other baptism apart from this one alone, which is the redemption [ⲠⲤⲰⲦ𝟼] into God, Father, Son, and Holy Spirit, when confession is made through faith in those names, which are a single name of the gospel, when they have come to believe what has been said to them, namely that they (Father, Son, and Holy Spirit) exist. From this they have salvation, those who have believed that they exist. (127,28–128,5)

There is only one true baptism "which transcends every voice," although it is given a variety of names (128,19–129,34).[58] It is the ritual *par excellence* which the author's community underwent as a seal, or in anticipation, of unity with the Father.[59] In this ritual, the Christians proclaim their confession of faith in

[55] These "lower psychics" are said to come from the inferior elements of the Logos (131,22–132,37).

[56] Luz arrives at a similar conclusion, in the context of his (questionable) argument that *The Tripartite Tractate* represents a Christianizing of Gnosticism: "Die Grenze des Gnostizismus ist m.E. auch dort erreicht, wo der Verfasser die Schranken zwischen 'wesenhaften' Pneumatikern und den aus der Umkehr, dem Gebet und der Hoffnung lebenden Psychikern—gewiss nicht ohne Selbstwidersprüche—abzubauen beginnt: Der schroffe anthropologisch-ontologische Dualismus wird wenigstens ansatzweise durchbrochen und in der Breite des Entscheidungsspielraums des 'Psychischen' aufgehoben" ("Der dreiteilige Traktat," 391).

[57] This worldly church is a reflection of the Church in the Pleroma (cf. 58,29; 94,21; 97,7). For reference to the Church in this section, see also 121,31.37; 122,7.12.30; 128,18; 135,26.

[58] This baptism is called, *inter alia*, "silence," "bridal chamber," "the light which does not set and is without flame," "the eternal life," and "all that which it is."

[59] Galatians 3:26–28 comes to mind when reading this passage, but Devoti overstates his case when he claims that "il *De creatione hominis* e il *De generibus tribus* sono un approfondimento della *Lettera ai Galati* di Paolo, in particolare dei capitoli 3 e 4" ("Una Summa," 340).

God, and God in turn allows them to share in his knowledge (128,14-19). Remarkable in this part of *The Tripartite Tractate* is the presence and importance of God as the Father, the Church as the body of believers and "gnostics," and baptism as the rite of union.

3.3.3.1

Sin is mentioned for the first time in 115,15. The passage in context is as follows (114,30-115,25):[60]

. . .ⲬⲈ (114,30).	
ⲠⲈⲈⲒ ⲠⲈ ⲈⲦⲈⲀⲠⲚ̄ⲤⲰⲦⲎⲢ ⲰⲰⲠⲈ	He it is who was our Savior
ⲘⲘⲀϥ ⲀⲂⲀⲖ Ⲍ̄Ⲛ̄Ⲛ ⲞⲨⲘⲚ̄ⲦⲰⲂⲎⲢ Ⲛ̄	in willing compassion,
ⲰⲰⲠ Ⲛ̄ⲔⲀⲌ ⲈϤⲞⲨⲰⲰⲈ ⲈⲦⲈ ⲠⲈⲦⲀⲨ	who is that which
ⲰⲰⲠⲈ ⲘⲘⲀϥ ⲠⲈ ⲬⲈ ⲈⲢⲈⲚ̄ⲚⲦⲀϥⲞⲨ	they were. For it was for
. . . .	their sake that he became
ⲰⲚ̄Ⲍ̄ ⲀⲂⲀⲖ ⲈⲦⲂⲎⲦⲞⲨ Ⲍ̄Ⲛ̄Ⲛ ⲞⲨⲠⲀⲐⲞⲤ (35).	manifest in an involuntary
Ⲛ̄ⲀⲦⲞⲨⲰⲰⲈ ⲀⲨⲰⲰⲠⲈ Ⲛ̄ⲤⲀⲢⲌ̄ Ⲍ̄Ⲓ̈ ⲮⲨ	suffering. They became flesh and
ⲬⲎ ⲈⲦⲈ ⲠⲈⲈⲒ ⲠⲈ ⲀⲚⲎⲌⲈ ⲈⲦⲈⲘⲀⲌⲦⲈ	soul,—that is, eternally—
. . . .	which (things) hold
ⲘⲘⲀⲨ ⲀⲨⲰ ⲘⲚ̄ Ⲍ̄Ⲛ̄ⲦⲈⲔⲞ	them and with corruptible things
ⲈϤⲀⲨⲘⲞⲨ ⲚⲈⲦⲀⲌ[Ⲱ]ⲰⲠ]Ⲉ ⲀⲈ Ⲍ̄ⲰⲰϥ . . .	they die. As for those who [came
[Ⲡ]ⲢⲰⲘⲈ [ⲚⲚ]ⲀⲦⲚⲈⲨ ⲀⲢⲀϥ Ⲍ̄ⲚⲚ ⲞⲨ (1)	into being], [the] invisible one
[Ⲙ]Ⲛ̄ⲦⲀⲦⲚⲈⲨ ⲀⲢⲀⳠ ⲀϥⲦⲤⲈⲂⲀⲨ ⲀⲢⲀϥ	taught them invisibly about
[Ⲍ]Ⲛ̄ ⲞⲨⲘⲚ̄ⲦⲀⲦⲚⲈⲨ ⲀⲢⲀⳠ ⲀⲚ ⲬⲈ ⲞⲨ	himself. Not only did he
ⲘⲞⲚⲞⲚ ⲀϥⲬⲒ ⲀⲢⲀⲞⲨ Ⲙ̄ⲠⲒⲘⲞⲨ Ⲛ̄ⲦⲈ[Ⲩ]	take upon ⟨himself⟩ the death
ⲞⲨ ⲚⲈⲦⲈⲀϥⲘⲈⲨⲈ ⲀⲢⲀⲞⲨ ⲀⲦⲢⲈϥⲦⲞⲨ (5)	of those whom he thought
. . . .	to save, but
ⲬⲀⲨⲞⲨ ⲀⲖⲖⲀ ⲦⲞⲨⲔⲈⲘⲚ̄ⲦⲰⳘⲘ Ⲁ[Ⲛ] . . .	he also accepted their smallness to
ⲠⲈⲚⲦⲀⲨⲈⲒ ⲀⲌⲢⲎ̈ ⲀⲢⲀⲤ ⲈⲀⲨⲚⲈⲤⲦⲞ[Ⲩ]	which they had descended when
ⲔⲀⲦⲀ ⲠⲤⲰⲘⲀ ⲘⲚ̄ ⲦⲮⲨⲬⲎ ⲀϥⲬ[ⲒⲦⲤ]	they were ⟨born⟩ in body
. . . .	and soul.
ⲀⲚ ⟨Ⲉ⟩ⲂⲞⲖ Ⲙ̄ⲠⲈⲈⲒ ⲬⲈ ⲀϥⲦⲢⲞⲨⲰ Ⲙ̄Ⲙ[Ⲁ]Ⲥ	(He did so) because he
. . . .	had let himself be
ⲀⲨⲰ ⲀϥⲦⲢⲞⲨⲘⲈⲤⲦϥ̄ Ⲛ̄ⲚⲞⲨⲖⲒⲖⲞⲨ Ⲛ̄(10)	conceived and born as an
. . . .	infant, in
ⲤⲰⲘⲀ ⲮⲨⲬⲎ ⲬⲈ Ⲍ̄ⲢⲎ̈ Ⲍ̄Ⲛ̄ Ⲛ̄ⲔⲈⲔⲀⲨⲈ.	body and soul. Among all
. . . .	the others
ⲦⲎⲢⲞⲨ ⲈⲚⲦⲀⲨⲢ̄ ⲔⲞⲒⲚⲰⲚⲒ ⲀⲢⲀⲨⲞⲨ ⲘⲚ̄	who shared in them
ⲚⲈⲚⲦⲀⳘⲀⲈⲒⲈ ⲀⲨⲰ ⲈⲨⲬⲒ Ⲙ̄ⲠⲞⲨⲞⲒ̈Ⲛ	and those who fell and received
ⲚⲈⲀϥⲈⲒ ⲈϥⲬⲀⲤⲒ Ⲛ̄Ⲍ̄ⲎⲦⲞⲨ ⲠⲈ ⲀⲂⲀⲖ.	the light, he came being exalted,
ⲬⲈ Ⲍ̄Ⲛ̄ ⲞⲨⲘⲚ̄ⲦⲀⲦⲢ̄ ⲚⲞⲂⲈ ⲀⲨⲰ Ⲍ̄Ⲛ̄Ⲛ ⲞⲨ(15)	because he had let himself
Ⲙ̄Ⲛ̄ⲦⲀⲦⲦⲰⲖⲘ̄ ⲀⲨⲰ Ⲍ̄Ⲛ̄ ⲞⲨⲘⲚ̄Ⲧ	be conceived without sin, stain
ⲀⲦⲬⲰⲌⲘ̄ ⲠⲈⲚⲦⲀϥⲦⲢⲞⲨⲰ Ⲙ̄ⲘⲀϥ	and defilement. He was

---

[60] The text and translation are from *Nag Hammadi Codex I*, 298-300.

ⲀⲨϪⲠⲟϥ ⲌⲘ̅ ⲠⲂⲒⲟⲤ ⲈϥϢⲟⲟⲠ ⲌⲘ̅ ⲠⲂⲒⲟⲤ ...... begotten in life, being in life
ⲀⲂⲀⲗ ϪⲈ Ⲛ̅ⲦⲀⲨ ⲘⲚ̅ ⲚⲈⲦⲘ̅ⲘⲈⲨ ⲌⲚ̅ ...... because the former and the latter
Ⲛ ⲞⲨⲠⲀⲐⲟⲤ ⲘⲚ̅Ⲛ ⲞⲨⲦⲚⲱⲘⲎ ⲈⲚⲤⲠⲀ(20).............. are in passion and
.... changing opinion
ⲚⲈ ⲀⲂⲀⲗ Ⲛ̅ⲦⲈ ⲠⲗⲟⲄⲟⲤ ⲈⲚⲦⲀⲌ2ⲔⲒⲘ .... from the Logos who moved,
ⲈⲚⲦⲀⲤⲦⲈⲌⲀⲨ ⲀⲦⲢⲟⲨⲱⲱⲠⲈ Ⲛ̅Ⲥⲱ .... who established them to be body
ⲘⲀ 2Ⲓ ⲮⲨⲬⲎ ⲠⲈⲈⲒ ⲇⲈ Ⲛ̅ⲦⲀϥ ‹ⲠⲈⲦ› ⲈⲀϥϪⲒ .... and soul. He it is
.... ‹who› has taken
ⲀⲢⲀϥ ⲘⲠⲢⲈϥⲈⲒ 2Ⲁ ⲚⲈⲦⲀⲚ̅Ⲣ ϢⲢⲠ̅ .... to himself the one who came from
.... those whom we previously
Ⲛ̅ϪⲟⲟⲨ .... (25) .... mentioned. ...

3.3.3.2

The argument is straightforward, though not as detailed in places as one would like. Immediately before this pericope (113,2–114,30) the author describes the Father's decision to send his son down to the world. The Father is "one . . . , invisible, unknowable, [and] incomprehensible" (114,22–26). He grants that he might be seen, known and comprehended, and ordains "the manifestation of salvation" (114,17). Through his compassion for humanity he sends his son, "our Savior," who also is eternal and unbegotten (113,36–37). The Hebrew prophets predicted certain aspects of the Savior's coming, though not having access to all the details.

The pericope quoted above concerns the Savior's incarnation and "immaculate conception." He allows himself to be conceived and born as an infant, in body and soul (ϪⲈ ⲀϥⲦⲢⲟⲨⲱ ⲘⲘⲀϥ ⲀⲨⲱ ⲀϥⲦⲢⲟⲨⲘⲈⲤⲦϥ Ⲛ̅Ⲛ̅ⲞⲨⲗⲒⲗⲟⲨ Ⲛ̅ⲤⲱⲘⲀ ⲮⲨⲬⲎ – 115,9–11). He receives his flesh (ⲦⲈϥⲤⲀⲢ2) from the pneumatic Logos (114,9–10), but shares in people's somatic and psychic natures. Yet he is different: "he appeared exalted" (ⲈϥϪⲀⲤⲒ). This is "because he had let himself be conceived without sin, stain and defilement." He resembles people, then, but is not quite like them either. He lives "in a state of not sinning" (ⲞⲨⲘⲚ̅Ⲧ̅ⲀⲦ̅Ⲣ̅ⲚⲟⲂⲈ), while they live "in passion and changing opinion" (2Ⲛ̅Ⲛ ⲞⲨⲠⲀⲐⲟⲤ ⲘⲚ̅Ⲛ ⲞⲨⲦⲚⲱⲘⲎ ⲈⲚⲤⲠⲀⲚⲈ). Sin, then, appears to be an intrinsic part of humanity's somatic and psychic existence, which derives from creation. Absence of sin is remarkable.

This does not tell us a great deal about sin, aside from its hold over humanity. What also is unclear is the part played by the psychics and pneumatics in the Savior's plan of salvation. The focus, though, is on the pneumatics, those who had "descended" and "fasted in body and soul." "And as for those who came into being [the pneumatics as 'the hidden race'?], the invisible one taught them invisibly about themselves" (114,39–115,2). The Savior's mission was to teach the pneumatics and take death off their shoulders (115,4).

3.3.4.1

Sin is mentioned again in 117,4. The passage in context is as follows (116,27–117,17):[61]

...ϫϵ ⲛ̄ (116,27) ....The Savior was
Ⲧⲁϥ ⲘⲈⲚ ⲠⲤⲰⲦⲎⲢ ⲚⲈⲞⲨⲌ̈ⲒⲔⲰⲚ ....an image
ⲠⲈ ⲚⲆⲈ ⲞⲨⲈⲈⲒ Ⲛ̄ⲞⲨⲰⲦ ⲈⲦⲈ Ⲛ̄ ....of the unitary one, he who
Ⲧⲁϥ ⲠⲈ ⲠⲦⲎⲢϥ̄ ⲔⲀⲦⲀ ⲠⲤⲰⲘⲀ (30) ....is the Totality in bodily form.
ⲈⲦⲂⲈ ⲠⲀⲈⲒ ⲀϥⲦⲞⲨϪⲞ ⲠⲤⲘⲀⲦ Ⲛ̄ ......Therefore, he preserved the form of
ⲦⲘ̄ⲚⲦⲀⲦⲠⲰⲒϫⲈ ⲦⲈⲈⲒ ⲈⲦⲈⲢⲈ ....indivisibility, from which
ⲦⲘ̄ⲚⲦⲀⲦⲠⲀⲐⲞⲤ ⲒϫⲞⲞⲠ ⲀⲂⲀⲖ Ⲛ̄ ....comes impassibility.
Ⲉ2ⲎⲦⲤ̄ ⲚⲀⲈⲒ Ⲛ̄ⲆⲈ Ⲛ̄ⲦⲀⲨ Ⲉ2Ⲛ̄Ⲉ̈ⲒⲔⲰ̄(Ⲛ) ....They, however, are images
ⲚⲈ Ⲛ̄ⲆⲈ ⲠⲞⲨⲈⲈⲒ ⲠⲞⲨⲈⲈⲒ ⲈⲦⲀⲈ (35) ....of each thing which
ⲞⲨⲰⲚ2̄ ⲀⲂⲀⲖ ⲈⲦⲂⲈ ⲠⲈⲈⲒ ⲤⲈ ....became manifest. Therefore, they
ϫⲒ ⲀⲢⲀⲨ Ⲙ̄ⲠⲒⲠⲰⲒϫⲈ ⲀⲂⲀⲖ Ⲉ̈ⲒⲦⲞⲞⲦϥ̄ Ⲙ̄ ....assume division from
ⲠⲤⲘⲀⲦ ⲈⲀⲨϫⲒ ⲘⲞⲢⲪⲎ ⲀⲠⲒϫⲰ ⲈⲦ ....the pattern, having taken form
....for the planting which
ⲒϫⲞⲞⲠ 2Ⲛ̄ ⲠⲤⲀ ⲚⲠⲒⲦⲚ̄ [ⲚⲦⲠ]Ⲉ ⲠⲈⲈⲒ ⲀⲚ ....exists beneath [the heaven].
....This also
[Ⲡ]ⲈⲦⲢ ⲔⲞⲒⲚ[ⲰⲚⲒ] ⲀⲦⲔⲀⲔⲒⲀ ⲈⲦⲒϫⲞⲞⲠ Ⲛ̄ (117,1) ....is what shares in
....the evil which exists
[2]ⲢⲎ̈ 2Ⲛ̄ Ⲛ̄Ⲧ[Ⲟ]ⲠⲞⲤ ⲈⲚⲦⲀⲨⲠⲰ2 ⲒϫⲀⲢⲞ .....in the places which they have
[Ⲟ]Ⲩ ⲈⲀⲠⲞⲨⲰϫⲈ ⲈⲀⲠⲞⲨⲰϫⲈ ⲄⲀⲢ ....reached. For the will held
ϪⲢⲰ ⲀⲢⲘ̄ ⲠⲦⲎⲢϥ̄ 2Ⲁ ⲠⲚⲀⲂⲈⲒ ϪⲈⲔⲀⲤⲈ ....the Totality under sin so that
2Ⲙ̄ ⲠⲞⲨⲰϫⲈ ⲈⲦⲘ̄ⲘⲈⲨ ⲈϤⲚⲀⲚⲀⲈ (5) ....by that will he might have mercy
Ⲙ̄ⲠⲦⲎⲢϥ̄ Ⲛ̄ⲤⲈⲚⲞⲨ2ⲘⲈ ⲈⲞⲨⲈⲈⲒ ⲞⲨ ....on the Totality and they might
....be saved, while a single one
ⲀⲈⲈⲦϥ̄ ⲠⲈⲦⲎⲒϫ Ⲁ† ⲰⲚ2 ⲠⲔⲈϫⲰϪⲠ ....alone is appointed to give
....life and all the rest
ⲦⲎⲢϥ̄ ⲈϥⲢ ϪⲢⲒⲀ Ⲙ̄ⲠⲚⲞⲨ2ⲘⲈ ⲈⲦⲂⲈ ....need salvation. Therefore,
ⲠⲈⲈⲒ ⲀⲂⲀⲖ 2Ⲛ̄ ⲚⲈⲈⲒ Ⲙ̄ⲠⲒⲢⲎⲦⲈ ⲠⲈⲚ ....it was from (reasons)
....of this sort that
ⲦⲁϥⲢ ⲀⲢϪⲈⲤⲐⲀⲒ Ⲛ̄ϪⲈ 2ⲘⲞⲦ Ⲁ† ⲚⲒⲦⲀ (10) ....it began to receive
....grace to give the
ⲈⲒⲞ ⲈⲚⲦⲀⲨⲦⲀϫⲈ ⲞⲈⲒϫ Ⲙ̄ⲘⲞϥ ⲀⲂⲀⲖ ....honors which were proclaimed
Ⲉ̈ⲒⲦⲞⲞⲦϥ̄ Ⲛ̄ⲒⲎ(ⲤⲞⲨ)Ⲥ ⲚⲈⲈⲒ ⲈⲦⲤⲘ̄ⲠⲘ̄ⲠⲒϫⲀ .by Jesus, which were suitable for
ⲀⲂⲀⲖ Ⲉ̈ⲒⲦⲞⲞ ‹ⲦⲞ› Ⲩ ⲀⲦⲢⲞⲨⲦⲀϫⲈ ⲀⲈⲒϫ Ⲙ̄ⲠⲔⲈϫⲰ ....him to proclaim to
ϪⲠ̄ ⲈϥⲔⲎ Ⲁ2Ⲣ̈Ⲏ Ⲛ̄ⳓⲒ ⲤⲠⲈⲢⲘⲀ Ⲛ̄ⲆⲈ ....the rest, since a seed of the
ⲠⲤϫⲠ ⲰⲠ Ⲛ̄ⲆⲈ ⲒⲎ(ⲤⲞⲨ)Ⲥ ⲠⲈϪⲢ(ⲒⲤⲦⲞ)Ⲥ ⲠⲈⲈⲒ Ⲛ̄ⲦⲀⲚⲠ̄ (15).....promise of
....Jesus Christ was set up, whom we have
ⲆⲒⲀⲔⲞⲚⲒ Ⲙ̄ⲠⲒⲞⲨⲰⲚ2̄ ⲀⲂⲞⲀ ⲘⲚ̄ ⲠⲒⲘⲞ[Ⲩ] ....served in (his) revelation
ϫⲈ ....and union.

3.3.4.2

This pericope answers an intriguing question posed by the author in 115,25–116,25 (which follows the first passage examined above). We know, he says, that both the Savior and "those who came with him [the pneumatics] took body and soul" (115,30), and that all came "from the Logos who had returned to himself after his movement from the organization" (115,27–29).[62] And we know that the pneumatics "received their bodily emanation along with the body of the Savior through the revelation and the mingling with him" (116,2–5). Why, then, if they emerged from the same source and share in the Savior's pneumatic body, do they "share in the passions" (116,20–21) as the psychics do, while the Savior does not? Why do the pneumatics resemble the psychics, who were "brought forth from passion," and not the Savior, "who did not share in the passions" (116,26–27)?

The two-fold response (116,28–117,36) is that the Father planned it that way and that in fact the Savior and the pneumatics are not identical. The divine plan requires that all humanity share "in the evil [ⲧⲕⲁⲕⲓⲁ] which exists in the places which they have redeemed," and it entails "a single one" giving life. For this script to be fulfilled, the pneumatics had to share in the passions of the world. Furthermore, the Savior "preserved the form of indivisibility, from which comes impassibility" (116,31–33) since he was "a bodily image of the unitary one" (116,28–29); while the pneumatics "assume division" since they are "images of each thing which became manifest" (116,34–37). The pneumatics, then, lack the indivisibility without which an escape from the passions is impossible.

Following this pericope is a discussion about the salvation brought to the pneumatics (117,17–36) and the psychics (117,37–118,14). To the former is given the promise of redemption, or "the return to what they were from the first, from which they possess a drop" (117,18–21). Knowledge of "the truth which existed before the ignorance came to be" (117,29–30) provides this redemption. To the psychics, or "those who have been brought forth in a lowly thought of vanity [by the Logos]" (117,37–38) and who live in evil, is given freedom through "the abundance of the [Father's] grace" (118,3–4). The Savior, then, offers redemption to both the pneumatics and the psychics.

How does sin fit into this construct? Part of God's plan of salvation entails holding "the Totality" (ⲡⲧⲏⲣϥ) under sin so that "he might have mercy on the Totality and they might be saved" (117,3–6). In the context of *The Tripartite Tractate*, ⲡⲧⲏⲣϥ signifies what is everlasting, including what is already part of the Pleroma and what is destined to be so. Accordingly, it can refer both to the aeons of the Pleroma (e.g. 107,31; 110,4) and to that part of humanity which will be saved (e.g. 124,34: "The Son himself, who has the position of redeemer of the Totalities"). Holding the Totality under sin, then, means keeping humanity

---

[62] Is ⲉⲛⲧⲁϥⲥⲧⲁϥ (a second perfect) to be read as a pluperfect ("had returned"), as Attridge and Mueller do in their translation, or as a simple past, as the editors of the *Tractatus Tripartitus* have done? Another way of stating it is, did the Logos return to the Pleroma before playing a part in the creation of the Savior and the pneumatics? Nothing in our tractate suggests this, so the latter reading is to be preferred.

temporarily under the control of passion, without unity and knowledge. Sin reflects this ignorance, division and "sharing in the passions."

3.3.5

The two occurrences of sin in *The Tripartite Tractate* complement one another. The first pericope makes it clear that sin is a fundamental part of the human condition, and that it is inextricably linked with passion and change. Indeed, an outstanding characteristic of the Savior's incarnation is his sinlessness. The second pericope explains why this sinful state applies even to the pneumatics, and states that sinlessness is only possible if God allows a person to have knowledge of the pre-cosmic golden age. Sin is part of ignorance, and entails being controlled by passions and evil. Since most of the discussion is geared to the pneumatics, it is unclear whether sin meant something else for the psychics. Yet the author's tendency to place these two groups in the same category suggests that sin would have applied equally to both.

3.4 *The Gospel of Philip*

3.4.1

The Gospel of Philip proclaims a simple and consistent message. People live in a world where both good and evil are present. After their death they will end up either in "the evil Middle," to suffer for the wrongs they did on earth, or in God's realm, where joy and serenity reign eternally. People's actions on earth determine their fate. Until recently they suffered since the evil powers controlled the world from its inception. Christ's descent to earth from the upper realm provided them with the information required to bypass the "Middle" realm and attain rest with God. However, such salvation after death demands perfection while on earth. Certain salvific rituals or sacraments allow this to occur. These, in turn, require outstanding conduct on the part of the "perfected" Christians, including a concerted effort to help others attain the same level of perfection. The focus of this work, then, is on personal salvation for as many as possible, especially through sacraments and personal example. Speculations about the Pleroma and Sophia are kept to a minimum, and the division of humanity into three natures or races is virtually absent.

Structurally, *The Gospel of Philip* does not fall into set categories. The initial scholarly descriptions of this work insisted that it was "without any definite plan of composition."[63] This stance was soon modified. Wilson, for instance,

---

[63] This quote is from Eric Segelberg, "The Coptic-Gnostic Gospel according to Philip and its Sacramental System," *Numen* 7 (1960) 191. Cf. also Jean Doresse's evaluation of *The Gospel of Philip*: "une simple épître, mais sans destinataire précisé, un véritable traité controversant de façon vague avec des adversaires jamais nommés. . . . Pas de plan précis" (*Les livres secrets des gnostiques d'Égypte*. I. *Introduction aux écrits gnostiques coptes découverts à Khénoboskion* [Paris: Librairie Plon, 1958], 240); Robert M. Grant, "Philip consists of materials which seem to be arranged chaotically, if one can speak of chaotic

claimed that *The Gospel of Philip* was organized so as to spiral inexorably towards the supreme mystery of the bridal chamber, while Ménard showed how linking words actually allowed for continuity and progression of thought.[64] Indeed, the means by which the author presents his message resembles, on a literary level, the embroidery of God's name and attributes by Muslim calligraphers. In both artistic media the units of expression, whether consonants and words or metaphors and images, blend into one another to produce variety and unity at the same time. This makes the structural analysis of the work difficult to undertake. But it certainly requires abandoning Schenke's initial division of *The Gospel of Philip* into 127 sayings (Sprüche) as Ménard suspected already in 1967 and Isenberg carried out a decade later.[65] What this means in practice is that the work must be treated as a whole. Yet one pericope cannot be understood necessarily by setting it into its immediate context. Accordingly, the full meaning of each pericope which discusses sin must be determined by examining the relevant issues in the entire work.

3.4.2.1
Sin is discussed first in 66,7–67,1. The passage is as follows:[66]

H N̄ϥϣⲱⲡⲉ 2M̄ ⲡⲉⲉⲓⲕⲟⲥⲙⲟⲥ H 2N̄ ⲧⲁⲛⲁ . . . . Either he will be in
. . . . this world or in the
ⲥⲧⲁⲥⲓⲥ H 2N̄ N̄ⲧⲟⲡⲟⲥ ⲉⲧ2N̄ ⲧⲙⲏⲧⲉ . . . . resurrection or in the places
. . . . in the middle.
MH ⲅⲉⲛⲟⲓⲧⲟ N̄ⲥⲉ2ⲉ ⲉⲣⲟⲉⲓ N̄2HTⲟⲩ ⲡⲉ . . . . God forbid that I be
. . . . found in them!
ⲉⲓⲕⲟⲥⲙⲟⲥ ⲟⲩM̄ ⲡⲉⲧⲛⲁⲛⲟⲩϥ N̄2HTϥ (10) . . . . . In this world there is good
ⲟⲩM̄ ⲡⲉⲑⲟⲟⲩ Nⲉϥⲡⲉⲧⲛⲁⲛⲟⲩⲟⲩ M̄ⲡⲉ . . . . and evil. Its good

---

arrangement" ("Two Gnostic Gospels," *JBL* 79 [1960] 2); and Hans-Martin Schenke: "unsere Schrift [ist] eine Art Florilegium gnostischer Sprüche und Gedanken" (*Koptische-gnostische Schriften aus den Papyrus-Codices von Nag-Hammadi* [with Johannes Leipoldt], TF 20 [Hamburg-Bergstedt: Herbert Reich Evangelischer Verlag, 1960], 33).

[64] Ménard, *L'Évangile selon Philippe*, 2–6; and Wilson: "a sort of spiral movement, gradually approaching the central and deepest mystery [the bridal chamber]" (*The Gospel of Philip*, 10). Wilson repeats this claim in his article on *The Gospel of Philip* in *The Interpreter's Dictionary of the Bible. Supplementary Volume* (Nashville: Abingdon Press, 1976), 664.

[65] Schenke, *Koptisch-gnostische Schriften*. Ménard includes Schenke's numbering in his translation and commentary, yet notes in his introduction, "il serait mieux de ne pas trop insister sur les divisions de Schenke et d'abandonner comme modèle de comparaison un ouvrage de type de l'*Évangile selon Thomas*" (*L'Évangile selon Philippe*, 6). Isenberg dropped Schenke's divisions altogether in *The Nag Hammadi Library*.

[66] The text is taken from Ménard, *L'Évangile selon Philippe*, 76–78 (who more freely reconstructs the text than Till does in *Das Evangelium nach Philippos*, 32–34). The translation is from *The Nag Hammadi Library*, 140. This pericope includes sayings 63–65 in Schenke's numeration.

ⲦⲚⲀⲚⲞⲨⲞⲨ ⲀⲚ ⲚⲈ ⲀⲨⲰ ⲚⲈϤⲠⲈⲐⲞⲞⲨ ϨⲘ ......is not good, and its evil
ⲠⲈⲐⲞⲞⲨ ⲀⲚ ⲚⲈ ⲞⲨⲚ̄ ⲠⲈⲐⲞⲞⲨ ⲆⲈ ⲘⲚ̄Ⲛ̄ ...not evil. But there is evil after
ⲤⲀ ⲠⲈⲈⲒⲔⲞⲤⲘⲞⲤ ⲈϨⲘ̄ⲠⲈⲐⲞⲞⲨ ⲚⲀⲘⲈ ⲚⲈ...this world which is truly evil —
ⲦⲈⲦⲞⲨⲘⲞⲨⲦⲈ ⲈⲢⲞⲤ ϪⲈ ⲦⲘⲈⲤⲞⲦⲎⲤ Ⲛ̄ⲦⲞϤ (15) ......what is called "the
....Middle." It
ⲠⲈ ⲠⲘⲞⲨ ϨⲰⲤ ⲈⲚϢⲞⲞⲠ ϨⲘ̄ ⲠⲈⲈⲒⲔⲞⲤ ....is death. While we are in
....this world
ⲘⲞⲤ ϢϢⲈ ⲈⲢⲞⲚ ⲈϪⲠⲞ ⲚⲀⲚ Ⲛ̄ⲦⲀⲚⲀⲤⲦⲀ ....it is fitting for us to
....acquire the resurrection for ourselves
ⲤⲒⲤ ϪⲈⲔⲀⲀⲤ ⲈⲚϢⲀⲔⲀⲀⲔⲚ ⲀϨⲎⲨ Ⲛ̄ⲦⲤⲀⲢϨ...........so that when we strip
....off the flesh
ⲈⲨⲚⲀϨⲈ ⲈⲢⲞⲚ ϨⲚ̄ ⲦⲀⲚⲀⲠⲀⲨⲤⲒⲤ Ⲛ̄ⲦⲚ̄ⲦⲘ̄ ....we may be found in rest
....and not walk
ⲘⲞⲞϢⲈ ϨⲚ̄ ⲦⲘⲈⲤⲞⲦⲎⲤ ϨⲀϨ ⲄⲀⲢ ⲤⲈⲢ̄ⲠⲖⲀ (20).........in the Middle. For
....many go astray
ⲚⲈⲤⲐⲈ ϨⲚ̄ ⲦϨⲒⲎ ⲚⲀⲚⲞⲨⲤ ⲄⲀⲢ ⲈⲈⲒ ⲈⲂⲞⲖ ....on the way. For it
....is good to come forth
ϨⲘ̄ ⲠⲔⲞⲤⲘⲞⲤ ϨⲀ ⲦⲈϨⲎ ⲈⲘⲠⲀⲦⲈⲠⲢⲰⲘⲈ.......from the world before one
Ⲣ̄ ⲚⲞⲂⲈ ⲞⲨⲚ̄ ϨⲞⲈⲒⲚⲈ ⲘⲈⲚ ⲞⲨⲦⲈ ⲤⲈⲞⲨⲰϢ)...........has sinned. Some
....neither desire (to sin)
ⲀⲚ ⲞⲨⲦⲈ ⲘⲚ̄ ϬⲞⲘ Ⲙ̄ⲘⲞⲞⲨ ϨⲚ̄ⲔⲞⲞⲨⲈ ⲆⲈ ...nor are able (to sin). Others,
ⲈⲨϢⲀⲚⲞⲨⲰϢ [Ⲙ]ⲘⲚ̄ ϨⲎⲨ ϢⲞⲞⲠ ⲚⲀⲨ ϪⲈ (25) ......(even) if they desire
....(to sin), are not better off
Ⲙ̄ⲠⲞⲨⲈⲒⲢⲈ ⲈⲦ[ⲞⲨⲞ]ⲨⲰϢ ⲄⲀⲢ ϤⲈⲒⲢⲈ Ⲙ̄ⲘⲞ ....for not having done it, for
....[this] desire makes
ⲞⲨ Ⲛ̄ⲢⲈϤⲢ̄ ⲚⲞⲂⲈ [Ⲡ]ⲦⲘⲞⲨⲰϢ ⲆⲈ ⲦⲀⲒ.........them sinners. But (even)
....if some do not desire (to sin),
ⲔⲀⲒⲞⲤⲨⲚⲎ ⲚⲀϨ2[Ⲱ]Ⲡ ⲈⲢⲞⲞⲨ Ⲙ̄ⲠⲈⲤⲚⲀⲨ ....righteousness will be concealed
....from them both — the desire-not
ⲀⲨⲰ ⲠⲞⲨⲰϢ ⲀⲚ [Ⲙ]Ⲛ̄ ⲠⲈⲒⲢⲈ ⲀⲚ ⲞⲨⲀⲠⲞ ....and the do-not. An
....a vision saw some people
ⲤⲦⲞⲖⲒⲔ[Ⲟ]Ⲥ [Ϩ]Ⲛ̄ [ⲞⲨ]ⲞⲠⲦⲀⲤⲒⲀ ⲀϤⲚⲀⲨ ⲀϨⲞ (30) ....apostolic man in
....a vision saw some people
ⲈⲒⲚⲈ ⲈⲨⲞⲦⲠ [Ϩ]Ⲛ̄ ⲞⲨⲎⲈⲒ Ⲛ̄ⲔⲰϨⲦ ⲀⲨ ....shut up in a house of fire and
ϢⲈ[Ⲩ]ⲘⲎⲢ ϨⲚ̄ [ⲞⲨⲎⲈⲒ] Ⲛ̄ⲔⲰϨⲦ ⲈⲨⲚⲎϪ ...bound with fiery [chains], lying
[ⲈⲨⲎⲈ]Ⲓ̈ Ⲛ̄ⲔⲰϨⲦ [ⲈⲨϪⲰ ϪⲞ]ⲞⲨ Ⲙ̄ⲘⲞⲞⲨ ϨⲚ̄ ......in flaming [ointment].
....They possessed
[ⲔⲰ]ϨⲦ[...]ⲀⲨⲰ ⲠⲈϪⲀⲨ ⲚⲀⲨ.............[...] And he said to them,
[ϪⲈ..... ⲘⲚ̄ Ϭ]ⲞⲘ Ⲙ̄ⲘⲞⲞⲨ ⲀⲚⲞⲨϨⲘ̄ ......(35) "[Why are they not able]
....to be saved?"
[Ⲙ̄ⲘⲞⲞⲨ ... ⲔⲀⲦⲀ] Ⲙ̄ⲠⲞⲨⲞⲨⲰϢ ⲀⲨϪⲒ.....[They answered], "They did
....not desire it. They received
[Ⲙ̄ⲠⲘⲞⲨ ⲚⲞⲨ]ⲔⲞⲖⲀⲤⲒⲤ ⲠⲀⲈⲒ ⲈⲦⲞⲨⲘⲞⲨⲦⲈ ....[this place as] a
....punishment, what is called

ϵⲣⲟϥ ϫⲉ ⲡⲕⲁⲕⲉ ⲉⲧ[ⲍ̅ⲓⲡⲥⲁⲛⲃⲟ]ⲗ ϫⲉ ϥ[. . .] (67,1) . . . . 'the [outer]
. . . . darkness,' because he is [thrown] out (into it)."

3.4.2.2

This pericope discusses the Christian's fate after death. It is set within the framework of a tripartite view of the cosmos: a world below, having good and evil elements to it; a middle realm (ⲧⲙⲉⲥⲟⲧⲏⲥ) where evil and punishment reign;[67] and the upper, spiritual realm "of the resurrection." Being perfect, or acquiring the resurrection, while on earth enables the Christian to bypass the Middle and proceed directly to the Father and his rest. This is salvation. On the other hand, sinning prevents the Christian from acquiring or maintaining the resurrection, and is destined to land a person in the Middle to endure everlasting punishment. This is damnation. These horrors are graphically described in the final part of the pericope (66,29–67,1), an apocalyptic vision of the punishment of those who remain in the Middle. This section surely was intended to encourage people to avoid sin at all costs.

Matthew's Sermon on the Mount comes to mind in this presentation of sin, with echoes of Hebrews as well. The imperfect state of the manuscript in 66,23–29 renders any understanding of the passage speculative to some degree,[68] yet the general sense is not obscured: sin includes desiring to do an evil act or actually doing it. As Matthew says, adultery is the act itself or merely looking "at a woman lustfully" (5:27). Furthermore, 66,21–23 suggests that just one sinful act or thought was enough to land a Christian in the Middle. This is reminiscent of the quest for perfection in Hebrews, and the threat: "For if we sin deliberately after receiving the knowledge of the truth, there no longer remains a sacrifice for sins, but a fearful prospect of judgment, and a fury of fire" (Heb 10:26–27). What needs to be explored is how one can avoid sin and acquire the resurrection while on earth. This requires moving beyond the confines of the pericope.

3.4.2.3

Several times the author states that people must attain the resurrection before their death (e.g. 56,15–20; 73,1–4). The point made in 66,7–23 is reiterated in 76,31–77,1: "it is necessary that we by all means become perfect men before we leave the world. He who has received everything and has not rid himself of these places will not be able to share in that place, but will go to the Middle as imperfect. Only Jesus knows the end of this person." Yet the author does not dangle

---

[67] For a similar ⲙⲉⲥⲟⲧⲏⲥ, cf. the *Pistis Sophia*, chapters 144–46. This contrasts with Irenaeus (*Adv. haer.* I,7,1), where the Valentinian μεσότης is Sophia's temporary abode, and will become the final abode for the Demiurge and some of the psychics.

[68] The translations of this section diverge considerably. Ménard has conveniently summarized earlier versions in his *L'Évangile selon Philippe*, 181.

the necessity of perfection before his audience in order to discourage them.[69] Rather, he stresses how participation in the sacraments allows them to acquire that resurrection. Indeed, it comes as no surprise that the author follows up his discussion of sin in 66,7-67,1 with an examination of the importance of the sacraments (67,2-30), culminating in the well-known sentence: "The Lord did everything in a mystery, a baptism and a chrism and a eucharist and a redemption and a bridal chamber" (67,27-30).

Much has been said about the sacraments in *The Gospel of Philip*.[70] We need only examine the author's main position. There seem to be five distinct rites in which the Christian can participate (67,27-30). These are arranged in ascending order (69,14-29) — so, for example, "the chrism is superior to the baptism" (74,12-13). Yet their distinctiveness is often blurred. Baptism can sometimes include redemption (69,25-26), and chrism the eucharist (74,36-75,11). In practice, the Christians of that community may have participated in at least the first three sacraments (baptism, chrism and eucharist) in the same ceremony. The "bridal chamber" (ⲚⲨⲘⲪⲰⲚ) is clearly the supreme rite in this work (e.g. 64,31-70,22), yet it is far from clear what the author intends by this.[71]

The double baptism is the author's principal concern. He insists that baptism, reinforced by chrism (the "second baptism," done with olive oil — 73,17-18), actually provides immortality. In these two rites, purification occurs visibly through water and invisibly through fire and light (57,22-28). Jesus has purified and perfected the water at baptism (77,7-9) and God has "dyed it" (63,25-30), yet it is still possible for someone to emerge from the water baptism without having received the Holy Spirit (64,22-31). So "it is fitting to baptize in the two, in the light and the water. Now the light is the chrism" (69,11-13). This dual baptism provides the resurrection (69,25-26) and perfection: "He who has been anointed possesses everything. He possesses the resurrection, the light, the cross, the Holy

---

[69] Ménard states: "La notion du péché dans l'*Évangile selon Philippe* est très pessimiste, parce qu'elle décrit l'état d'un psychique complètement livré à la εἱμαρμένη" (*L'Évangile selon Philippe*, 182). This claim needs correcting. Aside from the fact that the author is not dealing with "psychics," Ménard has downplayed this work's stress on the possibility of salvation, not on damnation or determinism.

[70] E.g. Eric Segelberg, "The Coptic-Gnostic Gospel"; "The Baptismal Rite according to the Coptic-Gnostic Texts of Nag Hammadi," in *Studia Patristica V*, ed. by F. L. Cross, TU 80 (Berlin: Akademie-Verlag, 1962), 117-28; D. H. Tripp, "The 'Sacramental System' of the Gospel of Philip," in *Studia Patrisica. Vol. XVII in Three Parts*, ed. by E. A. Livingstone, I (Oxford: Pergamon Press, 1982), 251-60; and Wilson, *The Gospel of Philip*, 17-23. See also note 28 of the following chapter.

[71] The most extensive study of the bridal chamber in *The Gospel of Philip* is by Jean-Marie Sevrin, "Les noces spirituelles dans l'Évangile selon Philippe," *Mus* 87 (1974) 143-93. This is part of his doctoral dissertation submitted to l'Université Catholique de Louvain in 1972. One of his concluding sentences reveals some of the problems: "Qu'il y ait ou qu'il n'y ait pas de rite spécifique de la chambre nuptiale est impossible à décider" (192).

Spirit" (74,18-21). In turn, this resurrection requires a spiritual flesh, which the eucharist provides (56,26-57,22; cf. also 75,14-24).[72]

This possession of the Holy Spirit provides the Christian with unity and life, and escape from death and duality (68,22-69,8). It also allows escape from the clutches of the archons, or evil powers (ⲚⲆⲨⲚⲀⲘⲒⲤ ⲘⲠⲞⲚⲎⲢⲞⲚ — 59,19), who do not want people to be saved (54,31-33). No unclean spirit will cleave to you, says the author, if you possess the Holy Spirit (66,2-3). All Christians, then, who undergo the two baptisms have at least a measure of control over these powers. If the control were total, however, the author would have no need to warn his audience of the fate which awaits them should they not die sinless.

This pericope reveals that a person's normal state is that of a sinner under the domination of evil powers, destined for eternal punishment in the Middle. With the Son's descent and the sacraments he leaves behind for Christians, a perfect, sinless existence becomes possible, resulting in access to the Father's realm after death.

3.4.3.1

Sin is discussed a second time in 77,15-78,12. The passage is as follows:[73]

. . . ⲠⲈⲦⲈⲨⲚⲦⲀϤ Ⲙ . . .	He who has
ⲘⲀⲨ ⲚⲦⲄⲚⲰⲤⲒⲤ ⲚⲦⲘⲈ ⲞⲨⲈⲖⲈⲨⲐⲈⲢⲞⲤ . . .	knowledge of the truth
. . .	is a free man,
ⲠⲈ ⲠⲈⲖⲈⲨⲐⲈⲢⲞⲤ ⲆⲈ ⲘⲀϤⲢ ⲚⲞⲂⲈ ⲠⲈ . . .	but the free man does not sin,
ⳁⲢⲈ ⲄⲀⲢ ⲘⲠⲚⲞⲂⲈ Ⲡ2Ⲙ̅2ⲀⲖ̅ ⲘⲠⲚⲞⲂⲈ . . .	for "he who sins is
. . .	the slave of sin."
ⲠⲈ ⲦⲘⲀⲀⲨ ⲦⲈ ⲦⲀⲖⲎⲐⲈⲒⲀ ⲦⲄⲚⲰⲤⲒⲤ ⲆⲈ . . .	Truth is the mother,
. . .	knowledge
ⲠⲈ ⲠⲦⲰⲦ ⲚⲈⲦⲈ ⲤⲦⲞ ⲚⲀⲨ ⲀⲚ ⲀⲢ̅ ⲚⲞⲂⲈ (20) . . .	the father. Those who
. . .	think that sinning does not apply to them
ⲈⲠⲔⲞⲤⲘⲞⲤ ⲘⲞⲨⲦⲈ ⲈⲢⲞⲞⲨ ⲬⲈ ⲈⲖⲈⲨ . . .	are called "free" by the world.
ⲐⲈⲢⲞⲤ ⲚⲀⲈⲒ ⲈⲦⲤⲦⲞ ⲚⲀⲨ ⲀⲚ ⲀⲢ̅ ⲚⲞⲂⲈ . . .	Knowledge of the truth
. . .	merely makes
ⲦⲄⲚⲰⲤⲒⲤ ⲚⲦⲀⲖⲎⲐⲈⲒⲀ ⲬⲒⲤⲈ Ⲛ2ⲎⲦ ⲈⲦⲈ . . .	such people arrogant, which
ⲠⲀⲈⲒ ⲠⲈ ⲤⲈⲒⲢⲈ ⲘⲘⲞⲞⲨ ⲚⲈⲖⲈⲨⲐⲈⲢⲞⲤ . . .	is what the words "it makes
. . .	them free" mean.
ⲀⲨⲰ ⲤⲦⲢⲞⲨⲬⲒⲤⲈ ⲈⲠⲘⲀ ⲦⲎⲢϤ ⲦⲀⲄⲀⲠⲎ (25) . . .	It even gives them a
. . .	sense of superiority over the whole world. But "love

---

[72] Against unnamed opponents, the author argues that people must be raised with flesh, while he argues against others that this flesh is of a different nature.

[73] The text is taken from Ménard, L'Évangile selon Philippe, 98-100 (cf. Till, Das Evangelium nach Philippos, 54-56). The translation is from The Nag Hammadi Library, 146-47. This pericope includes sayings 110-11. The English translation of 77,20 reads ⲠⲒⲰⲦ ("the father") instead of ⲚⲦⲰⲦ ("the union").

ⲆⲈ ⲔⲰⲦ ⲠⲈⲦⲀ2Ⲣ̄ ⲈⲖⲈⲨⲐⲈⲢⲞⲤ ⲆⲈ 21 . . . . builds up." In fact,
. . . . he who is really free through
ⲦⲚ̄ ⲦⲄⲚⲰⲤⲒⲤ ϤⲞ Ⲛ̄2Ⲙ2Ⲁ̄Ⲗ̄ ⲈⲦⲂⲈ ⲦⲀⲄⲀ . . . . knowledge is a slave
. . . . because of love
ⲠⲎ Ⲛ̄ⲚⲀⲈⲒ ⲈⲘⲠⲀⲦⲞⲨⲰ ϤⲒ Ⲉ2ⲢⲀ[Ⲓ̈ ⲚⲦⲈ . . . . for those who have not
. . . . yet been able to attain to the
ⲖⲈⲨⲐⲈⲢⲒⲀ Ⲛ̄ⲦⲄⲚⲰⲤⲒⲤ ⲦⲄⲚⲰ[ⲤⲒⲤ ⲆⲈ]. . . freedom of knowledge. Knowledge
ⲤⲈⲒⲢⲈ Ⲙ̄ⲘⲞⲞⲨ Ⲛ̄ⲱ)ⲒⲔⲀⲚⲞⲤ ⲈⲤ[ⲦⲢⲞⲨ]. . . . makes them capable of becoming
ⲱ)ⲱⲠⲈ Ⲛ̄ⲈⲖ[ⲈⲨⲐ]Ⲉ[ⲢⲞⲤ Ⲧ]ⲀⲄⲀⲠⲎ [ⲘⲀⲤ2Ⲓ] . . . . free. Love [never calls]
ⲖⲀⲀⲨ 2Ⲉ ⲠⲰ[Ⲥ ⲤⲚⲀ2Ⲓ ⲞⲨ]ⲞⲚ [ⲞⲨⲞⲚ ⲚⲒⲘ] . . . . something its own,
. . . . [and yet] it may actually possess [that very thing].
ⲠⲰⲤ ⲠⲈ ⲘⲀⲤ2[ⲞⲞⲤ 2Ⲉ ⲠⲀⲈⲒ ⲠⲰⲈⲒ ⲠⲈ] . . . . . It never [says "This is mine"]
Ⲏ ⲠⲀⲈⲒ ⲠⲰⲈⲒ ⲠⲈ [ⲀⲖⲖⲀ Ⲥ2Ⲱ ⲘⲘⲞⲤ 2Ⲉ ⲚⲀⲈⲒ] . . . . or "That is mine,"
. . . . [but "All these]
ⲚⲞⲨⲔ ⲚⲈ ⲦⲀⲄⲀⲠⲎ Ⲙ̄ⲠⲚⲈⲨⲘ[ⲀⲦⲒⲔⲎ] (35) . . . . are yours." Spiritual love
ⲞⲨⲎⲢⲠ ⲦⲈ 21 ⲤⲦⲞⲈⲒ ⲤⲈⲢ̄ⲀⲠⲞ[ⲖⲀⲨⲈ Ⲙ̄ . . . . is wine and fragrance.
ⲘⲞⲤ ⲦⲎⲢⲞⲨ Ⲛ6[Ⲓ Ⲛ]ⲈⲦⲚⲀⲦⲞ2ⲤⲞⲨ Ⲙ̄ⲘⲞⲤ (78,1) . . . . All those who anoint
. . . . themselves with it take pleasure in it.
ⲤⲈⲢ̄ⲀⲠⲞⲖⲀⲨⲈ 2ⲰⲞⲨ Ⲛ6Ⲓ ⲚⲈⲦⲀ2ⲈⲢⲀⲦⲞⲨ . . . . While those who
. . . . are anointed are present,
Ⲙ̄ⲠⲞⲨⲂⲞⲖ 2ⲰⲤ ⲈⲨⲀ2ⲈⲢⲀⲦⲞⲨ Ⲛ6Ⲓ ⲚⲈⲦ . . . . those nearby also profit
. . . . (from the fragrance).
ⲦⲞ2Ⲥ ⲚⲈⲦⲦⲀ2Ⲥ̄ Ⲛ̄ⲤⲞ6Ⲛ ⲈⲨⲱ)ⲀⲖⲞ ⲈⲦⲞⲨ . . . . If those anointed with
. . . . ointment withdraw from them
ⲱⲞⲨ Ⲛ̄ⲤⲈⲂⲰⲔ ⲱ)ⲀⲢⲈⲚⲎ ⲈⲤⲈⲦⲞ2Ⲥ ⲀⲚ (5) . . . . and leave, then those not
. . . . anointed,
ⲘⲞⲚⲞⲚ ⲈⲨⲀ2Ⲉ ⲈⲢⲀⲦⲞⲨ Ⲙ̄ⲠⲞⲨⲂⲀⲖ ⲱ)ⲀⲨ . . . who merely stand nearby, still
6Ⲱ ⲞⲚ 2Ⲙ̄ ⲠⲞⲨⲤ†ⲂⲰⲱⲚ ⲠⲤⲀⲘⲀⲢⲒⲦⲎⲤ . . . . remain in their bad odor.
. . . . The Samaritan
Ⲛ̄ⲦⲀϤ† ⲖⲀⲀⲨ ⲀⲚ ⲀⲠⲈⲦⲱ)ⲞⲞ6Ⲉ ⲈⲒⲘⲎ . . . . gave nothing but
ⲎⲢⲠ 21 ⲚⲈ2 ⲔⲈⲖⲀⲀⲨ ⲀⲚ ⲠⲈ ⲈⲒⲘⲎⲦⲒ Ⲁ . . . . wine and oil to the wounded
. . . . man. It is nothing other than
ⲠⲤⲞ6Ⲛ̄ ⲀⲨⲱ Ⲁ4ⲐⲈⲢⲀⲠⲈⲨⲈ Ⲛ̄Ⲙ̄ⲠⲖⲎⲄⲎ (10) . . . . . the ointment. It healed the
. . . . wounds,
ⲦⲀⲄⲀⲠⲎ ⲄⲀⲢ 2ⲰⲂⲤ Ⲛ̄ⲞⲨⲘⲎⲎⲱ)Ⲉ Ⲛ̄ⲚⲞ . . . . for "love covers a multitude
ⲂⲈ . . . . of sins. . . ."

3.4.3.2

This encouragement to focus on love rather than freedom is reminiscent of Paul's advice to the Corinthians in 1 Corinthians 8–14. There, the problems concern idol food and glossolalia, while here the issue is sin. In both cases the authors argue that the greater good of the community must take precedence over the freedoms gained through Christianity, and that ἀγάπη must be paramount.

It is correct, the author grants (as though, like Paul, he were answering a question), that the one who has knowledge of the truth is free, and that a free person does not sin. Then he makes two qualifications. The first is a minor one: the free person might not sin, but that does not mean that sinning does not apply to that person. This point implies that the freedom over sin is something which must be renewed constantly. The second qualification introduces his main point. Freedom from sin often leads to arrogance, and a sense of superiority to, and distance from, the world, but those who are really free do not remove themselves from the people in the world. On the contrary, their love for their fellow men and women requires that they do all they can to impart their newly-won freedom to others. "While those who are anointed are present, those nearby also profit (from the fragrance)" (78,2-3). So, "freedom from the world" still means continued involvement in the world.

Two terms are striking in this pericope: slave (2M̄2Ẍ) and love (ⲀⲄⲀⲠⲎ). Slave has a negative connotation in 77,18, where the author probably quotes John 8:34 ("he who sins is the slave of sin"); but it is used positively in 77,26-29: "he who is really free through knowledge is a slave because of love for those who have not yet been able to attain to the freedom of knowledge." We must not allow the familiar Pauline flavor of this last sentence to obscure the fact that this is the only positive use of "slave" in *The Gospel of Philip*. The author makes frequent use of the term slave, but always in combination with ignorance and in contrast to knowledge and freedom.[74] Perhaps he has deliberately altered his use of this term here for effect, as Paul sometimes did.

The author's use of love in this pericope, though, is consistent with his statements elsewhere. Previously he said:

> Faith receives, love gives. No one will be able to receive without faith. No one will be able to give without love. Because of this, in order that we may indeed receive, we believe, but it is so that we may love and give, since if one does not give in love, he has no profit from what he has given [61,36-62,5].[75]

And shortly after the pericope in question, he restates his views metaphorically:

> God's farming likewise has four elements — faith, hope, love, and knowledge. Faith is our earth, that in which we take root. And hope is the water through which we are nourished. Love is the wind through which we grow. Knowledge then is the light through which we ripen. Grace exists in four ways: it is earthborn; it is heavenly; it comes from the highest heaven; and it resides in truth [79,24-33].

In these passages the author connects love and knowledge. With the reception of ⲄⲚⲰⲤⲒⲤ through ⲠⲒⲤⲦⲒⲤ comes the requirement to give or to love.

---

[74] For the use of slave, cf. 52,2; 54,31; 62,30; 69,2; 72,17-20; 77,18; 79,14.17; 80,24.30; 81,12; 83,26; 84,10; 85,24.25.

[75] Love is also mentioned in 54,17, in connection with truth.

3.4.3.3

The paraenetical tone of this pericope is continued nearly to the end of the work, as one would expect in a letter rather than a Gospel. Two words of advice dominate: care for those who are not "perfect," and make the perfect "more perfect." Accordingly, the exhortation to love others given in 77,15–78,12 is continued in 79,33, where the audience is encouraged to comfort all and cause no one any distress. Similarly, they are told in 78,12–79,18 not to imitate the world, and in 82,30–84,14 to ensure that the root of evil lying within them is plucked out.

The implications of these exhortations are important. First, all people seem to be given a chance to receive salvation. This point is stated unequivocally in 52,35–53,23: Christ "redeemed the good people in the world as well as the evil" (53,13–14), for all are part of the same unity. "Light and darkness, life and death, right and left, are brothers of one another. They are inseparable" (53,14–16). The author expresses this point metaphorically in 85,5–10:

> For this reason the [Temple] veil was not rent at the top only, since it would have been open only to those above; nor was it rent at the bottom only, since it would have been revealed only to those below. But it was rent from top to bottom.

All were given a chance to enter. Second, salvation does not come through faith and knowledge alone. It also entails proper actions. "Those who sow in the winter reap in the summer. The winter is the world, the summer the other aeon" (52,25–26). Sin is a reality for those who are still under the domination of the evil spirits in the world, but it can also apply to those who have received the Holy Spirit. The Pauline view again seems to be the closest to that found in *The Gospel of Philip:* baptism in Christ gives one the opportunity to overcome the power of sin and be perfect, but it provides no guarantee.

3.4.4

Sin in *The Gospel of Philip*, then, is an intention or an act not in keeping with the divine realm. Such acts or intentions have drastic consequences. They result in horrible punishments after death, in an area called "the Middle," and exclusion from the divine realm. People sin because the evil powers control the world and do their utmost to encourage them to act improperly. The descent of Christ into the world countered the influence of the evil powers by revealing their true nature to people.[76] Through this saving knowledge provided by Christ, and the sacraments which he instituted, people can now withstand the evil powers, lead sinless lives, and avoid punishment after death. However, sin has not disappeared for the Christians. They are encouraged through love to interact with others who are still without the saving grace effected by baptism and chrism. And

---

[76] There is no mention of the atoning value of Christ's descent or death in *The Gospel of Philip*.

they are reminded of the dynamic nature of their own salvation which requires constant awareness of the presence of sin. Sin as a threat or sin as a reality—in either case, the author's Christian community would not have been indifferent to this concept.

3.5 *The Interpretation of Knowledge*

3.5.1

Klaus Koschorke divides this work into three parts.[77] He concentrates on Part 3 (15,16–21,34), saying nothing about Part 1 (1–8) and little about Part 2 (9–15,15.)[78] This focus reflects his interest in Church order among the gnostics, but it also reflects the badly-damaged state of the manuscript. So little remains of the first eight pages, for instance, that it really becomes a "part" by default, while pages 15–21 are better preserved and allow us to follow the argument. This tripartite division of the work, then, is helpful, but it may not reflect the author's intention. All that is evident from the work itself is that the last part of this letter addresses the dissatisfaction resulting from the distribution of spiritual gifts in his community.

Sin is mentioned seven times in four passages. Three of these (9,27–38; 12,25–29; 14,28–38) are in the second part, while the fourth closes the work (21,16–34). The dominance of sin in the last few verses points to its importance for the author. Unfortunately, the fragmentary nature of the text renders any reconstruction highly speculative. We are left with providing summaries of the second and third parts, and offering a few suggestions about the meaning of sin in this tractate.

3.5.2.1

The first occurrence of sin is in 9,27–38. The passage is as follows:[79]

... ⲧⲉϥⲥⲃⲱ ⲛ̄ⲇⲉ ⲧⲉ ⲧⲉ(9,27) .... Now this is his teaching:
ⲉⲓ ϫⲉ ⲙ̄ⲛ̄ⲙⲟⲩⲧⲉ ⲛⲏⲧⲛ̄ ⲁⲉⲓⲱⲧ ϩⲓϫⲛ̄ .... Do not call out to
.... a father upon the
ⲡⲕⲁϩ ⲟⲩⲉⲉⲓ ⲡ[ⲉ] ⲡⲉⲧⲛ̄ⲉⲓⲱⲧ ⲉⲟⲛ .... earth. Your Father,
.... who is in heaven,
ⲛ̄ⲙⲡⲏⲩⲉ ⲛ̄ⲧⲱⲧⲛ̄ ⲡⲉ ⲡⲟⲩⲁⲉⲓⲛ ⲙ̄ (30) .... is one. You are the
.... light of the world.
ⲡⲕⲟⲥⲙⲟⲥ ⲛⲁⲥⲛⲏⲩ ⲁⲩⲱ ⲛⲁϣⲃⲣ̄ .... They are my brothers and my
ⲕⲟⲓⲛⲱⲛⲟⲥ ⲛⲉⲧⲣⲉ ⲙ̄ⲡⲟⲩⲱϣⲉ .... fellow companions who do the will of

---

[77] Koschorke, "'Eine neugefundene gnostische Gemeindeordnung,'" 33.

[78] Koschorke summarizes Part 2 in a footnote ("Eine neugefundene gnostische Gemeindeordnung," 33–34).

[79] The text is from Turner's (unpublished) transcription; the translation from *The Nag Hammadi Library*, 430.

ⲙ̄[ⲡ]ⲉⲓⲱⲧ ⲉⲩ ⲛ̄ⲅⲁⲣ ⲡⲉ ⲫⲏⲩ ⲉⲕⲱⲁⲛ . . . . . . .the Father. For what use is it
† ⲍⲏⲩ ⲙ̄ⲡⲕⲟⲥⲙⲟⲥ ⲛ̄ⲕ†ⲁⲥⲓ ⲛ̄ⲧⲉⲕ . . . . .if you gain the world and you
. . . . .forfeit your soul?
ⲯⲩⲭⲏ ⲉⲛϣⲟⲟⲡ ⲛ̄ⲅⲁⲣ ⲍⲛ̄ ⲡⲕⲉⲕⲉⲓ (35). . .For when we were in the dark we
ⲛⲉⲛⲙⲟⲩⲧⲉ ⲁ2ⲁ2 ⲭⲉ ⲉⲓⲱⲧ ⲉⲛⲟⲉⲓ . . . . . .used to call many "father," since
ⲛ̄ⲁⲧⲥⲁⲩⲛⲉ ⲁⲡ[ⲉ]ⲓⲱⲧ ⲙ̄ⲙⲏⲉ ⲁⲩⲱ . . . . .we were ignorant of the true
. . . . .Father. And this is the great
ⲡⲉⲉⲓ ⲡⲉ ⲡⲛ̄[ⲁ]ϭ ⲛ̄ⲱ ⲛ̄ⲛⲁⲃⲉⲓ ⲧⲏ . . . . .conception of all the sins . . . .

3.5.2.2

The basic thrust of this passage is evident: being a Christian requires not merely believing in Christ, but doing the will of the Father (ⲡⲟⲩⲱϣⲉ ⲙ̄ⲡⲉⲓⲱⲧ – 9,32-33). This may be a continuation of the first eight pages, where one of the few detectable themes is the need to believe "that the Christ is alive in order that our faith may be holy and pure" (ⲉⲥⲟⲩⲁⲁⲃ ⲉⲥⲧⲟⲩⲃⲏⲩ – 1,23-25). A "holy thing is the faith to see the likeness" (2,16-17), and Jesus is that likeness (5,38). Doing the will of the Father entails being in the world yet not being of it.[80] Hence, the author exhorts his audience to be missionaries ("You are the light of the world" – 9,30-31), but not to concern themselves with worldly matters ("For what use is it if you gain the world and you forfeit your soul?" – 9,33-35). Their focus is to be on the "Father who is in heaven" (9,29).

3.5.2.3

The ethical nature of this pericope is striking, and even more so when it is set in the context of Matthew's Sermon on the Mount. One of the remarks (in 9,27-28) is a direct quote from the triple Synoptic tradition (Mk 8:26; Matt 16:26; Lk 9:25), but the entire passage fits most naturally into the context of Matthew 5-7. There also one finds the same dual focus on doing the will of the Father (e.g. 7:21) and not being "of the world" (e.g. 6:19-24). The need for missionary work also emerges, as well as the same verse, "You are the light of the world" (5:14); while the phrase which opens the pericope, "Your Father who is in heaven," is a *Leitmotiv* in the Sermon on the Mount (e.g. 5:16,45; 6:1,9,26,32; 7:11,21). The author of *The Interpretation of Knowledge* certainly had the ethical demands of Matthew 5-7 in mind when he composed 9,27-38. This short pericope is also an ethical statement. Perhaps, after the introductory section of this work, it was meant to serve as a corrective for those who placed too much emphasis on salvation through faith (and knowledge) alone.

3.5.2.4

The final phrase of this pericope introduces sin: "And this is the great conception of all the sins . . . ." There are two main problems with understanding

---

[80] This polemic against the world runs throughout the work. It is depicted as a bitter place (6,17) of unfaith and death (1,36-38), which is run by evil rulers and authorities (20,22), and in which Jesus was disgraced (10,22).

the author's intent. The first is that the following eight lines (on page 10) are not extant. The second is determining to what the demonstrative pronoun ⲛⲉⲉⲓ refers: is it the preceding phrase or the pericope as a whole? Sin could mean ignorance "of the heavenly Father," or a focus on worldly matters and the avoidance of the Father's will. To state the matter as sharply as possible, sin could be a state of mind or a moral lapse. It is impossible to be sure what the author intended to say, especially given the eight-line gap which follows. However, given the strong ethical tone of this pericope and its links with the Sermon on the Mount, it is best to link sin tentatively with ethics and with not doing the Father's will.

3.5.2.5

The author develops this point. At the beginning of page 9, Jesus is introduced as "the teacher" (ⲡⲥⲁϩ—9,15) who "spoke with the Church" (ⲱⲉϫⲉ ⲙⲛ ⲧⲉⲕⲕⲗⲏⲥⲓⲁ—9,18). The ethical remarks in 9,27-38 highlight part of his teaching (9,27), and this continues on pages 10–11. There Jesus is said to provide knowledge of humanity's true origin (with the Father) and the depths to which people have fallen (10,29-30). On earth, people have been led astray (ⲣ̄ⲡⲗⲁⲛⲁ) while being in "the flesh of condemnation" (ⲱⲟⲟⲡ ⲛ̄ⲥⲁⲣⲝ ⲛ̄ⲧⲉ ⲕⲁⲧⲁⲇⲓⲕⲏ—10,26-27). Even Jesus was clothed with this "garment of condemnation" when he descended to earth (11,27). These remarks are a continuation of 6,25-38 which describe the "nets of flesh" binding people, imprisoning the person within (ⲡⲣⲱⲙⲉ ⲉⲧϩⲓϩⲟⲩⲛ—6,33). This fleshly covering is a temporary dwelling given by "the rulers and authorities," who compel people to serve them and to suffer. Accordingly, ⲡⲣⲱⲙⲉ ⲉⲧϩⲓϩⲟⲩⲛ comes from the Father and would naturally do the Father's will, but the fleshly bodies which have been placed on this inner person have made it a handmaid of these rulers and authorities. In this context, sin is acting in accordance with the will of the rulers and would be virtually impossible to prevent. Only knowledge of one's true origin with the Father would encourage one to act differently, and provide true redemption.

3.5.3.1

The author then reflects on the redemption of the redeemer himself (page 12), and in this context the second reference to sin occurs (12,25-29).[81]

[ⲛ̄]ⲗⲉ ϩⲓⲧⲟⲟⲧϥ̄ ⲛ̄[ϭⲓ ⲡⲉⲉⲓ] ⲛ̄ⲧⲁϩϫⲓ ⲛⲁ ......And through [him] who was
ϭⲛϭ ⲧⲛ̄ϫⲓ ⲙ̄ⲡⲕ[ⲱⲉ ⲗⲃ]ⲗⲗ ⲛ̄ⲛ̄ⲁⲃⲓ ....disgraced we receive the
....forgiveness of sins.
ϩⲓⲧⲟⲟⲧϥ̄ ⲛ̄ⲗⲉ ⲛ̄ⲡ[ⲉⲛⲧ]ⲁϩⲟⲩⲛϭⲛⲟⲩ.......And through the one who was
ϭ ⲟ̄ [ⲙⲛ̄] ⲁ ⲩ ⲱ ⲡ ⲉ ⲛ ⲧ [ⲁ ϩ ⲟ ⲩ ⲥ]ⲁ ⲧ ϥ̄ ⲉ ⲛ ϫ ⲓ ⲛ̄ ......disgraced and the one who
ⲧⲭⲁⲣⲓⲥ ....was redeemed we receive grace.

---

[81] The text is from Turner's transcription; the translation from *The Nag Hammadi Library*, 431.

Jesus put on the "garment of condemnation" (11,28), appeared "as flesh" (12,18) and "was disgraced" (12,30). "But who is it that redeemed the one who was disgraced? It is the emanation of the name" (12,29–31; cf. 12,12), an aeon projected by ⲤⲞⲪⲒⲀ (12,33), that allowed Jesus to shed his fleshly garment. Thus redeemed himself, he allowed people in turn to "escape the disgrace of the carcass and be regenerated" (12,36–37).

In this context the forgiveness of sins and the reception of grace are connected with, or parallel to, this escape from the disgrace of the carcass and the regeneration. Why people's sins have to be forgiven is unclear, but the link between sin and the fleshly bodies is a continuation of 9,27–38.

3.5.4.1
Part two concludes with another reference to sin (14,28–38):[82]

ⲦⲀⲢⲞⲨⲦⲚ̄ⲚⲀⲨ ⳓⲈ Ⲙ̄ⲠⲚ̄[Ⲁ]ⳓ Ⲛ̄ⲱ̄ⲎⲢⲈ	Moreover, when the
	great Son was sent
Ⲛ̄ⲤⲀ ⲚⲈⳒⲤⲚⲎⲨ Ⲛ̄ⲔⲞ[Ⲩ]ⲈⲒ ⲀⳒⲠⲱⲢⲟ̄	after his small brothers,
	he spread
ⲀⲂⲀⲖ Ⲙ̄ⲠⲆⲒⲀⲦⲀⳒⲘⲀ Ⲙ̄ⲠⲒⲱⲦ ⲀⳒⲱⲱⲉ	abroad the edict of the Father and
Ⲙ̄ⲘⲀⳒ ⲈⳒⳆ Ⲁ2Ⲛ̄ ⲠⲦ[Ⲏ]Ⲣ̄Ⳓ ⲀⲨⲱ ⲀⳒ	proclaimed it, opposing the All.
ⳒⲒ Ⲙ̄Ⲡ𝕏ⲈⲒⲢⲞⳒⲢⲀⲪⲞⲚ Ⲛ̄ⲈⲤ ⲠⲀⲦⲔⲀ	And he removed the old bond of
	debt, the one of condemnation.
ⲦⲀⲆⲒⲔⲎ ⲠⲈⲈⲒ Ⲛ̄ⲆⲈ Ⲡ[Ⲉ Ⲡ]ⲆⲒⲀⲦⲀⳒⲘⲀ	And this is the edict that
ⲈⲚⲈⳒ𝕎ⲞⲞⲠ ⲠⲈ ⲚⲈ[Ⲛ]ⲦⲀ2ⲞⲨⲈⲈⲒⲦⲞⲨ	was: Those who reckoned
	themselves enslaved have
Ⲛ̄ⳓⲀⲞⲨⲀⲚ Ⲁ2ⲞⲨ𝕎[ⲱ]ⲠⲈ Ⲛ̄ⲔⲀⲦⲀⲆⲒ (35)	become condemned in
	Adam. They
ⲔⲞⲤ 2Ⲛ̄ ⲀⲆⲀⲘ Ⲁ2ⲞⲨⲚ̄ [Ⲧ]ⲞⲨ ⲀⲂⲀⲖ Ⲙ̄Ⲡ	have been brought from death,
ⲘⲞⲨ Ⲁ2ⲞⲨ𝕏Ⲓ Ⲙ̄ⲠⲔⲱ[Ⲉ] ⲀⲂⲀⲖ Ⲛ̄ⲚⲞⲨ	received forgiveness for their
ⲚⲀⲂⲒ ⲀⲨⲱ Ⲁ2ⲞⲨⲤⲱⲦⲈ Ⲙ̄ⲘⲀⲨ 2ⲒⲦⲚ̄	sins, and been redeemed by [. . .]

3.5.4.2
This passage repeats the point made in 9,27–38 and 12,25–29: the body of flesh, the "garment of condemnation," has enslaved people, but the Savior has "forgiven their sins" and redeemed them. They are now free to do the Father's will and follow the inclinations of the inner person.

What is new in this pericope is the claim that this "old bond of debt" goes back to Adam and resulted in death (cf. Rom 5:12). In addition, the "powers and authorities" are now called "the All" (ⲠⲦⲎⲢⳒ – 14,14.24.31).[83] Jesus, the "Head,"

---

[82] The text is from Turner's transcription; the translation from *The Nag Hammadi Library*, 432.

[83] This negative use of the "All" comes as a surprise since the term in Valentinianism usually is positive and refers to the heavenly Pleroma (e.g. *Val. Exp.* 22,19–35 *et passim*).

drew himself "up from the pit" (13,25–26), i.e. the fleshly world (10,30–31), at his crucifixion, and ascended to the Father. The "consummation" (ΤCΥΝΤΕΛΕΙΑ — 14,10) will occur later, when the "body" will be separated from the All and rise to join its "Head." Redemption and forgiveness of sins, then, anticipate this ascent, but the power of the All has not yet been overcome.

3.5.5

The final part of this work addresses two issues which disturbed the community. The first appears to be the most troublesome (15–19). It concerns the envy or jealousy (ΦΘΟΝΕΙ/ΦΘΟΝΟC – 15,29.30.38; 17,28.36; 18,31) felt by some Christians because of other members' "gifts" or charismata (2ΜΑΤ).[84] The author urges them not to envy a brother or sister who has a gift which they do not possess (16,20–27), including glossolalia (16,31–38). He reminds them that they are all members of one body, with Christ as the head, and that each has an important and unique role to play (17,18–22). Be thankful, he says, that you are part of this great body. Your jealousy merely shows your ignorance (17,27–29).

Again, these admonitions are ethical in nature. Even the possession of knowledge does not preclude the presence of envy or jealousy in some, and the reception of a gift can still result in improper conduct. This is reminiscent of Paul's argument in 1 Corinthians 12–14:[85] both authors stress unity within one body and condemn divisiveness. What is different is that Paul directs his remarks principally to the self-styled elite, while this author addresses the bitterness felt by the ordinary members of the community.

The second issue raised is persecution (20–21). He laments: "Why do they persecute men of this sort to death" (ΕΤΒΕ ΕΥ CΕΡΔΙΩΚΕ ΝCΑ ΝΙΡΩΜΕ Ν†ΜΙΝΕ ΝΩ2ΡΗΪ ΑΠΜΟΥ – 20,25–26)? "They are senselessly mad!" he exclaims (20,37), and ends on a note of support mixed with admonition. Referring to their special status he says that they ought to expect a more difficult life because they are "combatants for the Word" (ΝΩΛΕΙΧ ΜΠΛΟΓΟC – 21,28–29), not merely average folk (ΙΔΙΩΤΗC – 21,26). Then he reminds them that this special status entails extra responsibilities: "if we sin against [the Logos], we sin more than barbarians" (ΕΝΩΑΝ ΡΝΑΒΙ ΑΡΑΥ ΤΝ ΡΝΑΒΙ Ν2ΟΥΟ ΑΝΕΘΝΟC – 21,29–30). "But if we surmount every sin, we shall receive the crown of victory, even as our Head was glorified by the Father" (ΩΑΝΩΩΠΕ ΝΑΕ ΝΤΠΕ ΝΝΑΒ[Ι] ΝΙΜ ΤΝΝΑΧΙ ΜΠ[ΛΛ]ΚΛΑΜ ΜΠΧΡΟ ΝΘΕ ΝΤΝΑΠΕ ΝΤΑ2Χ[Ι] ΕΑΥ 2ΙΤΜ ΠΙΩΤ – 21,31–34).

---

[84] Koschorke argues that this ΦΘΟΝΟC applies to two groups: "auf der einen Seite als *eifersüchtige Missgunst* derer, die andern ihre Geistesgaben vorenthalten, so wie als *Neid der zu kurz Gekommenen* auf der anderen Seite" ("Eine neugefundene Gemeindeordnung," 34). In fact, the text reveals only hints of the former.

[85] The body-head metaphor, though, is characteristic of Ephesians and Colossians, not of the undisputed Pauline letters.

This final page of *The Interpretation of Knowledge* (21) reveals that these people can and do sin, and that they are concerned about it. As combatants for Christ they are expected to make an extra effort to lead sinless lives so as to "receive the crown of victory" and be glorified by the Father as Christ was. Sinlessness is the means to this end. It does not come naturally.

3.5.6
In this work, sinning means not acting in accordance with the Father's will. Since the descent and ascent of Christ, humanity is divided: on one side is the Church, the body of Christ; on the other, the outsiders. All are still under the domination of the powers and authorities (=the All), who continue to control people by means of their fleshly bodies and who encourage them to sin. The ascent of Christ has allowed the Father's children to recognize the nature of their "inner person" and the worthlessness of their bodies. Christ has forgiven their past sins and given them gifts and knowledge to withstand the force of the "powers" and to lead sinless lives. But the possibility of sinning remains real since the All is still active. It is fair to say that these Christians would have been more concerned with sin than their counterparts, the ΙΔΙΟΤΗC, for as combatants they had to withstand the All knowing full well the implications should they fail.

3.6 A Valentinian Exposition

3.6.1
This tractate is poorly preserved. One-third to one-half of each of its eighteen pages is missing. In addition, there is no way of determining for certain whether the five fragments which follow were originally part of the same work. As Ménard rightly states: "Vu l'état lacuneux du texte, il est parfois hasardeux ou hypothétique d'en faire un commentaire thématique."[86]
The second fragment contains the reference to sin. We analyze the fragment first on its own to determine what can be said about sin. The context then is expanded gradually to include the other fragments and finally the work as a whole. The first part of the analysis must bear the most weight, since it is possible that this fragment was not part of the preceding work.

3.6.2.1
The passage in which sin occurs at least twice (depending on the reconstruction) is short. Twenty-eight lines survive more or less intact, ten others are quite fragmentary, and at least nine are missing altogether. The pericope is as follows (40,30–41,38):[87]

Π[ϵϵΙ] Πϵ ΠΠΛΗΡѠΜΑ ΜΠΚϵ (30) . . . . [Tel] est le Plérôme du som-
ϕΑΛΛΙΟΝ ΝΤΓΝѠCΙC ΠϵϵΙ . . . . maire de la gnose qui
ΝΤ[Α]2ΟΥΑΝ2q̄ ΝϵΝ ΑΒΑΛ 2Ι . . . . nous [a] été révélé par

---

[86] Ménard, *L'Exposé valentinien*, 1.
[87] The text and translation are from Ménard, *L'Exposé valentinien*, 56–59.

ⲧⲛ̄ [ⲡⲉ]ⲛⲭⲗⲉⲓⲥ ⲓ̅ⲏ̅ⲥ̅ ⲡⲉⲭⲣⲏⲥⲧⲟⲥ .... [no]tre Seigneur Jésus le Christ,
ⲡⲓⲙⲟⲛⲟⲅⲉⲛⲏⲥ ⲛⲉⲉⲓ ⲛⲉ ⲛ̄ .... le Monogène. Ceux-ci sont
ⲃⲉⲃⲗⲓⲟⲛ ⲗⲩⲱ ⲛ̄ⲁⲛⲁⲅⲕⲁⲓ (35) .... sûrs et nécessai-
ⲟⲛ ⲭⲉⲕⲁⲥⲉ ⲉⲛⲁⲙⲁ2ⲉ ⲛ̄2 .... res, de sorte que nous marchions
ⲡⲏⲓ̈ ⲛ̄2ⲏⲧⲟⲩ ⲛⲉⲉⲓ ⲛ̄ⲁⲉ ⲛⲉ .... en eux. Et ils sont
ⲛⲁⲡⲱ̣ⲗⲁⲣⲡ̄ⲛ̄ ⲛ̄ⲃⲁⲡⲧⲓⲥⲙⲁ .... ceux du premier baptême
[9 lignes manquent de la p. 41] .... [...]
ⲡⲡ[ⲱ̣ⲗⲗ]ⲣⲛ[...] (10) .... le [pre]mier [...]
ⲃⲁⲡⲧⲓⲥⲙⲁ [ⲡⲉ ⲡⲕⲱⲉ ⲁ] .... baptême [est le rejet]
ⲃⲁⲗ ⲛ̄ⲛ̄ⲛⲁⲃⲓ[...ⲛ̄] .... des péchés[...]
ⲧⲁ2ⲭⲟⲟⲥ ⲭ[ⲉ...] .... qui a dit[...]
ⲙ̄ⲙ[ⲁ]ⲧⲛ̄ ⲁⲡ[...ⲛ̄ⲛⲉ] .... vous au[...]
ⲧⲛ̄[ⲛ]ⲁⲃⲓ ⲡⲡ. [...] (15) .... vos péchés. Le[...]
ⲡ[ⲉ] ⲛ̄ⲧⲩⲡⲟⲥ ⲙ̄ⲡ[...] .... es[t] un modèle de[...]
ⲅⲟ[...] ⲙ̄ⲡⲉⲭⲣⲏⲥⲧⲟ[ⲥ...] .... [...]du Christ[...]
ⲙ̄[ⲡ]ⲱ̣ⲱ̣ⲱ̣ ⲛ̄ⲛ̄ [...ⲛ̄2ⲡⲏ] .... [l'] égal des[...en]
ⲓ̈ ⲛ̄2ⲏⲧ̄ϥ̄ ⲙ̄ⲡ[...ⲕⲉ] .... lui[...le]
ⲫ[ⲁⲗⲗⲓⲟⲛ] ⲛ̄ⲅⲁⲣ ⲛ̄ⲓ̄ⲏ̄[ⲥ̄.] [..] (20) .... s[ommaire], en effet, de Jé[sus].
ⲙ̄[ⲙⲉⲛ] ⲡⲱ̣ⲁⲣⲡ̄ⲛ̄ ⲙ̄ⲡⲃ[ⲁⲡⲧⲓⲥ] .... De [plus], le premier bap[tê-]
[ⲙⲁ ⲛⲉⲉ]ⲓ ⲡⲉ ⲡⲕⲱⲉ [ⲁⲃⲁⲗ] .... [me, c'] est celui du [re]jet
[ⲛ̄ⲛ̄ⲛⲁⲃⲓ] ⲥⲉⲓⲛⲉ ⲙ̄ⲙ[ⲁⲛ ⲁⲃ] .... [des péchés. Nous sommes] emportés
[ⲁⲗ ⲍ̄ⲛ̄ ⲙ̄ⲙ]ⲁⲩ ⲁⲃⲁⲗ 2ⲓ[ⲧⲟⲟⲧ̄ϥ̄] .... [loin d'] eux par [lui]
[ⲁ2ⲟⲩ]ⲛ ⲁⲛⲁⲩⲛⲉⲙ [ⲉⲧⲉ ⲛⲉⲉⲓ] (25)...[dans] ce qui est de droite, [à savoir]
[ⲡⲉ ⲁ2]ⲟⲩⲛ ⲁⲧⲙⲛ̄ⲧⲁ[ⲧⲧⲉⲕⲟ] .... dans l'Impé[rissable],
[ⲉⲧⲉ ⲛⲉⲉ]ⲓ [ⲡ]ⲉ ⲡⲓⲟⲣⲇⲁ[ⲛⲏⲥ] .... c'est-à-dire le Jourd[ain].
[ⲁⲗⲗ]ⲁ ⲡⲓⲧⲟⲡⲟ[ⲥ] ⲡⲉ [ⲁⲃⲁⲗ 2ⲙ̄] .... [Mais] ce [lieu] est [du]
[ⲡ]ⲕ[ⲟ]ⲥⲙⲟⲥ ⲛ̄ⲧⲉ[ⲉⲓⲙⲓⲛⲉ ⲁⲩ] .... [mon]de. [Ainsi] nous avons [été]
ⲟ̄ⲉ ⲙ̄ⲙⲁⲛ ⲁⲃⲁ[ⲗ] ⲍ̄ [ⲙ̄ ⲡⲕⲟⲥ] (30) .... emportés du [mon-]
ⲙⲟⲥ ⲁ2ⲟⲩⲛ ⲁⲡⲁⲓⲱ[ⲛ ⲑⲉ] .... de dans l'Éo[n]. L'in-]
ⲣⲙⲏⲛⲓⲁ ⲅⲁⲣ ⲛ̄ⲓⲱ2[ⲁⲛⲛⲏⲥ] .... terprétation, en effet, de Je[an]
ⲡⲉ ⲡⲁⲓⲱⲛ ⲑⲉⲣⲙ[ⲏⲛⲓⲁ ⲛ̄] .... est l'Éon, l'inter[prétation],
ⲇⲉ ⲙ̄ⲡⲏ ⲉⲧⲉ ⲡⲓⲟⲣⲇ[ⲁⲛⲏⲥ] .... d'autre part, de ce qui est le Jourd[ain]
ⲡⲉ ⲧⲕⲁⲧⲁⲃⲁⲥⲓⲥ ⲉⲧ[...] (35) .... est la descente qui[...]
ⲙⲟⲥ ⲡⲉ ⲉⲧⲉ ⲡⲉⲉⲓ [ⲡⲉ ⲡ̄ⲛ̄ⲃⲱⲕ] .... à savoir [notre] ex[ode]
ⲁⲃⲁⲗ ⲍ̄ⲙ̄ ⲡⲕⲟⲥⲙⲟ[ⲥ ⲁ2ⲟⲩⲛ] .... du monde [dans]
ⲁⲡⲁⲓⲱⲛ .... l'Éon.

3.6.2.2

Three points stand out in this passage: baptism is decisive, it allows one to move from the material world to the heavenly aeon, and it entails a remission of sins. The introductory words highlight the first point. The author claims to be presenting a précis of a revelation received from ⲡⲉⲛⲭⲗⲉⲓⲥ ⲓ̅ⲏ̅ⲥ̅ ⲡⲉⲭⲣⲏⲥⲧⲟⲥ (40,31), and the "first baptism" emerges when he focuses on the actions which are "certain and necessary" (ⲂⲈⲂⲀⲒⲞⲚ ⲀⲨⲰ ⲚⲀⲚⲀⲄⲔⲀⲒⲞⲚ — 40,35-36). The second point is emphasized. The author mixes horizontal and vertical metaphors to describe a dualistic view of reality. "On the right" is John, the imperishable (ⲦⲘⲚⲦⲀⲦⲦⲈⲔⲞ — 41,26) and the aeon, while "on the left" stand people, the world and sins. But the author intends this horizontal line to be turned counter-clockwise ninety degrees. In this first baptism, one descends even further into the Jordan, only to emerge to be taken away from the world and up into the aeon (ⲚⲦⲈⲈⲒⲘⲒⲚⲈ ⲀⲨϬⲈ ⲘⲘⲀⲚ ⲀⲂⲀⲗ ⲌⲘ ⲠⲔⲞⲤⲘⲞⲤ ⲀⲌⲞⲨⲚ ⲀⲠⲀⲒⲰⲚ — 41,29-31). The Jordan, then, is a symbol of both the perishable and the imperishable.[88] If this first baptism indeed takes one ⲌⲘ ⲠⲔⲞⲤⲘⲞⲤ ⲀⲌⲞⲨⲚ ⲀⲠⲀⲒⲰⲚ, one wonders what role the second baptism can have.

The third point connects the first baptism principally with the remission of sins (ⲠⲔⲰϬⲈ ⲀⲂⲀⲗ ⲚⲚⲚⲀⲂⲒ — 41,22-23). Descent into the waters of the Jordan washes away our sins, and our ascent leads us far from them (ⲤⲈⲒⲚⲈ ⲘⲘⲀⲚ ⲀⲂⲀⲗ ⲌⲚ ⲘⲘⲀⲨ — 41,23-24). Sins are part of the "left" or the "lower" realm. No other details are provided.

3.6.3.1

The distinction drawn between the two levels of reality is accentuated in the fragment which follows (42,1-43,19), one which by its vocabulary and message is surely to be connected with the first fragment on baptism. The author uses a variety of examples to make his point. He claims that the first baptism results in a movement "from the carnal to the spiritual, from the physical to the angelic" (ⲀⲂⲀⲗ ⲌⲘ ⲠⲤⲀⲢⲔⲒⲔⲞⲚ ⲀⲌⲞⲨⲚ ⲀⲠⲠⲚⲈⲨⲘⲀⲦⲒⲔⲞⲚ ⲀⲂⲀⲗ ⲌⲚ ⲪⲨⲤⲒⲔⲞⲚ ⲀⲌⲞⲨⲚ ⲀⲦⲘⲚⲦⲀⲄⲄⲈⲗⲞⲤ — 42,13-16). This is also a movement "from slavery into sonship" (ⲀⲂⲀⲗ ⲌⲚ ⲞⲨⲘⲚⲦ2Ⲙ2Ⲁⲗ ⲀⲌⲞⲨⲚ ⲀⲨⲘⲚⲦⲰ)ⲎⲢⲈ — 42,19-21), and "from the bitterness of the world to the sweetness of God" (ⲀⲂⲀⲗ ⲌⲘ ⲠⲤⲒⲰ)Ⲉ ⲘⲠⲔⲞⲤⲘⲞⲤ ⲀⲌⲞⲨⲚ ⲀⲠ2Ⲁⲗⲟϭ ⲘⲠⲚⲞⲨⲦⲈ — 42,11-13). God in this passage is part of the upper world, and is not equated with the inferior Demiurge.[89] Through this baptism or bath (ⲤⲈⲒⲀⲨⲚⲈ — 42,31), Christ has saved us. We are now "in him" (42,36). This Pauline language is striking, and with Paul it is tempting to conclude that with such a baptism Christ has removed the power of sin.

---

[88] The author makes a play on words based on John's name. John, he states, stands for the aeon (in the baptism narratives): Ἰωάννης = Αἰών. Ménard also suggests (*L'Exposé valentinien*, 87) a second play on words in the same phrase: Ἰορδάνης = ⲦⲒ = descent. Both of these word plays, however, are not possible in Coptic; moreover, they require a knowledge of both Greek and Hebrew. Does this suggest a Greek-speaking Jewish Christian *Sitz* for this passage (and work?)?

[89] God elsewhere in *A Valentinian Exposition* is always identified with a member of the Pleroma (22,30; 24,34; 28,36; 38,11.14.21.33.37). The author's view of the Demiurge is not clear (37,33; [38,25;] 39,16).

3.6.3.2

Three other fragments remain to be examined. The last two concern the eucharist (43,20-38; 44,14-37). They are doxologies in which the author celebrates the eucharist (Ⲣ̄ ⲈⲨⲬⲀⲢⲒⲤⲦⲈⲒ – 43,21) by "giving thanks" (ⲱ̄ⲱⲡ 2ⲘⲀⲦ – 43,20) to the Father and praising his Son Jesus Christ.[90] It is striking that another sacrament is introduced immediately after baptism, and that both accord with other accounts of Valentinian sacramental life.[91] Another noteworthy feature of these verses is the statement that the author's community prided itself in accomplishing God's will (ⲞⲨⲰⲰⲈ – 43,31), claiming that the members were "complete in every spiritual gift and every purity" (ⲈⲨⲬⲎⲔ ⲀⲂⲀⲖ 2Ⲛ̄ ⲬⲀⲢⲒⲤ ⲚⲒⲘ 2Ⲓ ⲦⲞⲨⲂⲞ ⲚⲒⲘ – 43,34-36). As Paul would say: baptism removed their sins and gave them a new life in Christ, granting them the possibility to lead perfect lives. This did not remove the need to carry out God's will (and perhaps to struggle against sin). Rather, it gave the members the power to effect God's will perfectly.

The first fragment (40,1-29) concerns anointing (ⲦⲰ2Ⲥ – 40,13). It also is a doxology. The author glorifies the Father for sending his Son, Jesus Christ, to anoint them that they may "trample upon the snakes and the heads of the scorpions and all the power of the Devil" (ⲬⲈⲔⲀⲤⲈ ⲈⲚⲀⲱ6Ⲛ̄6ⲀⲘ Ⲛ̄ⲔⲀⲦⲀⲡⲀⲦⲈⲒ Ⲛ̄ⲦⲀⲡⲈⲚ̄Ⲛ̄2Ⲟϥ ⲀⲨⲰ Ⲛ̄ⲦⲀⲡⲈ Ⲛ̄ⲚⲞⲨⲞⲞ2Ⲉ ⲘⲚ̄ Ⲧ6ⲀⲘ ⲦⲎⲢⲤ̄ Ⲙ̄ⲡⲆⲒⲀⲂⲞⲖⲞⲤ – 40,14-17). This may be a reference to the Valentinian sacrament of "second baptism," as Ménard claims, but it is more likely that the fragment refers to their sacrament of anointing.[92] The "anointing" was performed either before the first baptism or simultaneously with it, given that this baptism removed sins and transported people from the bitterness of the world to the sweetness and gentleness of the divine realm — a realm with no Devil.

3.6.3.3

The text which precedes these fragments (22,4-39,39) is rich in detail concerning Valentinian speculation about the Pleroma, Sophia's fall, and her "repentance" (Ⲣ̄ⲘⲈⲦⲀⲚⲞⲈⲒ – 34,23). The description is strikingly similar to that found in the Fathers; yet, as Pagels and Ménard have both noted, it is not

---

[90] Note that this author distinguishes between the sacrament of eucharist, for which he has a Greek loan word, and the act of giving praise, for which he uses a Coptic expression.

[91] Cf. the phrase in *The Gospel of Philip:* "The Lord did everything in a mystery, a baptism and a chrism and a eucharist and a redemption and a bridal chamber" (67,28-30).

[92] So also Pagels and Turner (*The Nag Hammadi Library,* 435). Ménard's position is expressed in *L'Exposé valentinien,* 84. Against Ménard, note that (1) there is no reference to baptism in this fragment; (2) it precedes the discussion about first baptism, and does not follow it as one would expect if it were dealing with a second or higher baptism; (3) the word used for second baptism in the Fathers is usually ἀπολύτρωσις, not χρῖσμα as it is here; and (4) "baptism and a chrism and a eucharist" are the first three sacraments mentioned in *The Gospel of Philip* (67,28-29).

without some important differences.[93] *A Valentinian Exposition* as a whole is less useful in supplementing the information about sin in the second fragment. But the last three pages discuss worldly matters and are directly relevant to our inquiry, especially in the depiction of the Devil.

Three aspects about the world and humanity's place in it stand out in this work. The first concerns its creation. Sophia's fall results in a strain on the Pleroma, but her redemption leads to renewed unity. Her fall also leads eventually to the creation of the world (though the details are lacking). The world is created by God, who sometimes is called the Demiurge in this section (37-38), and who elsewhere is always part of the Pleroma (and usually equated with *Nous*). This is a far cry from Irenaeus's depiction of the Ptolemaic Demiurge.

The second aspect concerns the creation and constitution of humankind. People are created by the Demiurge (37,33 — or God in 38,21) "according to his image . . . and the likeness of those who exist from the first" (ⲔⲀⲧⲀ ⲦϤ2ⲒⲔⲰⲚ ⲘⲈⲚ ⲔⲀⲦⲀ ⲠⲒⲚⲈ ⲚⲆⲈ ⲚⲚⲈⲦⲱⲞⲞⲠ ⲬⲒⲚⲚ ⲱⲀⲠⲚ — 37,34-36). In "classical" Valentinianism, the Demiurge creates two humans, the sarkic (or hylic) and the psychic, and a pneumatic marrow is placed into the psychic one. This almost certainly is not the situation here.[94] For the comparison to work in this passage, the two "humans" would have to be psychic and pneumatic, which is never the case. In addition, there is no mention of a psychic "person" or "nature" anywhere in this tractate. Furthermore, the Demiurge in this work is divine, not merely partly so. To be sure, somebody deposited "seeds" (ⲤⲠⲈⲢⲘⲀ) into this person (37,36-38), but who it was and what results this had are not explained. People do not appear at first as lowly creatures.

The third aspect about the world is determinative. The Devil, one of the divine beings (ⲞⲨⲈⲈⲒ ⲠⲈⲚⲚⲀⲠⲚⲞⲨⲦⲈ — 38,13-14), falls from the Pleroma and rebels against God. Some angels join the rebellion. The Devil transfers his "root" or essence into "the bodies and carcasses of flesh," and these "cover the Man of God" (38,20-21). This results in Adam begetting sons who, in turn, fight with one another: "And Cain killed Abel his brother, for the [Devil?] breathed into them" (38,24-27).[95] From this ensues "the apostasy of angels and of humanity"

---

[93] Pagels in the introduction to this work in *The Nag Hammadi Library,* 435. Ménard emphasizes the continuity between this work and the other Valentinian ones, while also suggesting that *A Valentinian Exposition* could contain an earlier view of Valentinianism in which the triple human nature is downplayed (*L'Exposé valentinien*, 81).

[94] *Contra* Ménard, who claims: "d'abord il façonne l'homme à son image (κατ' εἰκόνα), c'est l'homme hylique, puis l'homme à la ressemblance (καθ' ὁμοίωσιν) des êtres célestes, l'homme psychique en formation" (*L'Exposé valentinien*, 79). This is consistent with Ménard's tendency to fit this work into the Valentinian mold.

[95] The key passage is missing. Ménard (following Turner in *The Nag Hammadi Library*) reconstructs the text as follows:

24 . . . 2ⲀⲔⲀⲒⲚ Ⲛ[ⲆⲈ ⲀϤⲘⲞ]Ⲩ[Ⲟ
25 [ⲨⲦ Ⲛ]ⲀⲂⲈⲗ ⲠⲈϤⲤⲀⲚ Ⲭ[Ⲉ Ⲁ.ⲏⲘⲒⲞ]
26 [ⲨⲢⲄⲞ]Ⲥ ⲄⲀⲢ ⲚⲒϤⲈ Ⲁ2ⲞⲨ[Ⲛ ⲀⲢⲀⲨ]

It makes little sense in context to have Cain killing his brother "because the Demiurge

(38,28–30), and the struggle between "those on the right with those on the left, and those in heaven with those on earth, the spirits with the carnal [ⲚⲚⲠⲚⲈⲨⲘⲀ ⲘⲚ ⲚⲤⲀⲢⲔⲒⲔⲞⲚ], and the Devil against God" (38,30–33). The world becomes the domain of the Devil, and humanity has been covered with the Devil's "flesh."

3.6.4

In this context, then, a person is made up of two basic parts. Sin means acting in accordance with the fleshly "covering," and this is contrary to one's divine nature. Since the devil is in combat with God and has taken control of the world, it becomes virtually impossible not to sin. Again, we are back essentially to a Pauline view of reality. The author of this tractate encourages his audience to be anointed in order to receive the power to trample on the Devil. And he encourages them to undergo their first baptism to be taken out of the carnal realm and into the spiritual aeon. Christ redeems their sins and frees them from the bondage of the Devil's flesh. The author talks of the need to move "upwards" and "to the right," away from "the left" and "the (lower) world." Yet he also is exhorting his audience to move "inwards" by gaining power over the outer fleshly layer. A focus on the inner self allows one to conform perfectly to God's will, and already to join in the sinless existence of the Pleroma.

3.7 *The Second Apocalypse of James*

3.7.1

The final three pages of this work (61–63) describe the martyrdom of James. This is a story that was often told among early Christians, and with many variants, as a wide range of sources reveals.[96] This particular version opens with the narrator recounting that James's oral presentation has not convinced ⲠⲖⲀⲞⲤ . . . ⲘⲚ ⲠⲘⲎⲎⲰⲈ (61,2–3). Undaunted, he re-enters the temple and continues to speak. From the content of the preceding narrative, one assumes

---

breathed his spirit into them." Their troubles derive from the "body and flesh" of the devil which they have inherited, as the author states five lines above this. In context, then, "devil" makes more sense than "Demiurge." Ⲭ[Ⲉ ⲀⲠⲀⲒⲀⲂⲞⲖⲞ]Ⲥ has one letter less than Ⲭ[Ⲉ ⲀⲆⲎⲘⲒⲞⲨⲢⲄⲞ]Ⲥ, but the state of the right margin of this manuscript easily allows this.

[96] E.g. Josephus, *Antiquities*, XX,200 (who sets the martyrdom of James in the year 62); and the accounts of Clement and Hegesippus recorded by Eusebius (*Hist. Eccl.* II,23). The parallels between Hegesippus's account and that found in *The Second Apocalypse of James* are explored by Böhlig, *Mysterion und Wahrheit*, 114–15; and Brown, "Jewish and Gnostic Elements," 227–31. Brown concludes: "In the version of the story preserved by Hegesippus, the interest in James the martyr has become centered on seeing his death as emulating the pattern of Jesus' death. In the rendition found in our apocalypse, we find that someone wished to emphasize that James was martyred according to the Jewish regulations for stoning" (231).

James's prayer in Hegesippus's account is short ("I beseech thee, O Lord, God and Father, forgive them, for they know not what they do"). It contains no reference to sin.

that the Messiahship of Jesus is at issue, but the only specific accusation is that James "has erred" (62,7).[97] At this point the priests decide to kill him.

The narrator's role as an insider, who in this situation can only hope to save himself by remaining silent, probably points to a redactional seam. It serves to connect the final part of the work with the opening words in 44,16 which identify the narrator as "Mareim, one of the priests." It also helps to give credence to the account he is about to narrate.

No trial is convened, nor is there even a debate. "You have erred" (ⲠⲈⲚⲦⲀ4ⲤⲰⲠⲘ̄), they declare, then they cast him down from the elevated part of the temple on which he is standing (61,25-26). Since this does not kill him, they try it again by stoning. The one large stone does not work, so they "made him dig a hole. They made him stand in it. After having covered him up to his abdomen, they stoned him in this manner" (62,8-12).[98] James does not go swiftly into the light.

3.7.2.1

This final stoning means the end for James, but he has time for an extended and dramatic prayer (62,16-63,29) before he "falls silent" (63,30). The narrator adds a personal touch to the story by saying that this particular prayer was different than usual (62,15).

The two references to sin occur here. The prayer, in its entirety, is as follows:[99]

. . . ⲠⲀⲚⲞⲨⲦⲈ ⲀⲨⲱ ⲠⲀⲒⲰⲦ (62,16)	My God and my Father,
ⲠⲈⲚⲦⲀ4ⲚⲀ2ⲘⲈⲦ ⲈⲂⲞⲖ 2Ⲛ̄	who saved me from
†2ⲈⲖⲠⲒⲤ ⲈⲤⲘⲞⲞⲨⲦ	this dead hope,
ⲠⲈⲚⲦⲀ4ⲦⲀⲚ2ⲞⲈⲒ 2Ⲛ̄Ⲛ ⲞⲨ	who made me alive through a
ⲘⲨⲤⲦⲎⲢⲒⲞⲚ Ⲛ̄ⲦⲈ ⲠⲈⲦⲈ 2ⲚⲀ4̄ (20)	mystery of what he wills,
ⲚⲈⲔⲦⲢⲈⲨⲰⲤⲔ̄ ⲚⲀⲒ Ⲛ̄ϬⲒ	do not let these days of this world
ⲚⲈⲒ2ⲞⲞⲨ Ⲛ̄ⲦⲈ ⲠⲈⲒⲔⲞⲤⲘⲞⲤ	be prolonged for me,
ⲀⲖⲖⲀ ⲠⲈ2ⲞⲞⲨ Ⲛ̄ⲦⲈ ⲠⲈⲔ	but the day of your
ⲞⲨⲞⲈ[ⲒⲚ . . .]Ⲛ̄ [. . .]ⲱⲞⳜⲚ̄	[light . . .] remains
Ⲛ̄2ⲎⲦ[. . .]Ⲩ (25)	in [. . .]
ⲱ [. . .]ⲱⲚ	[. . .]
ⲀⲚ[. . .]	[. . .]
[ⲞⲨ]ⳜⲀⲒ̈ ⲂⲞⲖⲦ̄ ⲈⲂⲞⲖ Ⲛ̄ⲤⲀⲂⲞⲖ Ⲙ̄ⲠⲈⲒ̈	salvation. Deliver me from this

[97] Mareim's report which opens the work describes how "a multitude [ⲞⲨⲘⲎⲎⳜⲈ] are disturbed . . . and angry [at him] . . . . For [he would] often say these words, and others also . . . while the multitude of people [ⲠⲀⲱⲀⲒ̈ Ⲛ̄ⲚⲖⲖⲞⲤ] were seated" (45,9-20). This paints a picture of a preacher who repeatedly presents his disturbing message in the temple.

[98] Brown ("Jewish and Gnostic Elements," 229-31) shows how this double process of stoning is consistent with the Mishnah's regulations.

[99] Both the text and the translation are taken from Hedrick's edition in *The Nag Hammadi Codices V,2-5 and VI,*144-49.

Μ[λ Ñ6]ΟΘΙλΘ ΜΠ̄Ρ̄ΤΡΘϤϢϢΧ̄Π ......[place of] sojourn! Do not let your

....grace be left behind

Ñ2ΗΤ Ñ6Ι ΠΘΚ2ΜΟΤ λλλλ Μλ̇.........................in me, but may

ΡΘϤϢϢΠΘ ΘϤΟΥλλΒ Ñ6Ι ΠΘΚ ....your grace become pure!

2ΜΟΤ Νλ2ΜΘΤ ΘΒΟλ Ñ̄ΝΟΥ (63,5) ....Save me from an

ΜΟΥ ΘϤ2ΟΟΥ λΝΙΤ ΘΒΟλ 2Ñ ....evil death! Bring me from

Ν ΟΥΜ̄2λΟΥ ΘΪΟΝ2̄ ΧΘ ϤΟΝ2̄ Ñ ....a tomb alive, because your grace—

2ΗΤ Ñ6Ι ΠΘΚ2ΜΟΤ ΠΘΡϢΣ.........................love—is alive in me

ΘΡ̄ 2ϢΒ Ñ̄ΟΥ2ϢΒ Ñ̄ΤΘ ΟΥΠλΗ..........to accomplish a work of fullness!

ΡϢΜλ Νλ2ΜΘΤ ΘΒΟλ 2Ñ̄Ν ΟΥ (10) ....Save me from

ΣλΡ2̄ Ñ̄ΝΟΒΘ ΧΘ λΪΤϢΤ Ñ ....sinful flesh, because I trusted in

2ΗΤΚ̄ 2Ñ Τλ6ΟΜ ΤΗΡΣ̄ ΧΘ Ñ̄ΤΟΚ.......you with all my strength! Because

ΠΘ ΠϢΝ2̄ Ñ̄ΤΘ ΠϢΝ2̄ Νλ2ΜΘΤ ....you are the life of the life, save me

ΘΒΟλ 2ΙΤΟΟΤ̄Ϥ Ñ̄ΝΟΥΧλΧΘ Ñ ....from a humiliating

ΡΘϤΟΒ̄ΒΙΟ ΝΘΚΤλλΤ ΘΤΟΟΤ̄Ϥ (15)...enemy! Do not give me into the hand

Ñ̄ΝΟΥΡΘϤ†2λΠ Ñ̄ΡΘϤΟϢϢΤ ....of a judge who is severe

ΘΒΟλ 2Μ̄ ΠΝΟΒΘ ΚϢ Νλϊ ΘΒΟλ ....with sin! Forgive me

Ñ̄ΝΗ ΘΤΘΡΟΪ ΤΗΡΟΥ Ñ̄ΤΘ ΝΘ ....all my debts of the

2ΟΟΥ ΧΘ †ΟΝ2̄ λΝΟΚ 2Ρλϊ Ñ ....days (of my life)! Because I am alive

2ΗΤΚ̄ ϤΟΝ2̄ Ñ̄2ΗΤ Ñ̄6Ι ΠΘΚ (20) ....in you, your grace is alive in me.

2ΜΟΤ λΪΡ̄λΡΝΙΣΘΘ Ñ̄ΟΥΟΝ ....I have renounced everyone,

ΝΙΜ Ñ̄ΤΟΚ ΔΘ λΪΟΥΟΝ2Κ̄ ΘΒΟλ................but you I have confessed.

Νλ2ΜΘΤ ΘΒΟλ 2Ñ̄Ν ΟΥΘλΙΨΙΣ ....Save me from evil

ΘΣ2ΟΟΥ †ΝΟΥ ΔΘ ΠΟΥΟ[ΘΙϢ)] ....affliction! But now is the [time]

ΠΘ λΥϢ ΤΟΥΝΟΥ ΤΘ ΠΙΠ̄[Ñλ̄] (25)................and the hour. O Holy

ΘΤΟΥλλΒ ΜλΤÑ̄ΝΟΟΥ 2λ[ΡΟϊ].......................[Spirit] send [me]

Ñ̄ΟΥΟΥΧ[λϊ . . .]ΠΟΥΟΘΙΝ[. . .] ....salvation [. . .] the light [. . .]

ΠΟΥΟΘΙΝ [. . .]Θ† . ΗϤ)[. . .] ....the light [. . .]

2Ñ ΟΥ6ΟΜ [. . .]Θ[. . .]ΚΟ Ñ[. . .]................in a power [. . .]

3.7.2.2

This prayer functions well in the narrative, regardless of what its original *Sitz* may have been![100] James is about to die, so naturally he reflects on the world he is leaving behind and the one which awaits him. As one would expect under these circumstances, the importance of the world is downplayed. James reminds himself of the world's transitory and inferior nature. He speaks of his "sojourn" (6ΟΘΙλΘ — 63,2) in "these days of the world" (62,22), and of the "sinful flesh"

---

[100] Funk, for instance, argues that the last section of this work (61–63) was not written by the same person who composed the first part (*Die zweite Apokalypse,* 193–98), and that the prayer probably had its own liturgical *Sitz im Leben* in some gnostic "Sterbesakrament bzw. eine Totenmesse" (219–20). Earlier, Böhlig argued for a Jewish-Christian *Sitz:* "Unser Text weist starke Vertrautheit mit jüdischer Gesetzlichkeit und Frömmigkeit aus" (*Mysterion und Wahrheit,* 118). We are concerned only with the final stage of this apocalypse. Whatever its original setting, the prayer was accepted by the (final) redactor.

(CλPϩ ÑNOBϬ—63,11) which he has been forced to wear. His thoughts, though, are riveted on his afterlife. Understandably, he prays to be taken up to "the day" of God's "light" (62,23-24). His final words, although not completely extant, give a good indication of this wish: "O Holy Spirit, send me salvation . . . the light . . . in a power" (63,25-29). He hopes that salvation will be granted to him since God's grace (ϩMOT) is alive in him. Yet, righteous as he may be, he is also terrified of undergoing punishments after he dies. Please save me from such a fate, he pleads in this prayer. "Save me from a humiliating enemy! Do not give me into the hand of a judge who is severe with sin! Forgive me all my debts of the days (of my life)!" (63,15-19). Remember, Father, that it is "you I have confessed. [So] Save me from evil affliction" (63,22-24).

Salvation and grace are the key concepts in this prayer. The Coptic version brings this out forcefully due to the verbal similarity between the words ϩMOT and NλϩMϬT (NOYϩM). All the occurrences of "grace" (63,3.4.8.21) and "save" (62,17; 63,5.10.13.23[101]) in the work are found in this prayer, and the four uses of ϩMOT form and effective counterpoint to the recurring formula NλϩMϬT ϬBOλ.[102]

This is not the prayer of a man who is confident and assured of resting soon with the Father. Placed in the mouth of "the righteous one,"[103] it becomes even more striking. James's worry about his sins also is remarkable. Although he considers himself to be "saved from this dead hope" (62,17-18) and filled with God's grace (63,2.4.7), he is still afraid of meeting "a judge who is severe with sin" (63,16-17)![104] He may be righteous (ΔIKλIOC), but he surely is not sinless![105] Furthermore, his plea to God to have all of his "debts" forgiven (KΩ NλÏ ϬBOλ

---

[101] Funk has emended the text in 63,16 to add another NλϩMϬT before ϬBOλ ϩM ΠNOBϬ. As it stands, the meaning of ÑPϬϥΩϣΩT ϬBOλ ϩM ΠNOBϬ is unclear. Hedrick's note expresses the problem well: "It can be understood in at least three ways. If one takes ϣΩϣΩT by itself and links ϬBOλ ϩM with ΠNOBϬ, it could be translated, 'one who torments through sin.' If one links ϬBOλ with ϣΩϣΩT and ϩM with ΠNOBϬ, it could be translated, 'one severe through sin' (Böhlig [Koptisch-gnostische Apokalypsen]). If one takes ϬBOλ ϩM with ϣΩϣΩT it could be translated, 'one who cuts off from sin' (Kasser ["Bibliothèque gnostique VI: Les deux apocalypses de Jacques," RTP 18 (1968) 163-86]). Funk emends the text by inserting NλϩMϬT before ϬBOλ ϩM ΠNOBϬ. I take ϬBOλ with ϣΩϣΩT" (Nag Hammadi Codices V,2-5 and VI, 146-47).

[102] Böhlig (Mysterion und Wahrheit, 116-17) structures the prayer in two parts, with the four instances of "save me" forming the framework of the second part.

[103] James is called ΔIKλIOC six times in the work: 44,13.17; 49,9; 59,22; 60,12; 61,14.

[104] Funk's reconstruction of the text (see note 101 above) does not alter the meaning of the passage. He writes NϬKTλλT ϬTOOTϥ ÑNOYPϬϥ†ϩλΠ ÑPϬϥϣΩϣΩT ‹NλϩMϬT› ϬBOλ ϩM ΠNOBϬ ("Du mögest mich nicht geben in die Hand eines strengen Richters! ‹Rette mich› aus der Sünde!"). The judge's "severity" in either case is based on the man's sins.

[105] Jesus is said to have lived "without blasphemy" (ΧΩPIC OYλ—47,24-25), and to have died by means of blasphemy. Since OYλ is a hapax legomenon, it is difficult to determine how close to "sin" the author considered "blasphemy" to be.

ⲚⲚⲎ ⲈⲦⲈⲢⲞⲒ̈ ⲦⲎⲢⲞⲨ ⲚⲦⲈ ⲚⲈϨⲞⲞⲨ – 63,17–19) almost certainly refers to the forgiveness of sins.[106] It is clear, then, that James has committed sins throughout his life, and that this will lead to punishment unless they are forgiven before he dies.

3.7.3.1

The closing pages of *The Second Apocalypse of James* stand well on their own, but they must also be understood in the light of the first part of this work. The full-blown Valentinian system described by Irenaeus could be read into this part of the work without doing much injustice to the text, but it does not emerge on its own.[107] Restricting ourselves to the work itself, the most notable feature is the dichotomy drawn between the creator God and the heavenly Father. This reveals that James's worry about which realm he will enter after death is consistent with the author's redactional tendency throughout the work.

The creator of the world, with whom the author associates "violence," "captivity," and "judgment," is inferior to the true and merciful God, "the Father who has compassion."[108] The inferior God exercises dominion over the cosmos only for the time allotted by the true God. During this period he "imprisons" the Father's children as well as his own (cf. 55,15–19), encouraging them to act improperly and allowing his "judges" to deal harshly with them when they die (53–54; 57,20–23; 58,2–6; 60,5–7). Jesus brings to people the knowledge of this state of affairs, and of their true home with the Father. After his death, he reveals this ⲄⲚⲰⲤⲒⲤ to James who, in turn, becomes "rich in knowledge" (47,7–8), "an illuminator and a redeemer" to those who belong to the Father (55,15–19).

Before this saving knowledge was provided, men and women acted improperly. But their evil actions were not their fault: "For (it is) not you who did them, but it is [your] Lord (who did them)" (59,6–10). Now that ⲄⲚⲰⲤⲒⲤ has been revealed, those who can must "hear and understand" (51,15). And they must act accordingly, which includes teaching others: "it is fitting that others know

[106] In Aramaic, one word was used for both "debt" and "sin": חובא. The variant readings of the Lord's Prayer in the NT (Matt 6:12/Lk 11:4) bear witness to the impossibility of keeping that dual meaning in Greek. The same holds true for Coptic.

[107] Böhlig cautiously placed this work in the Valentinian camp in his introductory comments to the *editio princeps:* "Die zweite Jakobusapokalypse hat ebenfalls gnostische Züge; doch fragt sich, ob hier nicht ein alter Text, der schwer einer bestimmten Schule zuzuweisen ist, den aber auch die Valentinianer gut verwendet konnten, überarbeitet wurde" (*Koptisch-gnostische Apokalypsen,* 28). Schenke and several others have simply called the work gnostic without connecting it with any group described by the Fathers. See Schenke's review of Böhlig's *Apokalypsen* in *OLZ* 61 (1966) 27; K. Rudolph, "Gnosis und Gnostizismus. Ein Forschungsbericht," *TRu* 34 (1969) 160; Brown, "Jewish and Gnostic Elements," 231; Funk, *Die zweite Apokalypse,* 4; and Hedrick, *Nag Hammadi Codices V,2–5 and VI,* 108.

[108] Funk (*Die zweite Apokalypse,* 199–209) presents a detailed examination of this question of two fathers in *The Second Apocalypse of James.*

through you" (51,11-13). Stringent ethical demands are implied rather than stated, yet the author insists that they "walk" (ⲘⲞⲞ(Ⲩ)Ⲉ) in the way of their true Lord: "[Renounce] this . . . way, which is (so) variable [and] walk in accordance with him who desires [that] you become free" (59,1-4; cf. also 52,18; 55,10).

3.7.3.2

The statements made by James about sin in 63,10-20 are consistent with the *Weltanschauung* depicted in the earlier chapters. The creator God is still active, encouraging people to act in a "fleshly" manner, and (as part of the vicious cycle) setting up judges to punish them for it when they die. James knows that he has not always acted properly, either before he received Jesus' revelation or afterwards. Walking in the way of the lower Lord is not difficult, but it leads to harsh judgment, while walking in the way of the true Lord is extremely difficult, though it holds the promise of salvation. ⲄⲚⲰⲤⲒⲤ provides the means of attaining that salvation, but it makes life on earth more difficult. In this context, James asks the Father to forgive his sins (debts) and allow him to pass by the judges who punish sinners mercilessly.

4. SUMMARY

4.1

The differences between these six works from the Nag Hammadi library is one of the striking features to emerge in this chapter. This points to the diversity within Valentinianism,[109] not to mention Christianity itself. For instance, the Logos replaces Sophia in *The Tripartite Tractate,* while in *A Valentinian Exposition* the true God creates men and women who, before the fall of the Devil, were not lowly creatures.

Most striking of all in this regard is the division of humanity. Valentinianism according to Irenaeus distinguishes between pneumatics, psychics and sarkics. Yet only *The Tripartite Tractate* clearly reflects this "classical" division. Indeed, in both *The Gospel of Philip* and *A Valentinian Exposition* all people seem to be treated the same. Actually, a bipartite rather than a tripartite division does more justice to these works on the whole. The distinction between "the children of the Father" and the "others" is clearly drawn in *The Gospel of Truth, The Second Apocalypse of James,* and *The Interpretation of Knowledge,* and the struggle between "those on the left" and "those on the right" is a feature of *A Valentinian Exposition.* Even in *The Tripartite Tractate* the psychics and the pneumatics are treated virtually as one group and set off from the hylics.

The diversity in these works is welcome since it probably reflects the wide range of options possible within Valentinianism. We have access to only a few

---

[109] This point holds even if some of these works are not in fact Valentinian since they all show marked differences from one another and from the patristic accounts (which themselves are not uniform).

primary sources for the study of early Christianity. In this case these six works may well represent the views of a large number of Christians in the second century.

4.2

Differences also emerge when one examines sin, but what is striking is the degree of overlap and the important role sin plays for each author. This overlap is not always extensive. The punishment awaiting the sinner after death is graphically described in *The Gospel of Philip* (where it is said to occur in the "Middle") and *The Second Apocalypse of James* (at the hands of the creator God), but it is not important in the other works. The connection between baptism and sin is more broadly based. In three works (*A Valentinian Exposition, The Tripartite Tractate* and *The Gospel of Philip*) baptism is the ritual *par excellence* which allows the Christian to overcome the power of sin, lead a sinless life and expect salvation after death. Without baptism sin cannot be checked.

On two issues the six works speak with one voice. The first is the cause of sin. People sin because they are encouraged to do so by an outside power hostile to God. This is taken to be the "devil" (*A Valentinian Exposition;* perhaps also *The Interpretation of Knowledge* — cf. 20,18), the "creator God" (*The Second Apocalypse of James*), or simply the "evil powers" (*The Gospel of Philip*). Other times the authors prefer to personify "error" (*The Gospel of Truth*) or "evil, "passion," and "ignorance" (*The Tripartite Tractate*). This outside instigator is far more powerful than people. This sounds a note of pessimism. Yet underlying this view is the understanding that people "deep down" do not want to sin, and that if the outside force can be countered a sinless existence is possible.

The second, and more important, issue to emerge in this chapter is the recognition that these Christians — all of them — are intent on "doing the Father's will." They definitely are not gnostics for whom actions have no significance and sin is of no concern whatsoever. Sin for them is an action not in keeping with the heavenly Father's will. They are worried about their salvation (cf. especially the moving prayer in *The Second Apocalypse of James*) and struggle to remain sinless in the hope that this will make the difference when they die. If anything, these Christians would have been more concerned than others about acting correctly and avoiding lapses. The frequent allusions to the ethical directives in the Sermon on the Mount are remarkable. Three works in particular show significant awareness of these chapters in Matthew: *The Gospel of Truth, The Gospel of Philip,* and *The Interpretation of Knowledge.* This buries the traditional claim that gnostics were not interested in ethics. In these works we encounter Christians who took sacraments quite seriously, who took to heart Matthew's Sermon on the Mount, and who were deeply concerned about not committing sins.

4
Conclusion

1. THE PROBLEM

1.1

We began this work by sketching the scholarly consensus on the role of sin in Valentinianism. This consensus has four main links. (1) Gnostics are redeemed by nature, not by actions, for the possession of *gnosis* brings freedom from worldly constraints. (2) Acting properly or improperly, then, has no salvific importance.[1] This affects their understanding of sin. One expects gnostics either to redefine sin, perhaps equating it with ignorance; or, more likely, to exclude the concept altogether—especially since in Christianity and Judaism it is tied so closely to ethics and salvation. (3) Valentinianism falls on this gnostic trajectory. Accordingly, the Judaeo-Christian understanding of sin, broadly defined, should play no significant role in this system. (4) This logical deduction is supported by the Fathers, since almost no mention is made of sin in their evidence for Valentinianism. Consequently, scholarly reconstructions of Valentinianism tend to refer only briefly to ethics and to include no discussion of sin.

1.2

In chapter 1 we noted three problems with this position. First, in religious systems ideals do not always conform to practice. Manicheism is a useful example in this regard, for it is decidedly gnostic in nature yet allows sin to play a vital role. A similar mix occurred centuries later with the Cathars. So sin could have been an integral part of Valentinianism. Second, Valentinianism falls not only on a gnostic but also on a Christian trajectory. Since Christians in the second century showed a great deal of concern for sin, it would be remarkable if Valentinians were completely different. So sin ought to have played some role in Valentinianism. Third, extensive new evidence warrants a reappraisal of this issue, especially since sin is mentioned several times in the Valentinian works from the Nag Hammadi library. So sin appears indeed to have been a factor in Valentinianism. The scholarly consensus on this issue, then, does not do justice to the evidence, both old and new.

---

[1] As Foerster states, "The ethics of the gnostics appear to be determined by the fact that they regarded themselves as 'saved by nature.' This leads to an indifference to ethical conduct" (*Gnosis,* 18).

2. THE RESULTS

2.1

The next step in our investigation was to determine the Valentinian understanding of sin by examining all of the sources individually and scrutinizing the relevant pericopes. Studying the patristic evidence in chapter 2, we focused on six passages (*Adv. haer.* I,21; *Exc. ex. Theod.* 51-52; *Ref.* VI, 41; Heracleon, Fragments 10, 40 41); and in chapter 3 we dealt with six Valentinian works from Nag Hammadi: *The Gospel of Truth, The Tripartite Tractate, The Gospel of Philip, The Interpretation of Knowledge, A Valentinian Exposition,* and *The Second Apocalypse of James.* Detailed exegeses of the appropriate passages confirmed our suspicion that sin played a more important role in Valentinianism than has previously been thought. This result is unquestionable, and is confirmed both by the patristic and the Nag Hammadi sources.

The precise meaning of sin in Valentinianism is more difficult to ascertain. No uniform picture has emerged. This is not surprising given the diversity within Christianity in its first two centuries. Even within the NT one finds no uniform view of sin. Nonetheless, a basic Valentinian position on sin does exist, and it is supported by a wide range of sources.

2.2

Sin in Valentinianism refers to a human act or thought not in harmony with the supreme God or Father. This view of sin is implied in the patristic sources and it is stated forcefully in the works from Nag Hammadi, where Christians are exhorted constantly to "do the Father's will." Moreover, as we have seen, the ethical directives of the Sermon on the Mount are often noted explicitly. This suggests that Valentinians were extremely concerned about acting and thinking correctly. Ethical indifference definitely is not a feature of Valentinianism.[2]

Sin concerns all people, but in different ways. Some are dominated by their hylic or sarkic nature and have no knowledge of the supreme God. They cannot refrain from sinning, and ignorance of the Father is no excuse. On the other hand, those who have acquired knowledge of their pneumatic nature recognize the Father's will and are naturally inclined to act in accordance with it. However, practice does not always live up to expectations, as the Nag Hammadi works reveal. For instance, James, in *The Second Apocalypse of James,* is a righteous individual who still admits to having sinned, and when faced with death is terrified by the consequences of his sinful acts. Similarly, *The Tripartite Tractate* explains how the Savior and the elect share a pneumatic nature, but insists that only the Savior can be sinless. Between these extremes lie the psychics, who are

---

[2] Cf. Rudolph: "the thesis . . . by the Church Fathers to the effect that the gnostic must be 'saved by nature' is to be taken *cum grano salis*. A life governed by gnostic principles is required of every true gnostic; this is not a matter of indifference to his salvation" (*Gnosis,* 261).

directed by their hylic nature yet at the same time are attracted to the *pneumatika*. These people tend to sin repeatedly, but there exists for them the possibility of change. The human condition, then, includes sinning, either constantly, repeatedly or infrequently. Why do people sin? The Valentinians offer two reasons. Ignorance of the Father is the basic one, for without knowledge of who the Father is and what he wants it is impossible to act properly.[3] However, even this *gnosis* is no guarantee of a sinless existence—or at least of one that is easily attainable—because people are faced with a powerful force which encourages them to act improperly. This outside power, whatever name it is given (e.g. the devil, error, evil), has settled in people's hylic part. In this way it poses a constant, internal threat.[4] People sin, then, because they are strongly urged to do so by an evil power residing within them, and ignorance of the Father for some makes the situation hopeless.[5]

Serious repercussions accrue from a sinless existence, for sinning in this age leads to exclusion from the age to come. The Valentinians stress the ultimate destruction of the hylics, and emphasize the need for the psychics to lead perfect lives if they are to share in some way the final "marriage feast." Even the pneumatics, who ought to be saved by nature alone, are expected to reflect this nature in their actions. This position is essentially Pauline. Paul often argues that salvation is not based on works, but insists at the same time that the Christian who is truly "in Christ" will live in accordance to God's law. Neither Paul nor the Valentinians, though, reveal how one can be "in Christ" or "pneumatic" while continuing to act improperly. Some Christians, then, may have argued that *gnosis* allowed them to do as they pleased (and there are hints of this already in 1 Corinthians), but the Valentinians were not among them. They insisted that the Father would reward only those who followed his will.

The crucial question for Valentinians is how one stops sinning. They claimed that outside help is required. The Son's descent brings *gnosis* to those able to receive it, thereby revealing the Father's will. Without this knowledge a sinless existence is not possible. Equally important, though, are the salvific rites

---

[3] Connecting sin with ignorance and righteousness with knowledge is also part of the Greek philosophical tradition. Cf. Plato's remarks in the Timaeus (86 D): οὐδεὶς ἑκὼν κακός.

[4] This view of an outside power is consistent with second century Christianity in general. Notable in virtually all the literature is the opposition drawn between the absolute power of God and the great power of Satan and evil. See J. J. Machielsen, "Le problème du mal selon les pères apostoliques," *ET* 62 (1981) 195-222.

[5] Cf. Pétrement's challenging remarks about Gnosticism as a whole: "La première idée sur laquelle semble se fonder le gnosticisme, ce n'est pas, comme on le croit souvent, que l'homme est divin par nature, mais au contraire, que l'homme est naturellement pécheur, naturellement esclave des grandes lois qui dominent le monde, esclave des 'forces'" (*Le Dieu séparé*, 287).

instituted by the Son, notably the baptism(s). As we read in *Excerpta ex Theodoto* 78,2, it is not only knowledge which makes us free, but also the "bath." Baptism in the spirit gives people the power to counter the evil force present in their hylic nature. The importance of this rite resulted in a proliferation of several types and degrees of baptisms and anointings among the Valentinians. Sinning, then, cannot be stopped without knowledge of how the Father expects us to act, and without the force to overcome evil obtained in baptism.

3. THE IMPLICATIONS

3.1

This understanding of sin has important repercussions on how we reconstruct Valentinianism. A comprehensive revision of the traditional picture is clearly in order, but it lies outside the purview of this study. We conclude instead by exploring three areas which now seem most in need of rethinking: the role of the psychics, the presence of sacraments, and the Christian nature of Valentinianism.

3.2.1

The traditional view of the psychics, which remains normative in modern scholarship, derives mainly from Irenaeus, and is supported by Clement of Alexandria.[6] Judith Kovacs reiterates the main points in the opening remarks of her thesis on Clement and the Valentinians: "The Valentinians claimed that most Christians were imperfect psychics, who worshipped the inferior god of the law, while they themselves were the perfect and spiritual children of the true Father."[7] According to this perspective, the "Valentinians" are an elite, highly restricted group of pneumatics[8] who are saved by their pneumatic seed which has been awakened by the Savior, and who can act exactly as they please. On the other side of the equation are the hylics, who form the bulk of humanity and whose actions also play no role in their salvation. The crucial difference is that the hylics are doomed to destruction regardless of what they do. The destinies of both the pneumatics and the hylics, then, are predetermined. The psychics fall in the middle in a triple division of humanity. They are the "Catholic Church" or the "Christians" who have no pneumatic element in them and can never expect

---

[6] Notably Irenaeus, *Adversus haereses* I,6,1–4; and Clement, *Stromata* II,10–15.

[7] Judith L. Kovacs, "Clement of Alexandria and the Valentinian Gnostics" (Ph.D. diss., Columbia, 1978), 1. Kovacs's argument is that Clement attempted to counter these (alleged) Valentinian charges, both openly, when he attacked them by name (i.e. in 14 passages in the *Stromata*), and implicitly in several other places. She also claims that Clement's position remained consistent, in spite of being influenced significantly by Valentinianism.

[8] Cf. Clement, *Excerpta ex Theodoto* 56,2: πολλοὶ μὲν οἱ ὑλικοί, οὐ πολλοὶ δὲ οἱ ψυχικοί· σπάνιοι δὲ οἱ πνευματικοί.

to live in the Pleroma. Without guidance, they are doomed with the hylics. But they are taught by the pneumatics that if they lead blameless lives they can expect to survive the final holocaust and dwell in the only region which will survive outside the Pleroma. In effect, the psychics replace the blacks in this form of apartheid, and they owe their future well-being to the guidance of their white masters. Not surprisingly, Irenaeus rejects this second-class standing, and launches an all-out attack against the Valentinian understanding of the psychics.

3.2.2
Theoretically, this depiction of the psychics is not without its problems, despite its solid backing by the earliest patristic sources. From a philosophical perspective, the psychics seem out of place in a dualistic system which posits the descent and reintegration of the pneuma followed by a final destruction of matter. What happens ultimately to the psychics who remain outside the Pleroma? Does the continued existence of an Ogdoad not contribute to instability? Would it not make more sense to assume that the psychics end up either in the Pleroma or as part of the final destruction? From a NT perspective one can argue that some humans will be excluded from salvation either through choice or through God's predetermined plan, but there is no textual support for the continued existence of a middle group—comparable in some ways to the "godfearers"—which keeps this intermediate status *ad infinitum*. If Valentinianism emerges out of second century Christianity, how does one explain this particular role of the psychics? From a sociological perspective the problems are even greater. How could the Valentinians expect to attract many adherents by arguing that only a tiny fraction of humanity qualified as pneumatics, and all the rest were doomed (by nature) to exclusion from the Pleroma? And why would Irenaeus be so worried about the defection of so many members of his own church to such a group? Would Christians have swarmed to join a dissident group which could transfer their status from "whites" to "blacks" in the age to come?

Several factors, then, point to the need to alter the accepted view of the psychics within Valentinianism in order to include the possibility of equal salvation for both psychics and pneumatics. The problem is how to interpret the patristic sources which strongly suggest otherwise. Scholars who have confronted this issue have approached it in two ways. One shows more sensitivity to redaction-critical concerns, the other to the separation and stratification of sources.

3.2.3
Elaine Pagels is the prime example of the former, and "Conflicting Versions of Valentinian Eschatology"[9] offers the most extensive discussion of her position.

---

[9] Elaine Pagels, "Conflicting Versions of Valentinian Eschatology: Irenaeus' Treatise vs. the Excerpts from Theodotus," *HTR* 67 (1974) 35–53.

She argues in this article that Irenaeus (*Adv. haer.* 1,7.1) and Clement (*Exc. ex Theod.*) present two different views of the role of the psychics in the end times. Irenaeus emphasizes the divisions between the psychics and the pneumatics, and claims that only the latter will enter the Pleroma. Clement emphasizes the unity of these groups. He distinguishes between the ψυχικοί and the πνευματικοί on the one hand and the ψυχικά and πνευματικά on the other, believing that in the end the ψυχικοί, stripped of their ψυχικά, will join the πνευματικοί in the Pleroma. Moreover, claiming that both Irenaeus and Clement tap into the same source for these views, Pagels argues that Clement has followed his source faithfully while Irenaeus has revised it considerably for polemical reasons. As she says:[10]

> Irenaeus' representation of Valentinian eschatology has so condi-
> tioned its subsequent interpretation that to challenge his interpretive
> structure requires nothing less than to reconceive our understanding
> of Valentinian soteriology . . . . Contrary to Irenaeus' version of
> Valentinian eschatology, the distinctions between psychics and pneu-
> matics are not eternally sustained. They have proven to be merely
> provisional—for the duration of the *oikonomia.* After this, all are
> restored into eternal equality and harmony; the Father has become
> "all in all" . . . . Existentially, then, throughout the *oikonomia,* there
> seems to be, as Irenaeus says, "two Gods" and three types of human
> beings. Ontologically—as the consummation will disclose—there is
> only *one* God, and *two* alternate human destinies—reprobation and
> redemption.

Pagels's hypothesis is appealing; the problem is that it does not enjoy suffi-
cient textual support, as several scholars have noted![11] J. F. McCue's points strike
at the heart of the matter:[12]

> 1) *Much* of Pagels's argument is based on parts of *Exc. Thdot.* that
> are not, by anyone's account, based upon the same source as the *Haer.*
> passage in question; and 2) . . . even these texts, as well as those that

---

[10] Pagels, "Conflicting Versions," 36, 50–51, 53. She also takes up this issue in *The Johannine Gospel in Gnostic Exegesis: Heracleon's Commentary on John,* SBLMS 17 (Nashville: Abingdon Press, 1973), 94–97, where she adds elements from Heracleon to support Theodotus and to counter Irenaeus.

[11] See William R. Schoedel's review of *The Johannine Gospel* in *JBL* 93 (1974) 316; Ekkehard Mühlenberg, "Wieviel Erlösungen kennt der Gnostiker Herakleon?" *ZNW* 66 (1975) 170–93; Robert Grant's review of *The Johannine Gospel* and *The Gnostic Paul* in *RSR* 3 (1977) 32; Kovacs, "Clement of Alexandria and the Valentinian Gnostics," 35–36; and James F. McCue, "Conflicting Versions of Valentinianism? Irenaeus and the *Excerpta ex Theodoto,*" in *The Rediscovery of Gnosticism,* I, 404–16.

[12] McCue, "Conflicting Versions," 405.

are based on the common source, give basically the same account of matters as does *Haer.* 1.7.1.

The distinction between the *pneumatikoi/psychikoi* and *pneumatika/psychika* does not emerge from this Clementine text (or any other),[13] and the *Excerpta* clearly end with the psychics rejoicing *in the Ogdoad* over the marriage shared by the pneumatics in the Pleroma. Clement indeed presents the psychics positively, as we saw in the second chapter, but both he and Irenaeus posit a lower level of salvation for them.

3.2.4

Quispel takes a different approach.[14] He interprets the role of the psychics by separating the Valentinian sources into Western and Eastern camps and by isolating an *Urlehre* deriving from Valentinus himself. Quispel claims that Valentinus "envisaged only the world dissolved and the πνεῦμα reintegrated,"[15] allowing salvation only for the pneumatics. Subsequently the "Western school" of the movement (represented by Ptolemy and Heracleon) allowed some psychics to be saved—but only partly so, and as a concession to other Christians, thereby introducing an element of instability. S. Pétrement modifies Quispel's position somewhat by making Valentinus himself responsible for the shift. She claims that Valentinus's original doctrine did not include psychics at all; only after his departure from the Roman church did he equate the psychics with the "Christians" he had left behind.[16] In either case, the partial salvation of the psychics is not considered part of Valentinus's original preaching.

The main problem with this approach is that it relies too heavily on speculation. Our sources do not allow us to separate documents—or even evidence—into Western and Eastern camps, or to decide what was part of Valentinus's own teaching (let alone to separate his teaching into early and later parts!).[17] When Quispel insists that "Valentinus himself recognized no such intermediate state of salvation [since he] was a consistent thinker,"[18] he is not only disparaging other Valentinian thinkers, but conveniently places on Valentinus a solution to the psychic problem for which he provides no textual support. Moreover, he is assuming that it is a solution which did not appeal to Valentinus's followers.

---

[13] Cf. especially Schoedel's review of *The Johannine Gospel,* 316; Mühlenberg, "Wieviel Erlösungen," 192; and McCue, "Conflicting Versions," 413.

[14] Gilles Quispel, "Valentinian Gnosis and the *Apocryphon of John,*" in *The Rediscovery of Gnosticism,* I, 124-25.

[15] Quispel, "Valentinian Gnosis," 130.

[16] Pétrement, *Le Dieu séparé,* 273-74.

[17] Quispel states that "an urgent task for Valentinian studies is the examination of differences between the Oriental and the Western schools" ("Valentinian Gnosis," 129), but this is a daunting task given the lack of evidence from the sources.

[18] Quispel, "Valentinian Gnosis," 130.

3.2.5

Our study of sin in Valentinianism has shed additional light on the psychics. The evidence from both groups of sources has pointed to the need to reassess the traditional view of these psychics. Surprisingly, the information provided by the Nag Hammadi sources in this regard has differed significantly from that provided by the Fathers.

The patristic sources emphasize the tripartite division of humanity,[19] enforcing the differences between the psychics and pneumatics. At the same time, the focus on sin has revealed the important role played by the psychics in this system. In the *Excerpta ex Theodoto,* for instance, more attention is placed on the psychics than on the pneumatics, and their salvation is one of the author's major concerns. Moreover, the patristic sources reveal few negative feelings towards the psychics; on the contrary, every effort is made to help them avoid destruction. This suggests (*contra* Pétrement) that the psychics as a group were not created as a way of dealing either polemically or patronizingly with the rest of the Christians. It also suggests that the Fathers have erred in making Valentinianism a movement of pneumatics alone, and perhaps also in emphasizing the distance between the psychics and pneumatics. Polemical and apologetic reasons probably are responsible for their revisionist presentation. The Fathers surely would have been insulted at being told that they were not on the pneumatic level (cf. Irenaeus's many sarcastic comments throughout his work).

The Nag Hammadi sources paint a different picture. The tripartite division of humanity does not stand out, and the psychics are placed side by side with the pneumatics "on the right side."[20] Actually, a bipartite division is the distinguishing feature of these works, and in some of them (e.g. *The Gospel of Philip, A Valentinian Exposition*) the left (or material) side is omitted altogether. What applies to the pneumatics tends to apply to the psychics as well, including a concern for proper actions and the avoidance of sin. This provides support for Pagels's hypothesis that the Valentinians envisaged the union of the pneumatics and the purified psychics in the Pleroma. What is difficult for her to prove using patristic sources becomes easier using those from the Nag Hammadi collection.

The portrayal of the psychics in the Nag Hammadi sources also suggests that the Valentinian understanding of people is essentially Pauline. The clearest expression of Paul's thought on this issue occurs in 1 Corinthians 2:6–3:3:

[6] σοφίαν δὲ λαλοῦμεν ἐν τοῖς τελείοις, σοφίαν δὲ οὐ τοῦ αἰῶνος τούτου οὐδὲ

---

[19] Cf. Sagnard's argument that this tripartite division "est constitutive de la gnose valentinienne" (*La gnose,* 478).

[20] A clear division between hylics, psychics and pneumatics occurs only in *The Tripartite Tractate.* Yet even in this work the psychics are portrayed positively and are said not to be "inclined to evil" (106,13). In addition, the main division in this work is between "those on the left" (the hylics) and "those on the right" (the others—132,9–10). The focus is on the latter. As well, the Savior is concerned with the salvation of "all those on the right" (132,8–9).

τῶν ἀρχόντων τοῦ αἰῶνος τούτου τῶν καταργουμένων· ἀλλὰ λαλοῦμεν θεοῦ σοφίαν ἐν μυστηρίῳ τὴν ἀποκεκρυμμένην, ἥν προώρισεν ὁ θεὸς πρὸ τῶν αἰώνων εἰς δόξαν ἡμῶν· . . . [12] ἡμεῖς δὲ οὐ τὸ πνεῦμα τοῦ κόσμου ἐλάβομεν ἀλλὰ τὸ πνεῦμα τὸ ἐκ τοῦ θεοῦ, ἵνα εἰδῶμεν τὰ ὑπὸ τοῦ θεοῦ χαρισθέντα ἡμῖν· [13] ἃ καὶ λαλοῦμεν οὐκ ἐν διδακτοῖς ἀνθρωπίνης σοφίας λόγοις ἀλλ' ἐν διδακτοῖς πνεύματος, πνευματικοῖς πνευματικὰ συγκρίνοντες. [14] ψυχικὸς δὲ ἄνθρωπος οὐ δέχεται τὰ τοῦ πνεύματος τοῦ θεοῦ· μωρία γὰρ αὐτῷ ἐστιν καὶ οὐ δύναται γνῶναι, ὅτι πνευματικῶς ἀνακρίνεται· [15] ὁ δὲ πνευματικὸς ἀνακρίνει [τὰ] πάντα, αὐτὸς δὲ ὑπ' οὐδενὸς ἀνακρίνεται. [16] τίς γὰρ ἔγνω νοῦν κυρίου, ὃς συμβιβάσει αὐτόν; ἡμεῖς δὲ νοῦν Χριστοῦ ἔχομεν. [3:1] κἀγώ, ἀδελφοί, οὐκ ἠδυνήθην λαλῆσαι ὑμῖν ὡς πνευματικοῖς ἀλλ' ὡς σαρκίνοις, ὡς νηπίοις ἐν Χριστῷ. [2] γάλα ὑμᾶς ἐπότισα, οὐ βρῶμα, οὔπω γὰρ ἐδύνασθε. ἀλλ' οὐδὲ ἔτι νῦν δύνασθε, [3] ἔτι γὰρ σαρκικοί ἐστε. ὅπου γὰρ ἐν ὑμῖν ζῆλος καὶ ἔρις, οὐχὶ σαρκικοί ἐστε καὶ κατὰ ἄνθρωπον περιπατεῖτε;

Yet among the mature we do impart wisdom, although it is not a wisdom of this age or of the rulers of this age, who are doomed to pass away. But we impart a secret and hidden wisdom of God, which God decreed before the ages for our glorification. . . . Now we have received not the spirit of the world, but the Spirit which is from God, that we might understand the gifts bestowed on us by God. And we impart this in words not taught by human wisdom but taught by the Spirit, interpreting spiritual truths to those who possess the Spirit. The unspiritual man does not receive the gifts of the Spirit of God, for they are folly to him, and he is not able to understand them because they are spiritually discerned. The spiritual man judges all things, but is himself to be judged by no one. "For who has known the mind of the Lord so as to instruct him?" But we have the mind of Christ. But I, brethren, could not address you as spiritual men, but as men of the flesh, as babes in Christ. I fed you with milk, not solid food; for you were not ready for it; and even yet you are not ready, for you are still of the flesh. For while there is jealousy and strife among you, are you not of the flesh, and behaving like ordinary men?

Those to whom these remarks are directed (Paul's opponents and others in the Corinthian community) could easily have reacted to this message the same way Irenaeus did to the Ptolemaic preaching, for Paul clearly states that he functions on the pneumatic level — that he has "the mind of Christ" — and only communicates fully with other πνευματικοί or τελείοι. Furthermore, he admits to being beyond human reproach, and reprimands the ψυχικοί for being drawn down by the σαρκικοί. Paul goes so far as to state that the ψυχικός "does not receive the gifts of the Spirit of God . . . and . . . is not able to understand them" (2:14). Yet these ψυχικοί include the Corinthians who are dear to him. In the same letter he says that God's Spirit dwells in them (3:16) and that they can expect to share equally in the coming salvation (15:42–58).

Paul considers the Christians in Corinth to be second-class Christians in terms of their ability to discern the spiritual truths, yet he also believes that they are far superior to the non-Christians who have no chance for salvation. He groups the ψυχικοί and πνευματικοί, and takes it for granted that both would be saved. Moreover, Paul suggests that the ψυχικοί could progress to the pneumatic level, and believes that the non-Christian can become a ψυχικός if and when God allows it.[21] The Valentinian understanding of the psychics was probably simply Pauline —sometimes stressing the unity of all Christians which is such a *Leitmotiv* in Paul's letters, other times accentuating the differences between the ψυχικοί and πνευματικοί as Paul himself occasionally does.

3.3

> Parler de la sacramentaire gnostique semble un paradoxe. Gnose et sacrement devraient s'exclure. Comment en effet concilier la médiation de rites matériels et contingents avec la nécessité d'un salut qui s'accomplit dans une connaissance simple et immédiate, illumination par l'ineffable d'où il est issu, de l'esprit égaré en ce monde? Les sacrements sont incongrus dans le gnosticisme pour cette raison qu'au dire d'Irénée avançaient certains valentiniens: "On ne doit pas accomplir le mystère de la Puissance inexprimable et invisible au moyen de créatures visibles et corruptibles, ni le mystère des réalités irreprésentables et incorporelles au moyen de choses sensibles et corporelles. La 'rédemption' parfaite, c'est la connaissance même de la Grandeur inexprimable" [*Adv. haer.* I.21.4].[22]

J.-M. Sevrin's remarks are based on two important facts: in theory, sacraments ought to play no role in Valentinianism, and the Fathers often underline this point. For these reasons, studies of Valentinianism usually downplay or deny the importance of sacraments.[23]

The patristic sources themselves, though, allow for another interpretation of Valentinian *praxis*. Most notable in this regard are the references to Valentinian

---

[21] Romans 9–11 highlights the deterministic pole of Paul's thought. He argues in this pericope that God deliberately hardened the hearts of the Jews in order to allow the Gentiles an opportunity for salvation.

[22] This is the opening paragraph of Jean-Marie Sevrin's *Le dossier baptismal séthien. Études sur la sacramentaire gnostique*, BCNHSE 2 (Québec: Les Presses de l'Université Laval, 1986), 1. Sevrin's fine study explores the importance of baptism in Sethianism.

[23] Jonas (*The Gnostic Religion*, 175) argues that Valentinianism establishes "the elaborate position of *gnosis* in the soteriological scheme: from being a qualifying condition for salvation, still requiring the co-operation of sacraments and of divine grace, from being a means among means, it becomes the adequate form of salvation itself." So also Foerster (*Gnosis*, 17): "For the gnostics a sacrament was strictly superfluous." Notable recent exceptions to this position are Rudolph, *Gnosis*, 204–47; and Green, "Ritual in Valentinian Gnosticism," 109–24.

rituals found sprinkled in a variety of contexts. These rituals are not always considered sacramental in nature—i.e. providing access to, or manifesting, salvation[24] —and they are sometimes applied only to the psychics, but the frequency with which they occur in patristic discussions of Valentinianism and the variants which appear in each Father strongly allude to their importance and widespread use. Marcus, for instance, is accused of deception and knavery by both Irenaeus and Hippolytus (*Adv. haer.* I.21,1-5; *Ref.* 6,41), but one must not overlook the eucharistic setting of these Marcosian practices. We have also seen how baptism stands out in virtually every patristic account of Valentinianism examined in this study. In effect, then, the Fathers have argued against their own position that "visible and corruptible" rites have nothing to do with "the mystery of incorporeal realities."

The student of Valentinianism must also be aware of certain limitations inherent in the patristic sources' presentation of sacraments. W. Bousset appreciated this at the turn of the century.[25]

> Freilich ist das Material, das sich uns hier bietet, nun nicht so reichhaltig, wie man es nach dem Charakter der Gnosis erwarten sollte. Das liegt aber nur an der Art unserer Quellen. Die Kirchenvätern sind an der religiösen Praxis der gnostischen Sekten, die wohl auch vielfach mit Erfolg geheimgehalten wurde, gleichgültig vorübergegangen. Sie interessierte im wesentlichen nur das bunte Rankenwerk der gnostischen religiösen Gedanken und Vorstellungen; auf den Kern der Dinge drangen sie nicht. Daher sind Notizen über die sakramentale Praxis und Frömmigkeit der Gnostiker uns nur gelegentlich erhalten.

Before the Nag Hammadi documents were published, then, the sources presented a sketchy and sometimes contradictory picture of Valentinian sacramentality. The little that was said about the subject on the one hand suggested that rituals and sacraments were unimportant to Valentinians, but on the other hand strongly hinted that sacraments were a vital part of that movement.

The Nag Hammadi works have reinforced the presence and importance of sacraments in the Valentinian communities. The list most commonly used occurs in *The Gospel of Philip:* "The Lord did everything in a mystery: baptism, chrism, eucharist, redemption and bridal chamber" (67,27-30). These appear to be listed in ascending order in this work. It is far from certain, though, whether all of these were separate sacraments,[26] and whether they applied to most Valentinian

---

[24] For this definition, see Sevrin, *Le dossier baptismal,* 2.

[25] Wilhelm Bousset, *Hauptprobleme der Gnosis,* FRLANT 10 (Göttingen: Vandenhoeck & Ruprecht, 1907), 278 (which is part of his chapter on sacraments; 276-319). Cf. also Sevrin's remarks, *Le dossier baptismal,* 2-3.

[26] Sevrin questions the sacramental nature of the "bridal chamber," and argues that the author of *The Gospel of Philip* may not have been thinking of a separate sacrament when he used this expression. See also his study "Les noces spirituelles."

communities. As Rudolph observes, the Nag Hammadi sources "have revealed nothing dramatically new . . . , apart from insights into the piety and cultic practice of the gnostic communities and what they thought of themselves."[27]

The Gospel of Philip provides the most information about Valentinian sacramentalism,[28] but other works are not silent on this issue.[29] The three sacraments which often recur are baptism, chrism and eucharist. The first two especially are frequently linked.[30] Recently, in Sevrin's words, "l'idée d'un complexe initiatique limité au baptême, à l'onction et à l'eucharistie gagne du terrain."[31] The fundamental importance of baptism in this "initiation complex" is indisputable. In this regard, the Nag Hammadi works have reinforced the patristic evidence.[32]

Much has been written about second century Christian baptism,[33] and the

---

[27] Rudolph, *Gnosis,* 208.

[28] Much has been written about sacraments in *The Gospel of Philip* (see notes 70–71 of the previous chapter). Cf. especially three unpublished doctoral dissertations: H.-G. Gaffron, "Studien zum koptischen Philippusevangelium unter besonderer Berücksichtigung der Sakramente" (Bonn, 1969); J.-M. Sevrin, "Pratique et doctrine des sacrements dans l'Évangile selon Philippe" (Louvain, 1972); and E. T. Rewolinski, "The Use of Sacramental Language in the Gospel of Philip (CG II,3)" (Harvard, 1978).

[29] E.g. *A Valentinian Exposition* includes sections on eucharist and baptism; *The Tripartite Tractate* discusses baptism (e.g. 127,30–34); and *The Gospel of Truth* mentions chrism (36,13–20).

[30] In this context Rudolph's remarks do justice to the Valentinian works from Nag Hammadi: "Anointing with oil has a greater representation than baptism in Gnosis and in some texts is even regarded as more significant. In general, however, it is taken closely with the baptismal ceremony—the anointing taking place either before or after the baptism . . . . Often the anointing is taken as a 'sealing,' the ointment as a 'seal,' i.e. it is a protective act and a declaration of property . . . . In the foreground however is the concept of redemption, the gift of immortality which is transmitted by anointing" (*Gnosis,* 228–29). The Pauline communities also may have combined chrism with water baptism. Cf. 2 Corinthians 1:21–22 and Ephesians 1:13–14; 4:30 which connect the "sealing with the Spirit" and baptism.

[31] Sevrin, *Le dossier baptismal,* 4 (referring to Rewolinski's thesis for support).

[32] A pericope from *The Testimony of Truth* (55–56) may incorporate an anti-Valentinian polemic. The text is too fragmentary to be certain. What is particularly intriguing is the possibility that the polemic is directed at Valentinian baptismal practices. The Valentinians seem to be accused of practicing a water baptism, which (in the eyes of the critic) is really "a baptism of death" (cf. also 30,30–31,33; 69,7–24). See Pearson, *Nag Hammadi Codices IX and X,* 107–16; and "Anti-Heretical Warnings in Codex IX from Nag Hammadi," in *Essays on the Nag Hammadi Texts in Honor of Pahor Labib,* ed. by M. Krause (Leiden: Brill, 1975), 145–54.

[33] Franz Dölger's works are still useful. Cf. especially *Der Exorzismus im altchristlichen Taufritual. Eine religionsgeschichtliche Studie,* SGKA 3 (Paderborn: Verlag von Ferdinand Schöningh, 1909), 70–193; *Sphragis. Eine altchristliche Taufbezeichnung in ihren Beziehungen zur profanen und religiösen Kultur des Altertums,* SGKA 5 (Paderborn: Verlag von Ferdinand Schöningh, 1911). He showed in *Der Exorzismus* how baptism for

Valentinian practices — as far as they can be discerned — are decidedly Christian. Fortunately, a detailed first-hand account of baptism has survived in *The Apostolic Tradition* of Hippolytus (chapters 15–21).[34] Although the Christian sources (both Valentinian and non-Valentinian) reveal some fluidity in the baptismal practices,[35] the process described in *The Apostolic Tradition* is consistent with that found elsewhere, and can serve as a rough tool for gauging what occurred in Valentinian communities. The initiation process described in this work is long and complicated. It begins with the candidate's decision to become a Christian and usually ends three years later with an elaborate baptism ceremony, immediately followed by a eucharist and the convert's proclamation that he or she will go forth in the world to do good works. The baptism itself is preceded by a two-day fast and an all-night vigil, then by a priestly anointing (with one type of oil) which is part of the exorcism process. The candidate is then immersed fully in water three times, each time followed by a question-and-answer exchange. Afterwards the person emerges from the water and is anointed "with the oil of thanksgiving" (24) by the priest, then again by the bishop in the church. This is followed by a eucharist where each Christian tastes from one of three cups. Baptism and chrism clearly are intertwined in this particular ritual, and the eucharist concludes the ceremony. Multiple chrisms are intended to ensure that the evil powers are completely removed. The final acknowledgment that the Christian can finally go out and act properly reveals how sinful acts were linked to control by evil powers, and how baptism cleansed the candidate of sins and removed him or her from this control by the evil powers.

Valentinians incorporated sacraments into their communities. This is undeniable, especially since the Nag Hammadi evidence has come to light. The one sacrament most frequently mentioned, and perhaps the most significant, was baptism, which included chrism(s) and probably also the Christian's first eucharist. In this regard, the Valentinian practices are consistent with those found among other Christians in the second century, and the variations detected in the sources and highlighted by the Fathers are no more significant than those found, for instance, between Justin's *First Apology* and Hippolytus's *Apostolic Tradition*.

3.4
    Nobody disputes the presence of a strong Christian component in Valentinianism, regardless of what view one holds on the origins of Gnosticism.[36] The

---

many Christians entailed rebirth (παλιγγενεσία), sealing (σφραγίς), enlightenment (φώτισμα) and the exorcisms of evil spirits. Cf. also Sagnard, *Extraits de Théodote,* Appendice F ("Le baptême au deuxième siècle et son interprétation valentinien"), 229–39.

[34] Bernard Botte, *Hippolyte de Rome. La tradition apostolique,* SC 11bis (Paris: Les Éditions du Cerf, 1968).

[35] Cf. Sagnard, *Extraits de Théodote,* 229–39.

[36] Notwithstanding the *Refutatio*'s argument that Valentinian ideas are fundamentally Platonic and Pythagorean, not Christian. This is part of Hippolytus's redactional

role played by the psychics and the importance of sacraments, as we have just seen, reinforces this Christian nature. Unquestionable also is the formative role played by the NT writings, especially the letters of Paul and the Gospel of John. Indeed, the Valentinian use of the NT was both coherent and sophisticated, as several of Pagels's studies have illuminated.[37] Sagnard's remarks on this matter are *apropos:*[38]

> En somme, c'est de l'Église *vivante,* qu'ils sortent, de l'Église telle qu'elle a pu se présenter entre 120 et 150. . . . Cependant, plus qu'à Justin ou au *Pasteur,* plus qu'à la vie contemporaine de l'Église, c'est aux Écrits de la Bible, et surtout au Nouveau Testament, que les Valentiniens recourent sans cesse. . . . Cet emploi constant de l'Écriture Sainte est un des caractères les plus saillants de la gnose *valentinienne.* Quant même nous ne saurions absolumment rien de la vie de ses promoteurs, un fait s'impose avec évidence: ils étaient au sein du christianisme.

On the other hand, the non-Christian and gnostic elements of the movement also are often underscored. These are sometimes considered to be an advantage, sometimes a disadvantage. The Church Fathers were the first to stress the deformative nature of these "pagan intrusions." Irenaeus especially claims that Valentinus "adapted the principles of the so-called gnostic heresy [i.e. that described in I.29–31] to his own teachings" (*Adv. haer.* I,11,1). Christian scholars still often view Valentinianism as a debased form of Christianity. Sagnard's remarks again are fitting, especially in this paragraph which follows his words quoted above:[39]

> Cherchons à pénétrer davantage le choix de ces textes: nous allons découvrir, non sans étonnement, que ce sont d'ordinaire des textes *de valeur authentiquement mystique et très profonde,* qui jouaient à plein dans la vie de l'Église, car le contact avec le Christ était encore très présent: mais cette mystique a été déformée, distendue, et finalement vidée de sa substance, sous l'apport d'éléments païens essayant d'entrer avec elle dans un impossible syncrétisme.

For others, especially the members of the *religionsgeschichtliche Schule,* this "pagan"-Christian syncretism allowed a breath of fresh (i.e. non-Jewish) air to

---

tendency: aligning the Valentinians with the Greek philosophical traditions allows him to refute their claims.

[37] Cf. especially *The Johannine Gospel* (1973); *The Gnostic Paul* (1975); "'The Mystery of the Resurrection': A Gnostic Reading of 1 Corinthians 15," *JBL* 93 (1974) 276–88; "A Valentinian Claim to Esoteric Exegesis of Romans as Basis for Anthropological Theory," *VC* 26 (1972) 241–58; and "Conflicting Versions of Valentinian Eschatology: Irenaeus' Treatise vs. the Excerpts from Theodotus," *HTR* 67 (1974) 35–53.

[38] Sagnard, *La gnose,* 603–04.

[39] Sagnard, *La gnose,* 604–05.

be brought into Christianity by a pre-Christian and predominantly Iranian gnostic stream. R. Reitzenstein and W. Bousset laid the foundation for this viewpoint at the turn of the century, and it is a view which has had a profound effect on NT scholarship through its advocacy by R. Bultmann.[40] Jonas and Rudolph subsequently emphasized the coherence of this "syncretism."[41]

Our study has shown that the Valentinian understanding of sin is fundamentally Christian in nature, and that it emerges naturally out of Pauline speculations about sin. Moreover, we have seen how Valentinian ethics in general reflect the gospel injunctions in the NT, notably those in Matthew's Sermon on the Mount. This position is at odds with that often expressed by scholars. Ménard's analysis of a passage in *The Gospel of Truth* (34,35–35,29) is a good example of the common view:[42]

> C'est une des rares fois où il est fait mention de péché dans notre opuscule. Submergé dans un contexte de mystique hellénistique, le "péché" y a perdu son sens moral. Le ἁμαρτάνειν de la mystique hellénistique, c'est la fatalité, la εἱμαρμένη, où la volonté de l'homme n'est pas mise en jeu, mais où elle est l'enjeu de ces deux forces métaphysiques opposées, la γνῶσις et l'ἄγνοια. C'est le sens de "péché" qu'on rencontre dans le *Corpus Hermeticum* et les religions à mystères: le destin y a remplacé la responsabilité.

Ménard is working within an Irenaean framework which considers Valentinianism to be a form of Christianity that has been distorted and essentially transformed by external, "pagan" influences. The Valentinian understanding of sin which emerges from our study strongly suggests that in fact this was not the case. One need not go to the *Corpus Hermeticum* to understand the Valentinians; the NT is the most useful *Sitz.*

Paul believed that the death of Christ removed the power of sin from people, allowing them to lead sinless lives; at least in theory, for in practice, Christians continued to act improperly, as Paul's letters reveal. Sin remained a vital concern

---

[40] Richard Reitzenstein argued that Gnosticism was not necessarily a Christian phenomenon — in *Poimandres. Studien zur griechisch-ägyptischen und frühchristlichen Literatur* (Leipzig: B. G. Teubner, 1904). Later, he became convinced that the roots of Gnosticism lay in Iran, due to Bousset's study, *Hauptprobleme der Gnosis.* Bousset separated Gnosticism into its component parts, and found pre-Christian analogies to each one. This led to his claim that Gnosticism was a syncretistic combination of pre-Christian elements which crystallized around an Iranian Savior myth. Carsten Colpe submits this "school" to a critical review in *Die religionsgeschichtliche Schule. Darstellung und Kritik ihres Bildes vom gnostischen Erlösermythus,* FRLANT 60 (Göttingen: Vandenhoeck & Ruprecht, 1961). Colpe argues that the evidence does not support the existence of a pre-Christian gnostic redeemer myth. He prefers instead (194–208) to see this myth evolving out of primitive Christian texts rather than having had an influence on them.

[41] Jonas, *The Gnostic Religion;* Rudolph, *Gnosis.*

[42] Ménard, *L'Évangile de vérité,* 167.

for the Pauline communities. The Valentinians claimed that gnosis from the Father removed the power of sin, making the "gnostics" theoretically free from sin. In practice, however, they too continued to be concerned with sin. Salvation through unmerited grace, and even the overthrow of evil, does not lead to "gnostic licentiousness" and ethical indifference for Paul. Neither is this the case for the Valentinians, although for both the possibility of abuse was built into the system.

Actually, one of the few fragments remaining from Valentinus's writings has a decidedly Pauline flavor. Valentinus's argument in Fragment 2 (*Strom.* 2, 114,3–6) is that the evil spirits attached to a person's heart do not allow it to be pure, and lead to improper desires (and, by implication, to improper actions). Providentially, and through no merit of that person, the Father chooses to sanctify a heart. Such a person is blessed because he or she shall see God. Clement objects to this, arguing that a soul never has evil spirits appended to it, and also that it can only be saved through obedience to the law. Clement continues: a Christian must first overcome these fleshly passions if there is to be a chance to withstand the evil spirits. In this argument Valentinus's emphasis on the human need for external and unmerited help is far more Pauline than Clement's plea to Christians to follow the law and struggle to overcome their fleshly passions on their own.[43]

3.5

Valentinianism is a form of second century Christianity,[44] and from a historical perspective it is no less or no more "authentic" than other contemporary expressions of Christianity.

This fundamentally Christian nature of Valentinianism presents a challenge to the historian of early Christianity. If, for instance, the Nag Hammadi works

---

[43] H. Langerbeck emphasizes the Platonic aspects of Gnosticism, but also argues that in matters of faith, gnosis, and evil Valentinus was on a Pauline trajectory; that there was no "Auseinandersetzung zwischen Gnosis und Pistis"—"Die Anthropologie der alexandrischen Gnosis: Interpretationen zu den Fragmenten des Basilides und Valentinus und ihrer Schulen bei Clemens von Alexandrien und Origenes," in his *Aufsätze zur Gnosis: Aus dem Nachlass*, AbhAkGöttingen 69 (Göttingen: Vandenhoeck & Ruprecht, 1967), 44. Cf. also his statement: "Für diese Aufgabe wäre natürlich die Feststellung, dass die Gnosis eine systematische Entfaltung der paulinischen Theologie ist, von Wichtigkeit" (81).

[44] Pétrement argues (in *Le Dieu séparé*) that *all* of Gnosticism, including Valentinianism, emerges out of Christianity. One of her summary statements presents her case well: "Nous avons tenté de faire voir qu'on peut se représenter la formation progressive du gnosticisme en considérant le développement d'une branche du christianisme, la branche paulinienne et johannique. Il nous a semblé que le gnosticisme se dessine peu à peu, à travers une série d'étapes, à partir des tendances gnosticisantes qu'on discerne dans le Nouveau Testament, jusqu'au moment où apparaît nettement, au début du IIe siècle, le gnosticisme proprement dit; et qu'on peut ensuite se représenter l'évolution de celui-ci, sans rupture, jusqu'au moment où il a produit parfois des spéculations qui semblent très différentes du christianisme que nous connaissons" (657).

were read in a Pachomian monastery, how does one explain their acceptance by these fourth century Egyptian monks? More pressing, though, is the need to explain Irenaeus's vehement rejection of these "false brethren." If Valentinus was essentially "au sein du christianisme" (using Sagnard's words), and if we need not go to any outside religious source to understand it, what does this say about Irenaeus and the other heresiologists? Did they seriously misinterpret the Valentinians? Or were they merely "church politicians" afraid of losing their grip on their churches? Other factors surely must be involved. And what does this say about our understanding of Valentinianism? Which aspects of this movement were considered the most threatening, not only to their contemporaries but also to later writers who themselves never encountered a living "Valentinian?" In this regard, our examination of sin in Valentinianism, though narrowly focused, has raised wide-ranging questions about the nature of second century Christianity, which continues to reveal its diversity and creativity.

Bibliography

Primary Sources and Tools of Research

Acta Iohannis. By Eric Junod and Jean-Daniel Kaestli. 2 vols. Corpus Christianorum: Series Apocryphorum, 1–2. Brepols: Turnhout, 1983.

The Ante-Nicene Christian Library. Edinburgh: T. & T. Clark, 1867–97. American edition: *The Ante-Nicene Fathers. Translations of the Writings of the Fathers down to A.D. 325.* 1885–1906. Reprint. Grand Rapids: Wm. B. Eerdmans Publishing Company, 1956–68.

The Apologies of Justin Martyr. Ed. by A. W. F. Blunt. Cambridge: Cambridge University Press, 1911.

The Apostolic Fathers. Ed. and trans. by Kirsopp Lake. 2 vols. Loeb Classical Library. London: William Heinemann, 1912–13.

The Books of Jeu and the Untitled Text in the Bruce Codex. Ed. by Carl Schmidt. Trans. by Violet MacDermot. Nag Hammadi Studies, 13. Leiden: Brill, 1978.

Clemens Alexandrinus. Erster Band. *Protrepticus und Paedagogus.* Hrsg. von Otto Stählin. 3. Auflage von Ursula Treu. Die griechischen christlichen Schriftsteller der ersten drei Jahrhunderte, 12. Berlin: Akademie-Verlag, 1972.

Clemens Alexandrinus. Zweiter Band. *Stromata Buch I–VI.* Hrsg. von Otto Stählin. 4. Auflage von Ludwig Früchtel und Ursula Treu. Die griechischen christlichen Schriftsteller der ersten drei Jahrhunderte, 52 (1. Auflage, 15). Berlin: Akademie-Verlag, 1985.

Clemens Alexandrinus. Dritter Band. *Stromata Buch VII und VIII. Excerpta ex Theodoto. Eclogae Propheticae. Quis dives salvetur. Fragmente.* Hrsg. von Otto Stählin. 2. Auflage von Ludwig Früchtel und Ursula Treu. Die griechischen christlichen Schriftsteller der ersten drei Jahrhunderte, 17^2 (1. Auflage, 17). Leipzig: Akademie Verlag, 1970.

Clemens Alexandrinus. Vierter Band. *Register.* Hrsg. von Otto Stählin. Die griechischen christlichen Schriftsteller der ersten drei Jahrhunderte, 39. Leipzig: J. C. Hinrichs'sche Buchhandlung, 1936. Supplemented by U. Treu, *Clemens Alexandrinus IV. Register I: Zitatenregister, Testimonienregister, Initienregister, Eigennamenregister.* Berlin: Akademie-Verlag, 1980.

Clément d'Alexandrie. Extraits de Théodote. Par François-M.-M. Sagnard. Sources chrétiennes, 23. 2ième éd. Paris: Les Éditions du Cerf, 1970.

Clément d'Alexandrie. Le Pédagogue. Livre I. Par Henri-Irénée Marrou. Trad. par Marguerite Harl. Sources chrétiennes, 70. Paris: Les Éditions du Cerf, 1960.

Clément d'Alexandrie. Le Pédagogue. Livre II. Par Claude Mondésert. Notes de Henri-Irénée Marrou. Sources chrétiennes, 108. Paris: Les Éditions du Cerf, 1965.

Clément d'Alexandrie. Le Pédagogue. Livre III. Par Claude Mondésert et Chantal Matray. Notes de Henri-Irénée Marrou. Sources chrétiennes, 158. Paris: Les Éditions du Cerf, 1970.

Clément d'Alexandrie. Le Protreptique. Par Claude Mondésert. 2ième éd. avec André Plassart. Sources chrétiennes, 2. Paris: Les Éditions du Cerf, 1949.

Clément d'Alexandrie. Les Stromates. Stromate I. Par Marcel Caster. Introduction de Claude Mondésert. Sources chrétiennes, 30. Paris: Les Éditions du Cerf, 1951.

Clément d'Alexandrie. Les Stromates. Stromate II. Par Claude Mondésert. Notes et introduction de P. Th. Camelot. Sources chrétiennes, 38. Paris: Les Éditions du Cerf, 1954.

Clément d'Alexandrie. Les Stromates. Stromate V. Par Alain le Boulluec et Pierre Voulet. 2 vols. Sources chrétiennes, 278-79. Paris: Les Éditions du Cerf, 1981.

Clement of Alexandria. The Exhortation to the Greeks. The Rich Man's Salvation and To the Newly Baptized. Trans. by G. W. Butterworth. 2 vols. Loeb Classical Library. London: William Heinemann, 1919.

A Coptic Dictionary. Compiled by W. E. Crum. Oxford: Clarendon Press, 1939.

Coptic Gnostic Papyri in the Coptic Museum at Old Cairo. Ed. by Pahor Labib. Cairo: Cairo Government Press, 1956.

Corpus Hermeticum. Ed. and trans. by Arthur Darby Nock and André Marie Jean Festugière. 4 vols. Association Guillaume Budé. Paris: Société d'Édition "Les Belles Lettres," 1945-54.

De resurrectione (Epistula ad Rheginum). Codex Jung f. XXII^r–f. XXV^v (p. 43-50). Ed. by Michel Malinine, Henri-Charles Puech, Gilles Quispel, Walter Till, Robert McL. Wilson, and Jan Zandee. Zürich/Stuttgart: Rascher Verlag, 1963.

Die drei Versionen des Apocryphon des Johannes im Koptischen Museum zu Alt-Kairo. Hrsg. von Martin Krause und Pahor Labib. Abhandlung des Deutschen Archäologischen Instituts Kairo, Koptische Reihe, Band I. Wiesbaden: Otto Harrassowitz, 1962.

Epiphanius. Erster Band. Ancoratus und Panarion haer. 1-33. Hrsg. von Karl Holl. Die griechischen christlichen Schriftsteller der ersten drei Jahrhunderte, 25. Leipzig: J. C. Hinrichs'sche Buchhandlung, 1915.

Epiphanius. Zweiter Band. Panarion haer. 34-64. Hrsg. von Karl Holl.

2. Auflage hrsg. von Jürgen Dummer. Die griechischen christlichen Schriftsteller der ersten drei Jahrhunderte, 31. Berlin: Akademie-Verlag, 1980.

Epiphanius. Dritter Band. Panarion haer. 65–80. De Fide. Hrsg. von Karl Holl. Die griechischen christlichen Schriftsteller der ersten drei Jahrhunderte, 37. Leipzig: J. C. Hinrichs'sche Buchhandlung, 1933.

The Epistle to Rheginos. A Valentinian Letter on the Resurrection. Ed. by Malcolm Lee Peel. New Testament Library. London/Philadelphia: SCM/Westminster, 1969. Revised German translation: *Gnosis und Auferstehung. Die Brief an Rheginus von Nag Hammadi.* Trans. by W.-P. Funk. Neukirchen-Vluyn: Neukirchener Verlag, 1974.

"*Das Evangelium nach Philippus.* Ein Evangelium der Valentinianer aus dem Funde von Nag-Hamadi." Hrsg. von Hans-Martin Schenke. *Theologische Literaturzeitung* 84 (1959): 1–26.

Das Evangelium nach Philippos. Hrsg. von Walter Till. Patristische Texte und Studien, 2. Berlin: Walter de Gruyter, 1963.

Evangelium Veritatis. Codex Jung f. VIII^v–XVI^v (p. 16–32) / f. XIX^r–XXII^r (p. 37–43). Ed. by Michel Malinine, Henri-Charles Puech, and Gilles Quispel. Studien aus dem C. G. Jung-Institut, VI. Zürich: Rascher Verlag, 1956.

Evangelium Veritatis. Codex Jung f. XVII^r–f. XVIII^v (p. 33–36). Ed. by Michel Malinine, Henri-Charles Puech, Gilles Quispel and Walter Till. Studien aus dem C. G. Jung-Institut, VI. Zürich: Rascher Verlag, 1961.

L'Évangile de Vérité. Rétroversion grecque et commentaire. Par Jacques-É. Ménard. Paris: Letouzey & Ané, 1962.

L'Évangile de Vérité. Par Jacques-É. Ménard. Nag Hammadi Studies, 2. Leiden: E. J. Brill, 1972.

L'Évangile selon Philippe. Introduction, texte, traduction, commentaire. Par Jacques-É. Ménard. Paris: Letouzey & Ané, 1967.

The Excerpta ex Theodoto of Clement of Alexandria. Ed. by Robert Pierce Casey. London: Christophers, 1934.

L'Exposé valentinien. Les fragments sur le baptême et sur l'eucharistie (NH XI,2). Par Jacques-É. Ménard. Bibliothèque copte de Nag Hammadi, Section «Textes», 14. Québec: Les Presses de l'Université Laval, 1985.

The Facsimile Edition of the Nag Hammadi Codices. Ed. by James M. Robinson et al. 11 vols. Leiden: Brill, 1972–79.

The Fragments of Heracleon. Ed. by Alan England Brooke. Texts and Studies, vol. 1, no. 4. Cambridge: University Press, 1891.

Gnosis. A Selection of Gnostic Texts. Ed. by Werner Foerster. Trans. and ed. by Robert McL. Wilson. 2 vols. Oxford: Clarendon, 1972–74.

The Gnostic Treatise on the Resurrection from Nag Hammadi. Ed. by Bentley Layton. Harvard Dissertations in Religion, 12. Missoula, MT: Scholars Press, 1979.

Gnostische und hermetische Schriften aus Codex II und Codex VI. Hrsg. von Martin Krause und Pahor Labib. Abhandlung des Deutschen Archäologischen Instituts Kairo. Koptische Reihe, Band 2. Glückstadt: Verlag J. J. Augustin, 1971.

"The Gospel of Philip." Trans. by C.-J. de Catanzaro. *Journal of Theological Studies* 13 (1962): 35-71.

The Gospel of Philip. Ed. by Robert McL. Wilson. London: A. R. Mowbray & Co. Limited, 1962.

A Greek-English Lexicon. Compiled by Henry George Liddell, Robert Scott, Henry Stuart Jones, and Roderick McKenzie. 9th ed. Oxford: The Clarendon Press, 1968.

A Greek-English Lexicon of the New Testament and Other Early Christian Literature. Compiled by Walter Bauer. Trans. by William F. Arndt and F. Wilbur Gingrich. 2nd edition revised and augmented by F. Wilbur Gingrich and Frederick W. Danker. Chicago: University of Chicago Press, 1979.

Hermetica. The Ancient Greek and Latin Writings which contain Religious or Philosophic Teachings ascribed to Hermes Trismegistus. Ed. and trans. by Walter Scott (the final volume with the assistance of A. S. Ferguson). 4 vols. Oxford: Clarendon Press, 1924-36.

Hippolyte de Rome. La tradition apostolique d'après les anciennes versions. Par Bernard Botte. 2ième édition. Sources chrétiennes, 11bis. Paris: Les Éditions du Cerf, 1968.

Hippolytus. Refutatio omnium haeresium. Ed. by Miroslav Marcovich. Patristische Texte und Studien, 25. Berlin: Walter de Gruyter, 1986.

Hippolytus Werke. Dritter Band. *Refutatio omnium haeresium.* Hrsg. von Paul Wendland. Die griechischen christlichen Schriftsteller der ersten drei Jahrhunderte, 26. 1916. Reprint. Hildesheim/New York: Georg Olms Verlag, 1977.

Index du Corpus Hermeticum. Par L. Delatte, S. Govaerts, et J. Denooz. Lessico Intellettuale Europeo, 13. Roma: Edizioni dell'Ateneo & Bizzarri, 1977.

Index Patristicus sive clavis patrum apostolicorum operum. Edidit Edgar J. Goodspeed. 1907. Reprint. Naperville, IL: Alec R. Allenson, Inc., 1960.

Index Tertullianeus. Par Gösta Claesson. 3 vols. Paris: Études Augustiniennes, 1974-75.

Irénée de Lyon. Contre les hérésies. Livre I. Par Adelin Rousseau et Louis Doutreleau. 2 vols. Sources chrétiennes, 263-64. Paris: Les Éditions du Cerf, 1979.

Irénée de Lyon. Contre les hérésies. Livre II. Par Adelin Rousseau et Louis Doutreleau. 2 vols. Sources chrétiennes, 293-94. Paris: Les Éditions du Cerf, 1982.

Irénée de Lyon. Contre les hérésies. Livre III. Par Adelin Rousseau et Louis Doutreleau. 2 vols. Sources chrétiennes, 210-11. Paris: Les Éditions du Cerf, 1974 (replaces the previous edition by F.-M.-M. Sagnard, Sources chrétiennes 34, 1952).

Irénée de Lyon. Contre les hérésies. Livre IV. Par Adelin Rousseau, Bertrand Hemmerdinger, Louis Doutreleau, et Charles Mercier. 2 vols. Sources chrétiennes, 100. Paris: Les Éditions du Cerf, 1965.

Irénée de Lyon. Contre les hérésies. Livre V. Par Adelin Rousseau, Louis Doutreleau, et Charles Mercier. 2 vols. Sources chrétiennes, 152–53. Paris: Les Éditions du Cerf, 1969.

Irénée de Lyon. Contre les hérésies: Dénonciation et réfutation de la gnose au nom menteur. Trad. par Adelin Rousseau. 2ième édition. Paris: Les Éditions du Cerf, 1985.

Koptisch-gnostische Apokalypsen aus Codex V von Nag Hammadi im Koptischen Museum zu Alt-Kairo. Hrsg. von Alexander Böhlig und Pahor Labib. Halle-Wittenberg: Wissenschaftliche Zeitschrift der Martin-Luther-Universität, 1963.

Koptisch-gnostische Schriften. Erster Band. *Die beiden Bücher des Jeû. Unbekanntes altgnostisches Werk.* Hrsg. von Carl Schmidt. 2. Auflage hrsg. von Walter Till. Die griechischen christlichen Schriftsteller der ersten drei Jahrhunderte, 45. Berlin: Akademie-Verlag, 1959.

Koptische-gnostische Schriften aus den Papyrus-Codices von Nag-Hammadi. Hrsg. von Hans-Martin Schenke und Johannes Leipoldt. Theologische Forschung, 20. Hamburg-Bergstedt: Herbert Reich Evangelischer Verlag, 1960.

The Letter of Peter to Philip. Text, Translation, and Commentary. Ed. by Marvin W. Meyer. SBL Dissertation Series, 53. Chico, CA: Scholars Press, 1981.

La Lettre de Pierre à Philippe. Par Jacques-É. Ménard. Bibliothèque copte de Nag Hammadi, Section «Textes», 1. Québec: Les Presses de l'Université Laval, 1977.

Nag Hammadi Codex I (The Jung Codex). Ed. by Harold W. Attridge. 2 vols. Nag Hammadi Studies, 22–23. Leiden: Brill, 1985.

Nag Hammadi Codices V, 2–5 and VI with Papyrus Berolinensis 8502, 1 and 4. Ed. by Douglas M. Parrott. Nag Hammadi Studies, 11. Leiden: Brill, 1979.

Nag Hammadi Codices IX and X. Ed. by Birger Pearson and Soren Giversen. Nag Hammadi Studies, 15. Leiden: Brill, 1981.

The Nag Hammadi Library in English. Ed. by James M. Robinson. New York: Harper and Row, 1977.

Nag-Hammadi-Register. Wörterbuch zur Erfassung der Begriffe in den koptisch-gnostischen Schriften von Nag-Hammadi. Angf. von Folker Siegert. Wissenschaftliche Untersuchungen zum Neuen Testament, 26. Tübingen: J. C. B. Mohr, 1982.

Nestle-Aland Novum Testamentum Graece. Edidit Kurt Aland *et al.* 26. Auflage. Stuttgart: Deutsche Bibelstiftung, 1979.

New Testament Apocrypha. Ed. by Edgar Hennecke. 3rd edition ed. by Wilhelm Schneemelcher. ET ed. by R. McL. Wilson. 2 vols. Philadelphia: Westminster Press, 1963–65.

Oracles Chaldaïques. Avec un choix de commentaires anciens. Par Édouard des Places. Collection Guillaume Budé. Paris: Société d'Édition "Les Belles Lettres," 1971.

Oratio Pauli Apostoli. Codex Jung f. LXXII (?) (p. 143?–144?). Ed. by Rodolphe Kasser, Michel Malinine, Henri-Charles Puech, Gilles Quispel, Jan Zandee, Werner Vycichl, and Robert McL. Wilson. Bern: Francke Verlag, 1975.

Origène. Commentaire sur Saint Jean. Par Cécile Blanc. 4 vols. Sources chrétiennes, 120, 157, 222, 290. Paris: Les Éditions du Cerf, 1966–82.

Origenes Werke. Hrsg. von P. Koetschau *et al.* 12 vols. Die griechischen christlichen Schriftsteller der ersten drei Jahrhunderte. Leipzig: J. C. Hinrichs'sche Buchhandlung, 1889–1941.

Origenes Werke. Vierter Band. *Der Johanneskommentar.* Hrsg. von Erwin Preuschen. Die griechischen christlichen Schriftsteller der ersten drei Jahrhunderte, 10. Leipzig: J. C. Hinrichs'sche Buchhandlung, 1903.

The "'Panarion" of Epiphanius of Salamis. Book I (Sects 1–46). Trans. by F. Williams. Nag Hammadi Studies, 35. Leiden: Brill, 1986.

A Patristic Greek Lexicon. Ed. by B. W. H. Lampe. Oxford: Clarendon Press, 1961–68.

Philosophumena or the Refutation of all Heresies. Trans. by F. Legge. 2 vols. London: Society for Promoting Christian Knowledge, 1921.

Pistis Sophia. Ed. by Carl Schmidt. Trans. by Violet MacDermot. Nag Hammadi Studies, 9. Leiden: Brill, 1978.

Plotin. Ennéades. Par Émile Bréhier. 6 vols. Collection Guillaume Budé. Paris: Société d'Édition "Les Belles Lettres," 1924–38.

Plotini Opera. Editio major. Edidit Paul Henry et Hans-Rudolf Schwyzer. 3 vols. Museum Lessianum Series Philosophica, 33–35. Paris: Desclée de Brouwer et Cie, 1951–73.

Plotini Opera. Edidit Paul Henry et Hans-Rudolf Schwyzer. 2 vols. Scriptorum Classicorum Bibliotheca Oxoniensis. Oxford: Clarendon Press, 1964–77.

Plotinus. Trans. by A. H. Armstrong. 3 vols. Loeb Classical Library. London: William Heinemann, 1966–67.

Ptolemaeus. Brief an die Flora. Hrsg. von Adolf Harnack. Kleine Texte für theologische Vorlesungen und Übungen, 9. Bonn: Marcus und Weber, 1904.

Ptolémée. Lettre à Flora. Par G. Quispel. Sources chrétiennes, 24. Paris: Les Éditions du Cerf, 1949.

Quellen zur Geschichte der christlichen Gnosis. Hrsg. von Walther Völker. Sammlung ausgewählter kirchen- und dogmengeschichtlicher Quellenschriften, neue Folge. Tübingen: J. C. B. Mohr, 1932.

Quinti Septimi Florentis Tertulliani Opera. Pars III ("Pseudo-Tertullian," pp. 213–26). Edidit Aemilii Kroymann. Corpus Scriptorum Ecclesiasticorum Latinorum, 47. Vindobonae: F. Tempsky, 1906.

Sancti Filastrii Episcopi Brixiensis. Diversarum hereseon liber. Edidit Fridericus Marx. Corpus Scriptorum Ecclesiasticorum Latinorum, 38. Vindobonae: F. Tempsky, 1898.

Sancti Irenaei. Libros quinque adversus haereses. Edidit W. Wigan Harvey. 2 vols. 1857. Reprint. Ridgewood, NJ: Gregg Press Incorporated, 1965.

Tertullien. Traité de la prescription contre les hérétiques. Par R. F. Refoulé. Sources chrétiennes, 46. Paris: Les Éditions du Cerf, 1957.

Tertullien. La chair du Christ. Par Jean-Pierre Mahé. 2 vols. Sources chrétiennes, 216–17. Paris: Les Éditions du Cerf, 1975.

Tertullien. Contre les valentiniens. Par Jean-Claude Fredouille. 2 vols. Sources chrétiennes, 280–81. Paris: Les Éditions du Cerf, 1980–81.

Tractatus Tripartitus. I. *De supernis. Codex Jung f. XXVI^r-f. LII^v (p. 51–104).* II. *De creatione hominis.* III. *De generibus tribus. Codex Jung f. LII^v-f. LXX^v (p. 104–140).* Ed. by Rodolphe Kasser, Michel Malinine, Henri-Charles Puech, Gilles Quispel, Jan Zandee, Werner Vycichl, and Robert McL. Wilson. Bern: Francke Verlag, 1973–75.

Le traité sur la résurrection. Par Jacques-É. Ménard. Bibliothèque copte de Nag Hammadi, Section «Textes», 12. Québec: Les Presses de l'Université Laval, 1983.

Die zweite Apokalypse des Jakobus aus Nag-Hammadi-Codex V. Hrsg. von Wolf-Peter Funk. Texte und Untersuchungen, 119. Berlin: Akademie-Verlag, 1976.

Secondary Literature

Aland, Barbara. "Erwählungstheologie und Menschenklassenlehre. Die Theologie des Herakleon als Schlüssel zum Verständnis der christlichen Gnosis?" In *Gnosis and Gnosticism. Papers Read at the Seventh International Conference on Patristic Studies (Oxford, September 8th–13th 1975),* ed. by Martin Krause, 148–81. Nag Hammadi Studies, 8. Leiden: Brill, 1977.

Aland, Barbara. "Gnosis und Kirchenväter: Ihre Auseinandersetzung um die Interpretation des Evangeliums." In *Gnosis. Festschrift für Hans Jonas,* hrsg. von by Barbara Aland, 158–215. Göttingen: Vandenhoeck & Ruprecht, 1978.

Aleith, Eva. *Paulusverständnis in der alten Kirche.* Beihefte zur Zeitschrift für die neutestamentliche Wissenschaft und die Kunde in der älteren Kirche, 18. Berlin: A. Töpelmann, 1937.

Angus, Samuel. *The Mystery Religions and Christianity. A Study in the Religious Background of Early Christianity.* 1925. Reprint. New Hyde Park, NY: University Books, Inc., 1966.

Arai, Sasagu. *Die Christologie des Evangelium Veritatis. Eine religionsgeschichtliche Untersuchung.* Leiden: Brill, 1964.

Bardy, Gustave. "Clément d'Alexandrie." In the *Dictionnaire d'Histoire et de Géographie Ecclésiastique,* vol. 12, 1953, 1423–28.

Bardy, Gustave. "Origène." In the *Dictionnaire de Théologie Catholique,* vol. XI/2, 1932, 1489–1565.

Barnes, Timothy. *Tertullian. A Historical and Literary Study.* Oxford: Clarendon Press, 1971.

Beaucamp, E. "Péché. I. Dans l'Ancien Testament." In the *Dictionnaire de la Bible. Supplément,* vol. 7, 1966, 407–71.

Becker, Jürgen. *Das Heil Gottes. Heils- und Sündenbegriffe in den Qumrantexten und im Neuen Testament.* Studien zur Umwelt des Neuen Testaments, 3. Göttingen: Vandenhoeck & Ruprecht, 1964.

Benoit, A. "Irénée et l'hérésie. Les conceptions hérésiologiques de l'évêque de Lyon." *Augustinianum* 20 (1980): 55–67.

Betz, O. "Das Problem der Gnosis seit der Entdeckung der Texte von Nag Hammadi." *Verkündigung und Forschung* 21 (1976): 46–80.

Bianchi, Ugo. "Péché originel et péché antécédent." *Revue de l'histoire des religions* 170 (1966): 117–26.

Bianchi, Ugo. "Gnostizismus und Anthropologie." *Kairos* 11 (1969): 6–13.

Bianchi, Ugo. "Anthropologie et conception du mal; les sources de l'exégèse gnostique." *Vigiliae Christianae* 25 (1971): 197–204.

Bianchi, Ugo. *Selected Essays on Gnosticism, Dualism and Mysteriosophy.* Studies in the History of Religions, 38. Leiden: Brill, 1978.

Blackman, A. M. "Sin. Egyptian." In the *Encyclopaedia of Religion and Ethics,* vol. 11, 1920, 544–45.

Blanc, Cécile. "Le commentaire d'Héracléon sur Jean 4 et 8." *Augustinianum 15 (1975): 109*–16.

Bonsirven, Joseph. "Le péché et son expiation selon la théologie du judaisme palestinien au temps de Jésus-Christ." *Biblica* 15 (1934): 213–36.

Bonsirven, Joseph. *Le judaisme palestinien au temps de Jésus-Christ.* 2 vols. Paris: Beauchesne, 1934–35.

Borchert, Gerald L. "An Analysis of the Literary Arrangement and Theological Views in the Coptic Gnostic Gospel of Philip." Th.D. diss., Princeton Theological Seminary, 1967.

Bousset, Wilhelm. *Hauptprobleme der Gnosis.* Forschungen zur Religion und Literatur des Alten und Neuen Testaments, 10. Göttingen: Vandenhoeck & Ruprecht, 1907.

Brooke, Alan England. *The Commentary of Origen on S. John's Gospel.* 2 vols. Cambridge: University Press, 1896.

Brown, S. Kent. "Jewish and Gnostic Elements in the Second Apocalypse of James (CG V,4)." *Novum Testamentum* 17 (1975): 225–37.

Brox, Norbert. *Offenbarung, Gnosis und gnostischer Mythos bei Irenaeus von Lyon.* Salzburg: Pustet, 1966.

Büchler, A. *Studies in Sin and Atonement in the Rabbinic Literature of the First Century.* 1927. Reprint. New York: KTAV, 1967.

Camelot, Pierre-Thomas, and Étienne Cornelis. "Gnose et Gnosticisme." In the *Dictionnaire de Spiritualité,* vol. 6, 1967, 508–41.

Caster, Marcel. *Lucien et la pensée religieuse de son temps.* Collection Guillaume Budé. Paris: Société d'Édition "Les Belles Lettres," 1937.

Colpe, Carsten. "Gnosis II (Gnostizismus)." In the *Reallexikon für Antike und Christentum*, vol. 11, 1981, 537-659.

Crouzel, Henri. "Les 'études valentiniennes' du P. Orbe." *Bulletin de littérature ecclésiastique* 60 (1960): 138-42.

Crouzel, Henri. *Origène et la "connaissance mystique."* Museum Lessianum, Section théologique, 56. Bruges: Desclée de Brouwer, 1961.

Crouzel, Henri. *Bibliographie critique d'Origène.* Instrumenta Patristica, 8. Steenbrugis: Abbatia Sti Petri, 1971.

Crouzel, Henri. "Origène." In the *Dictionnaire de Spiritualité,* vol. 11, 1982, 933-61.

De Faye, Eugène. *Introduction à l'étude du gnosticisme au IIe et au IIIe siècle.* Paris: Leroux, 1903.

De Faye, Eugène. *Clément d'Alexandrie. Étude sur les rapports du christianisme et de la philosophie grecque au IIe siècle.* Bibliothèque de l'École des Hautes Études, Sciences religieuses, 12. Paris: Ernest Leroux, 1906.

De Faye, Eugène. "De l'influence du gnosticisme sur Origène." *Revue de l'histoire des religions* 87 (1923): 181-235.

De Pablo Maroto, Daniel. "Pecado y santidad en la iglesia primitiva." *Revista de Espiritualidad* 32 (1973): 135-61.

Des Places, Édouard. "Péché. II. Dans la grèce antique." In the *Dictionnaire de la Bible. Supplément,* vol. 7, 1966, 471-80.

Devoti, Domenico. "Una Summa di teologia gnostica: il 'Tractatus Tripartitus'." *Revista di Storia e Letteratura Religiosa* 13 (1977): 326-53.

Dibelius, Otto. "Studien zur Geschichte der Valentinianer." *Zeitschrift für die neutestamentliche Wissenschaft und die Kunde des Urchristentums* 9 (1908): 230-47.

Dillon, John. *The Middle Platonists. A Study of Platonism, 80 B.C. to A.D. 220.* London: Duckworth, 1977.

Dodd, E. R. *The Greeks and the Irrational.* The Sather Classical Lectures, 25. 1951. Reprint. Berkeley/Los Angeles: University of California Press, 1968.

Dölger, Franz Josef. *Der Exorzismus im altchristlichen Taufritual. Eine religionsgeschichtliche Studie.* Studien zur Geschichte und Kultur des Altertums, 3. Paderborn: Verlag von Ferdinand Schöningh, 1909.

Dölger, Franz Josef. *Sphragis. Eine altchristliche Taufbezeichnung in ihren Beziehungen zur profanen und religiösen Kultur des Altertums.* Studien zur Geschichte und Kultur des Altertums, 5. Paderborn: Verlag von Ferdinand Schöningh, 1911.

Dölger, Franz Josef. "Die Sünde in Blindheit und Unwissenheit. Ein Beitrag zu Tertullian *De baptismo* I." In his *Antike und Christentum. Kultur und religionsgeschichtliche Studien,* Band 2, 222-29. Münster: Aschendorff, 1930.

Donovan, Mary Ann. "Irenaeus' Teaching on the Unity of God and His Immediacy to the Material World in Relation to Valentinian Gnosticism." Ph.D. diss., Institute of Christian Thought, St. Michael's College, 1977.

Donovan, Mary Ann. "Irenaeus in Recent Scholarship." *The Second Century* 4 (1984): 219–41.

Doresse, Jean. *Les livres secrets des gnostiques d'Égypte.* I. *Introduction aux écrits gnostiques coptes découverts à Khénoboskion.* Paris: Librairie Plon, 1958.

Doutreleau, Louis, and Lucien Regnault. "Irénée de Lyon." In the *Dictionnaire de Spiritualité,* vol. 7, 1969, 1923–69.

Dubarle, A.-M. "Le péché originel: recherches récentes et orientations nouvelles." *Revue des sciences philosophiques et théologiques* 53 (1969): 81–113.

Farina, R. *Bibliografia Origeniana 1960*-1970. Biblioteca del "Salesianum," 77. Torino: Società Editrice Internazionale, 1971.

Festugière, André Marie Jean. *L'Idéal religieux des grecs et l'évangile.* Études bibliques. Paris: J. Gabalda et Cⁱᵉ, 1932.

Festugière, André Marie Jean. *La révélation d'Hermès Trismégiste.* 4 vols. Études bibliques. Paris: J. Gabalda et Cⁱᵉ, 1943–54.

Floyd, W. E. G. *Clement of Alexandria's Treatment of the Problem of Evil.* Oxford Theological Monographs. Oxford: University Press, 1971.

Foerster, Werner. *Von Valentin zu Herakleon. Untersuchungen über die Quellen und die Entwicklung der valentinianischen Gnosis.* Beihefte zur Zeitschrift für die neutestamentliche Wissenschaft und die Kunde der älteren Kirche, 7. Gießen: Alfred Töpelmann, 1928.

Frend, W. H. C. "The Gnostic Sects and the Roman Empire." *Journal of Ecclesiastical History* 5 (1954): 25–37.

Frickel, Josef. *Hellenistische Erlösung in christlicher Deutung. Die gnostische Naassenerschrift.* Nag Hammadi Studies, 19. Leiden: Brill, 1984.

Früchtel, Ludwig. "Clemens Alexandrinus." In the *Reallexikon für Antike und Christentum,* vol. 3, 1957, 182–88.

Gaffron, H.-G. "Studien zum koptischen Philippusevangelium unter besonderer Berücksichtigung der Sakramente." Doctoral diss., Bonn, Rheinische-Friedrich-Wilhelms-Universität, 1969.

Gager, John G. *Kingdom and Community. The Social World of Early Christianity.* Englewood Cliffs, NJ: Prentice-Hall, Inc., 1975.

García Bazán, Francisco. *Plotino y la gnosis.* Buenos Aires: Fundación para la Educación, la Ciencia y la Cultura, 1981.

Good, Deirdre J. "Sophia in Valentinianism." *The Second Century* 4 (1984): 193–201.

Goulon, A. "Le malheur de l'homme à la naissance. Un thème antique chez quelques Pères de l'Église." *Revue des études augustiniennes* 18 (1972): 3–26.

Grant, Robert M. Review of *The Johannine Gospel in Gnostic Exegesis* and *The Gnostic Paul,* by Elaine H. Pagels. *Religious Studies Review* 3 (1977): 30–35.

Green, Henry A. "Gnosis and Gnosticism: A Study in Methodology." *Numen* 24 (1977): 95–134.

Green, Henry A. "Ritual in Valentinian Gnosticism: A Sociological Interpretation." *The Journal of Religious History* 12 (1982): 109–24.

Green, Henry A. *The Economic and Social Origins of Gnosticism*. SBL Dissertation Series, 77. Atlanta: Scholars Press, 1985.

Greer, Rowan A. "The Dog and the Mushrooms. Irenaeus's view of the Valentinians Assessed." In *The Rediscovery of Gnosticism*. Proceedings of the International Conference on Gnosticism at Yale, March 28–31, 1978. I. *The School of Valentinus*, ed. by Bentley Layton, 146–75. Studies in the History of Religions, 41. Leiden: Brill, 1980.

Grobel, Kendrick. *The Gospel of Truth. A Valentinian Meditation on the Gospel*. New York/Nashville: Abingdon Press, 1960.

Gross, Julius. *Entstehungsgeschichte der Erbsündendogmas von der Bibel bis Augustin*. München/Basel: Ernst Reinhardt Verlag, 1960.

Hartman, Louis F. "Sin in Paradise." *Catholic Biblical Quarterly* 20 (1958): 26–40.

Helderman, Jan. *Die Anapausis im Evangelium Veritatis. Eine vergleichende Untersuchung des valentinianisch-gnostischen Heilsgutes der Ruhe im Evangelium Veritatis und in anderen Schriften der Nag-Hammadi Bibliothek*. Nag Hammadi Studies, 18. Leiden: Brill, 1984.

Hey, O. "Ἁμαρτία. Zur Bedeutungsgeschichte des Wortes." *Philologus* 83 (1927/28): 1–17; 137–63.

Hilgenfeld, Adolf. *Die Ketzergeschichte des Urchristenthums*. Leipzig: Fues's Verlag, 1884.

Hirsh, Emmanuel. *Schöpfung und Sünde*. Tübingen: J. C. B. Mohr, 1931.

Huftier, M. "La philosophie plotinienne du péché et l'utilisation qu'en fait Saint Augustin." In *Études d'histoire littéraire et doctrinale*, 137–88. Université de Montréal, Publications de l'Institut d'études médiévales, 19. Montréal: L'Institut d'études médiévales, 1968.

Hurd, John Coolidge, Jr. *The Origin of I Corinthians*. 1965. Reprint. Macon, GA: Mercer University Press, 1983.

Janssens, Yvonne. "Héracleon: Commentaire sur l'Évangile selon saint Jean." *Le Muséon* 72 (1959): 101–51; 277–99.

Kinder, E. "Sünde und Schuld. V. Dogmengeschichtlich." In *Die Religion in Geschichte und Gegenwart*, vol. 6, 1962, 489–94.

Koepgen, G. *Die Gnosis des Christentums*. 3. Auflage. Occidens, 4. Trier: Spee Buchverlag, 1978.

Koschorke, Klaus. *Hippolyts Ketzerbekämpfung und Polemik gegen die Gnostiker. Eine tendenzkritische Untersuchung seiner 'Refutatio omnium haeresium.'* Göttingen Orientforschungen, VI Reihe: Hellenistica, 4. Wiesbaden: Harrassowitz, 1975.

Koschorke, Klaus. "Eine neugefundene gnostische Gemeindeordnung. Zum Thema Geist und Amt im frühen Christentum." *Zeitschrift für Theologie und Kirche* 76 (1979): 30–60.

Koschorke, Klaus. "Gnostic Instructions on the Organization of the Congregation: The Tractate Interpretation of Knowledge from CG XI." In *The Rediscovery of Gnosticism. Proceedings of the International Conference on Gnosticism at Yale, March 28–30, 1978.* II. *Sethian Gnosticism,* ed. by Bentley Layton, 757–69. Studies in the History of Religions, 41. Leiden: Brill, 1981.

Koschorke, Klaus. "Patristische Materialen zur Spätgeschichte der valentinianischen Gnosis." In *Gnosis and Gnosticism. Papers Read at the Eighth International Conference on Patristic Studies (Oxford, September 3rd–8th 1979),* ed. by Martin Krause, 120–39. Nag Hammadi Studies, 17. Leiden: Brill, 1981.

Koschorke, Klaus. *Die Polemik der Gnostiker gegen das kirchliche Christentum. Unter besonderer Berücksichtigung der Nag-Hammadi-Traktate "Apokalypse des Petrus" (NHC VII,3) und "Testimonium Veritatis" (NHC IX,3).* Nag Hammadi Studies, 12. Leiden: Brill, 1978.

Kovacks, Judith Lee. "Clement of Alexandria and the Valentinian Gnostics." Ph.D. diss., Columbia University, 1978.

Krause, Martin, ed. *Gnosis and Gnosticism. Papers Read at the Seventh International Conference on Patristic Studies (Oxford, September 8th–13th 1975).* Nag Hammadi Studies, 8. Leiden: Brill, 1977.

Lampe, G. W. H. *The Seal of the Spirit. A Study in the Doctrine of Baptism and Confirmation in the New Testament and the Fathers.* 2nd edition. London: S.P.C.K., 1967 (1951).

Langbrandtner, Wolfgang. *Weltferner Gott oder Gott der Liebe: Der Ketzerstreit in der johanneischen Kirche. Eine exegetisch-religionsgeschichtliche Untersuchung mit Berücksichtigung der koptisch-gnostischen Texte aus Nag-Hammadi.* Beiträge zur biblischen Exegese und Theologie, 6. Frankfurt am Main: Peter Lang, 1977.

Langerbeck, H. "Die Anthropologie der alexandrinischen Gnosis: Interpretation zu den Fragmenten des Basilides und Valentinus und ihrer Schulen bei Clemens von Alexandrien und Origenes." In his *Aufsätze zur Gnosis: Aus dem Nachlass,* 38–82. Abhandlungen der Akademie der Wissenschaften in Göttingen, philologisch-historische Klasse, dritte Folge, 69. Göttingen: Vandenhoeck & Ruprecht, 1967.

Layton, Bentley. "The Soul as a Dirty Garment [NH Codex II, Tract. 6]." *Le Muséon* 91 (1978): 155–64.

Lebreton, Jules. "Clément d'Alexandrie." In the *Dictionnaire de Spiritualité,* vol. 2, 1953, 950–61.

Leroux, G. *Mythe et mystère du péché originel chez saint Irénée de Lyon.* Montréal: Institut d'études médiévales, 1967.

Lilla, Salvatore R. C. *Clement of Alexandria. A Study in Christian Platonism and Gnosticism.* Oxford Theological Monographs. Oxford: University Press, 1971.

Logan, A. H. B., and A. J. M. Wedderburn, eds. *The New Testament and Gnosis. Essays in Honour of Robert McL. Wilson.* Edinburgh: T. & T. Clark Limited, 1983.

Loi, Vincenzo, ed. *Ricerche su Ippolito.* Studia Ephemeridis "Augustinianum," 13. Rome: Institutum Patristicum "Augustinianum," 1977.

Luedemann, Gerd. *Paul. Apostle to the Gentiles. Studies in Chronology.* Trans. by F. Stanley Jones. Philadelphia: Fortress, 1984.

Luz, Ulrich. "Der dreiteilige Traktat von Nag Hammadi." *Theologische Zeitschrift* 33 (1977): 384-92.

Lyonnet, S. "Péché. III. Dans le judaisme. IV. Dans le Nouveau Testament." In the *Dictionnaire de la Bible. Supplément,* vol. 7, 1966, 480-85; 486-567.

Machielsen, J. J. "Le problème du mal selon les pères apostoliques." *Église et théologie* 62 (1981): 195-222.

Magne, J. "Ouverture des yeux, connaissance et nudité dans les récits gnostiques du paradis." *Vigiliae Christianae* 34 (1980): 288-301.

Mair, A. W. "Sin. Greek." In the *Encyclopaedia of Religion and Ethics,* vol. 11, 1920, 545-56.

McCue, James F. "Conflicting Versions of Valentinianism: Irenaeus and the *Excerpta ex Theodoto.*" In *The Rediscovery of Gnosticism. Proceedings of the International Conference on Gnosticism at Yale, March 28-31, 1978.* I. *The School of Valentinus,* ed. by Bentley Layton, 404-16. Studies in the History of Religions, 41. Leiden: Brill, 1980.

McGuire, Anne Marie. "Valentinus and the *Gnostike Haeresis:* An Investigation of Valentinus' Position in the History of Gnosticism." Ph.D. diss., Yale, 1983.

Méhat, André. *Études sur les "Stromates" de Clément d'Alexandrie.* Patristica Sorbonensia, 7. Paris: Les Éditions du Seuil, 1966.

Méhat, André. "Clemens von Alexandrien." In the *Theologische Realenzyklopädie,* vol. 8, 1981, 101-13.

Meihering, E. P. "Some Observations on Irenaeus' Polemics against the Gnostics." *Nederlands theologisch tijdschrift* 27 (1973): 26-33.

Mortley, Raoul, and Carsten Colpe. "Gnosis I (Erkenntnislehre)." In the *Reallexikon für Antike und Christentum,* vol. 11, 1981, 446-537.

Mouson, J. "Jean-Baptiste dans les fragments d'Héracléon." *Ephemerides Theologicae Lovanienses* 30 (1954): 301-22.

Mühlenberg, Ekkehard. "Das Verständnis des Bösen in neuplatonischer und frühchristlicher Sicht." *Kerygma und Dogma* 15 (1969): 226-38.

Mühlenberg, Ekkehard. "Wieviel Erlösungen kennt der Gnostiker Herakleon?" *Zeitschrift für die Neutestamentliche Wissenschaft und die Kunde der älteren Kirche* 66 (1975): 170-93.

Nautin, Pierre. *Hippolyte et Josipe. Contribution à l'histoire de la littérature chrétienne du troisième siècle.* Études et textes pour l'histoire du dogme de la trinité, 1. Paris: Les Éditions du Cerf, 1947.

Neusner, Jacob. *The Idea of Purity in Ancient Judaism: The Haskell Lectures, 1972-1973*. Studies in Judaism in Late Antiquity, 1. Leiden: Brill, 1973.

Neusner, Jacob. "The Idea of Purity in Ancient Judaism." *Journal of the American Academy of Religion* 43 (1975): 15-26.

Orbe, Antonio. *Hacia la primera teologia de la procesión del verbo. Estudios valentinianos.* Vol. 1 (in 2 parts). Analecta Gregoriana, 99-100; Series Facultatis Theologicae, Sectio A, 17-18. Romae: Apud Aedes Universitatis Gregorianae, 1958.

Orbe, Antonio. *En los arbores de la exegesis Iohannea (Ioh. 1, 3). Estudios valentinianos.* Vol. 2. Analecta Gregoriana, 65; Series Facultatis Theologicae, Sectio A, 11. Romae: Apud Aedes Universitatis Gregorianae, 1955.

Orbe, Antonio. *La unción del verbo. Estudios valentinianos.* Vol. 3. Analecta Gregoriana, 113; Series Facultatis Theologicae, Sectio A, 19. Roma: Libreria Editrice dell' Università Gregoriana, 1961.

Orbe, Antonio. *La teología del Espíritu Santo. Estudios valentinianos.* Vol. 4. Analecta Gregoriana, 158; Series Facultatis Theologicae, Sectio A, 20. Roma: Libreria Editrice dell' Università Gregoriana, 1966.

Orbe, Antonio. *Los primeros herejes ante la persecución. Estudios valentinianos.* Vol. 5. Analecta Gregoriana, 83; Series Facultatis Theologicae, Sectio A, 15. Romae: Apud Aedes Universitatis Gregorianae, 1956.

Orbe, Antonio. "El Primer testimonio del Bautista sobre el Salvador, según Heracleón y Orígenes." *Estudios eclesiasticos* 30 (1956): 20-35.

Orbe, Antonio. *Antropología de S. Ireneo.* Madrid: Editorial Católica, 1969.

Pagels, Elaine. *The Johannine Gospel in Gnostic Exegesis: Heracleon's Commentary on John.* SBL Monograph Series, 17. Nashville: Abingdon Press, 1973.

Pagels, Elaine. "A Valentinian Interpretation of Baptism and Eucharist—And its Critique of 'Orthodox' Sacramental Theology and Practice." *Harvard Theological Review* 65 (1972): 153-69.

Pagels, Elaine. "The Valentinian Claim to Esoteric Exegesis of Romans as Basis for Anthropological Theory." *Vigiliae Christianae* 26 (1972): 241-58.

Pagels, Elaine. "Conflicting Versions of Valentinian Eschatology: Irenaeus' Treatise vs. the Excerpts from Theodotus." *Harvard Theological Review* 67 (1974): 35-53.

Pearson, Birger A. and James E. Goehring, eds. *The Roots of Egyptian Christianity.* Studies in Antiquity and Christianity. Philadelphia: Fortress, 1986.

Perkins, Pheme. "Irenaeus and the Gnostics. Rhetoric and Composition in *Adv. haer.,* Book 1." *Vigiliae Christianae* 30 (1976): 193-200.

Pétrement, Simone. "Valentin est-il l'auteur de l'épître à Diognète?" *Revue d'histoire et de philosophie religieuse* 46 (1966): 34-62.

Pétrement, Simone. *Le Dieu séparé. Les origines du gnosticisme.* Paris: Les Éditions du Cerf, 1984.

Poirier, Paul-Hubert. "La bibliothèque copte de Nag Hammadi: sa nature et son importance." *Studies in Religion/Sciences Religieuses* 15 (1986): 303-16.

Porúbčan, Stefan. *Sin in the Old Testament. A Soteriological Study.* Aloisiana scritti publicati sotto la direzione della pontificia facoltà teologica napolitana "San Luigi," 3. Roma: Herder, 1963.

Prunet, Olivier. *La morale de Clément d'Alexandrie et le Nouveau Testament.* Études d'histoire et de philosophie religieuses, 61. Paris: Presses universitaires de France, 1966.

Puech, Henri-Charles. *En quête de la Gnose.* I. *La Gnose et le temps et autres essais.* Bibliothèque des Sciences Humaines. Paris: Gallimard, 1978.

Puech, Henri-Charles. *Sur le manichéisme et autres essais.* Paris: Flammarion, 1979.

Quasten, Johannes. *Patrology.* I. *The Beginnings of Patristic Literature.* II. *The Ante-Nicene Literature after Irenaeus.* Westminster, MD: The Neuman Press, 1950-1953.

Quispel, Gilles. "The Original Doctrine of Valentinus." *Vigiliae Christianae* 1 (1947): 43-73. (Now reprinted in his *Gnostic Studies* I, 27-36. Istanbul: Nederlands Historisch-Archaeologisch Instituut in het Nabije Oosten, 1974.)

Quispel, Gilles. "La conception de l'homme dans la gnose valentinienne." *Eranos Jahrbuch* 15 (1947; publ. 1948): 249-286. (Now reprinted in his *Gnostic Studies* I, 37-57.)

Quispel, Gilles. "L'inscription de Flavia Sophè." In *Mélanges Joseph de Ghellinck, S.J.,* 1951, 201-214. (Now reprinted in his *Gnostic Studies* I, 58-69.)

Quispel, Gilles. "Origen and the Valentinian Gnosis." *Vigiliae Christianae* 28 (1974): 29-42.

Rahner, Karl. "Sünde als Gnadenverlust in der früchristlichen Literatur." *Zeitschrift für katholische Theologie* 60 (1936): 471-510.

Rambaux, Claude. *Tertullien face aux morales des trois premiers siècles.* Collection Guillaume Budé. Paris: Société d'Édition "Les Belles Lettres," 1979.

Richard, Marcel. "Hippolyte de Rome." In the *Dictionnaire de Spiritualité,* vol. 7, 1969, 531-71.

Roncaglia, M. *Histoire de l'église copte.* I. *Les origines du christianisme en Égypte. Du judéo-christianisme au christianisme hellénistique (Ier et IIe siècles);* II. *Le didascalée (IIe s.).* Beyrouth: Dar Al-Kalima, 1966-69.

Rondet, H. "Le péché originel dans la tradition." *Bulletin de littérature ecclésiastique* 66 (1965): 241-71; 67 (1966): 115-48; 68 (1967): 20-43.

Rondet, H. *Le péché originel dans la tradition patristique et théologique.* Paris: A. Fayard, 1967. (ET: *Original Sin. The Patristic and Theological Background.* London: Ecclesia Press, 1972.)

Rordorf, W. "La rémission des péchés selon la Didaché." *Irenikon* 46 (1973): 283-97.

Rudolph, Kurt. *Gnosis. The Nature and History of Gnosticism.* 2nd ed. Trans. and ed. by Robert McL. Wilson. San Francisco: Harper and Row, 1983.

Sagnard, François-M.-M. *La gnose valentienne et le témoignage de saint Irénée.* Études de philosophie médiévale, 36. Paris: Librairie Philosophique J. Vrin, 1947.

Saïd, S. *La faute tragique.* Paris: François Maspéro, 1978.

Schenke, Hans-Martin. *Die Herkunft des sogenannten Evangelium Veritatis.* Göttingen: Vandenhoeck & Ruprecht, 1959.

Schneemelcher, Wilhelm. "Epiphanius von Salamis." In the *Reallexikon für Antike und Christentum,* vol. 5, 1962, 909-27.

Schoedel, William R. Review of *The Johannine Gospel in Gnostic Exegesis: Heracleon's Commentary on John,* by Elaine H. Pagels. *Journal of Biblical Literature* 93 (1974): 315-16.

Schultz, Donald R. "The Origin of Sin in Irenaeus and Jewish Apocalyptic Literature." Ph.D. diss., McMaster University, 1972.

Schultz, Donald R. "The Origin of Sin in Irenaeus and Jewish Pseudepigraphal Literature." *Vigiliae Christianae* 32 (1978): 161-90.

Segelberg, Eric. "The Coptic-Gnostic Gospel according to Philip and its Sacramental System." *Numen* 7 (1960): 189-200.

Segelberg, Eric. "The Baptismal Rite according to some of the Coptic-Gnostic Texts of Nag-Hammadi." In *Studia Patristica, Vol. V: Papers presented to the Third International Conference on Patristic Studies held at Christ Church, Oxford, 1959; Part III: Liturgica, Monastica et Ascetica, Philosophica,* ed. by F. L. Cross, 117-28. Texte und Untersuchungen, 80. Berlin: Akademie-Verlag, 1962.

Sevrin, Jean-Marie. "Les noces spirituelles dans l'Évangile selon Philippe." *Le Muséon* 87 (1974): 143-93.

Sevrin, Jean-Marie. *Le dossier baptismal séthien. Études sur la sacramentaire gnostique.* Bibliothèque copte de Nag Hammadi, Section «Études», 2. Québec: Les Presses de l'Université Laval, 1986.

Smith, Morton. "The History of the Term *Gnostikos.*" In *The Rediscovery of Gnosticism. Proceedings of the International Conference on Gnosticism at Yale, March 28-31, 1978. II. Sethian Gnosticism,* ed. by Bentley Layton, 796-807. Studies in the History of Religions, 41. Leiden: Brill, 1981.

Standaert, B. "'L'Évangile de Vérité': Critique et lecture." *New Testament Studies* 22 (1976): 243-75.

Stead, G. C. "In Search of Valentinus." In *The Rediscovery of Gnosticism. Proceedings of the International Conference on Gnosticism at Yale, March 28-31, 1978. I. The School of Valentinus,* ed. by Bentley Layton, 75-102. Studies in the History of Religions, 41. Leiden: Brill, 1980.

Stewart, R. A. "The Sinless High-Priest." *New Testament Studies* 14 (1967-68): 126-35.

Story, Cullen I. K. *The Nature of Truth in "The Gospel of Truth" and in the Writings of Justin Martyr. A Study of the Pattern of Orthodoxy in the Middle of the Second Christian Century.* Supplements to *Novum Testamentum,* 25. Leiden: Brill, 1970.

Strobel, A. *Erkenntnis und Bekenntnis der Sünde in neutestamentlicher Zeit.* Arbeiten zur Theologie, 1, 37. Stuttgart: Calwer, 1968.

Tardieu, Michel. "Le Congrès de Yale sur le gnosticisme (28-31 mars 1978)." *Revue des Études Augustiniennes* 24 (1978): 188-209.

Tardieu, Michel, et Jean-Daniel Dubois. *Introduction à la littérature gnostique. I. Histoire du mot "gnostique," Instruments de travail, Collections retrouvées avant 1945.* Initiations au christianisme ancien. Paris: Les Éditions du Cerf, 1986.

Teichtweier, G. *Die Sündenlehre des Origenes.* Regensburg: Pustet, 1958.

Thomassen, Einar. "The Structure of the Transcendent World in the Tripartite Tractate (NHC I,5)." *Vigiliae Christianae* 34 (1980): 358-75.

Thomassen, Einar. "The Tripartite Tractate from Nag Hammadi. A New Translation with Introduction and Commentary." Ph.D. diss., St. Andrews, 1982.

Thompson, Alden L. *Responsibility for Evil in the Theology of IV Ezra. A Study Illustrating the Significance of Form and Structure for the Meaning of the Book.* Missoula, MT: Scholars Press, 1977.

Tripp, D. H. "The 'Sacramental System' of the Gospel of Philip." In *Studia Patristica. Vol. XVII in Three Parts,* ed. by E. A. Livingstone, I, 251-60. Oxford: Pergamon Press, 1982.

Tröger, Karl-Wolfgang. "Die gnostische Anthropologie." *Kairos* 23 (1981): 31-42.

Vallée, Gérard. *A Study in Anti-Gnostic Polemics. Irenaeus, Hippolytus, and Epiphanius.* Studies in Christianity and Judaism, 1. Waterloo: Wilfrid Laurier Press, 1981.

Van den Broek, R. "The Present State of Gnostic Studies." *Vigiliae Christianae* 37 (1983): 41-71.

Veilleux, Armand. "Monachisme et gnose." *Laval théologique et philosophique* 40 (1984): 275-94; 41 (1985): 3-24.

Völker, Walther. *Der wahre Gnostiker nach Clemens Alexandrinus.* Texte und Untersuchungen zur Geschichte der altchristlichen Literatur, 57. Berlin: Akademie-Verlag, 1952.

Whittaker, J. "Valentinus Fr. 2." In *Kerygma und Logos. Beiträge zu den geistesgeschichtlichen Beziehungen zwischen Antike und Christentum. Festschrift für Carl Andresen zum 70. Geburtstag,* hrsg. von A. M. Ritter, 455-60. Göttingen: Vandenhoeck & Ruprecht, 1979.

Wilson, Robert McL. *The Gnostic Problem. A Study of the Relation between Hellenistic Judaism and the Gnostic Heresy.* London: A. R. Mowbray, 1958.

Wilson, Robert McL. "Twenty Years After." In *Colloque international sur les textes de Nag Hammadi (Québec, 22-25 août 1978),* ed. by Bernard Barc. Bibliothèque copte de Nag Hammadi, Section «Études», 1. Québec: Les Presses de l'Université Laval, 1981.

Wisse, F. "Prolegomena to the Study of the New Testament and Gnosis." In *The New Testament and Gnosis. Essays in Honour of Robert McL. Wilson,* ed. by A. H. B. Logan and A. J. M. Wedderburn, 138-45. Edinburgh: T. & T. Clark Limited, 1983.

Zandee, J. "Gnostic Ideas on the Fall and Salvation." *Numen* 11 (1964): 13-74.

Index nominum

Index locorum

A. Canonical Early Christian Writings

Matthew

5:1-7:29	37-38, 78-80, 94, 101-02, 114n, 116, 131
11:9-14	54
12:29	38
20:20	30

Luke

10:19	38
12:50	30

John

1:18-29	51-56
4:34	54
4:46-53	56-60
8:21	60-62
8:34	98
8:44	61-62

Romans

5:12	103
7:9-13	59
7:23	34n, 37
9:1-11:36	126n

1 Corinthians

2:6-3:3	124-26
3:16	125
8:1-14:40	97
12:1-14:40	72, 104
15:42-58	125

2 Corinthians

1:21-22	128n
3:2-3	83

Galatians

3:26-28	86n

Ephesians

1:13-14	128n
4:30	128n

Hebrews

10:26-27	94

B. Non-Canonical Early Christian Writings

The Acts of John
chaps. 94-102,
109   7

The (First) Apocalypse of
   James   73

The (Second) Apocalypse of
   James   73-74, 110-115
44,11-60,24   114-15
61,1-63,32   110-14